Treasures

Treasures

the stories women tell
about the things they keep

UNIVERSITY OF
CALGARY
PRESS

K.V. Cairns and E.L. Silverman

© 2004 Kathleen Cairns
Third printing 2009
Published by the University of Calgary Press
2500 University Drive NW Calgary, Alberta, Canada T2N 1N4
www.uofcpress.com

National Library of Canada Cataloguing in Publication

Cairns, Kathleen V
  Treasures : the stories women tell about the things they keep / K.V.
Cairns and E.L. Silverman.

Includes bibliographical references.
ISBN 1-55238-073-4

  1. Souvenirs (Keepsakes) 2. Women—Canada—History.
I. Silverman, Eliane Leslau II. Title.

AM313.C33 2004   305.4'0971   C2004-901887-6

We acknowledge the financial support of the Government of Canada
through the Book Publishing Industry Development Program (BPIDP)
for our publishing activities. We acknowledge the support of the Alberta
Foundation for the Arts for this published work.

Canada   Canada Council   Conseil des Arts
           for the Arts   du Canada

Printed and bound in Canada by AGMV Marquis
∞This book is printed on acid-free paper
Cover, page design and typesetting by Mieka West.

Contents

This book arises from our interest in a little-discussed process by which women create a personal and collective history and support their own development as individuals and as members of a women's culture. By acting as the archivists of their own lives and the lives of others who are central to their self-definition – principally their children, sisters, aunts, mothers, grandmothers, and great-grandmothers – they build a record of personal development, a history that places them in time and place, and confirms their most deeply held values and sources of meaning. This process has occurred quietly in our own lives, in the lives of our female friends and family members, and in the lives of the research participants whose stories make up this book.

We set out to learn more about women as archivists by talking with women from many backgrounds about the things they keep, as well as why and how they keep them, listening with fascination as they shared the stories contained in their artefacts and explained how they use them to sustain themselves. Our youngest participant was fourteen years old, our oldest ninety-two. We spoke with women who had been were born and raised in Canada, who emigrated here from various other places, and who came to Canada as refugees. We spoke with employed and unemployed women; able-bodied and disabled women; heterosexuals and lesbians; women who had never married, who had divorced or been widowed, who had children or did not. As far as was possible within the limits of our social context, we worked to ensure that we would hear the voices of women from many different backgrounds rather than privileging the experiences of white, middle-class women.

In part, we looked for this diversity in our participants because doing so is increasingly important to feminist scholars as a matter of principle. We wanted to know whether and how differences in age, sexual orientation, social class, residency, and other forms of diversity in women's lives would affect the pattern we wanted to study. We wondered whether treasuring personal memorabilia was a shared practice among women – a part of women's collective culture – or whether it might be a luxury made possible only for some women by political stability; personal circumstances that provided a relatively predictable and stable life pattern; or luxuries of time, space, and money that made it possible for them to indulge a merely sentimental predilection.

In the end, it was clear to us that the process itself, the pattern of keeping and treasuring personally meaningful objects, is one shared by women. We do not claim, of course, that all women participate in this process, but we do find it remarkable that, try as we might, we could not find one who had no such collection. The choice of object might vary with a woman's experience, with what she finds important in her own life, and occasionally with the comparatively rich or impoverished relational history she has experienced. But even refugee women have invariably managed to bring a few items with them from their early lives – a doll, a small collection of photographs, a stamped identity card – and have almost always been able, with the help of their female friends and family still living in the country of origin, to retrieve other important things. In fact, reclaiming these things was essential, and having the collection intact again was a source of great comfort.

The number of items kept by individual women, however, varied enormously. The relatively small number in some women's collections was often due to some sort of tragedy: a ship bringing personal belongings from Australia sank, a home burned, an angry man destroyed them. Women who have lost many of their objects in these ways still weep for them, still feel dislocated without them, still fantasize about their recovery. Other women keep a great many items, but few or none came from a grandparent, parent, or other relative; rather, they originated with the woman herself or were given by friends – a pattern we saw exclusively in women who came from very unhappy, tumultuous, and often abusive families.

Our interest in this process, and the approach we used to try to understand it, was an outgrowth of feminist scholarship, which seeks to understand women's lives by listening to women's own voices and by bringing those voices to the attention of the world. Like other feminist scholars, we see women as fascinating individuals whose life stories, mostly unheard, resonate with the evidence of unacknowledged talent, intelligence, perceptiveness, achievement, strength, and persistence in the face of often overwhelming life circumstances.

The stories the participants shared with us, and which we have documented in this book, show the great richness of women's lives and the complexity and diversity of women's experiences. We believe, with Carolyn Heilbrun, that "as long as women are isolated one from the other, not allowed to offer other women the most personal accounts of their lives, they will not be part of any narrative of their own" (1988, 46). Through this research, we hoped to contribute to the emergence of women's voices, to witness and record lost personal narratives.

We sought to understand each woman as the authority on her own life, to enter as fully as possible into that life, to hear her own version of herself and how she uses valued objects to give her life meaning and coherence. We hoped to provide a glimpse of the objects we use to make our lives "visible" to ourselves and to add to the feminist literature that makes "ordinary" women's lives visible to others. At the same time, we wanted to understand the meanings women create and the purposes that women, as individuals and as members of a women's culture, achieve through this process – to understand "women as purveyors of heritage" (Josselson 1987, 42).

As we completed more and more interviews, we became convinced that the pattern of treasuring special possessions and of using them in ritualized ways is a widely shared one among women, one that does not seem to be influenced by social class, ethnicity, or relational history. We completed over a hundred lengthy, tape-recorded, and transcribed individual interviews; collected written responses to our requests for information from additional women about the objects they treasure; and tape-recorded discussions with large groups of women in various contexts. In none of these contexts did we hear a woman say that she had no treasured object to describe to us. There might be initial embarrassment about the kinds of things she kept – often a disclaimer to the effect that she had nothing to show us that the world would consider valuable. But once we had made it clear that we were interested in what was valuable to her and not in what others might value, the floodgates of conversation and reminiscence opened.

Most women, we found, had so many objects that were important to them that it was very difficult for them to choose which ones they would talk to us about. We asked each of them to show us and/or tell us about four to six of their most treasured possessions – the things they would save first in a disaster – but they often showed us many more. They told us about the agony of trying to decide what to bring and, as an interview progressed, about the central importance of "something else I should have brought." When the interview was held in the woman's own home, choosing among items was less of a problem – more things could easily be brought out. When it was held elsewhere, we were often invited to come to the house sometime so that we could see the many other important things that made up a collection.

In addition to completing interviews and studying the transcripts and other written records, we looked through diverse sources in women's studies, history, psychology, sociology, anthropology, and even consumer research for writings that studied the role and significance of personal possessions in women's lives. Most of the research we found, and there wasn't a great deal, focused on the meaning of possessions to particular groups of people, such as the role of possession loss or maintenance in the adjustment of elderly women and men moving into nursing homes. These studies usually commented on the correlations between the presence of treasured items and stable adjustment, or on a ubiquitous pattern of gender differences in the kinds and numbers of possessions that individuals saved.

Among this group of studies, the ones that interested us most were those such as Dittmar's (1991) study of the meanings of material possessions as reflections of identity. Comparing the valued material possessions of men and women, for example, she reports that "men cherish self-referent objects of action and women prefer objects of contemplation referring to memories and the immediate family" (161). The women in her study talked about their emotional reasons for treasuring objects, most often referring to their role in providing emotional security, symbolizing relatedness to others, and acting as a locus for self-continuity (168). One of the participants in Dittmar's study commented: "Possessions are a means to an end for me and not something in themselves" (168). It is precisely this purposeful use of cherished possessions to sustain a sense of self that interested us and that seems to us to describe an important and unique process in women's lives. How and where objects are kept, how they are used, and how they are shared with others varies widely, but the fact of a collection and its emotional significance is stable.

The women we spoke with keep many different sorts of objects and keep them in various ways. Some participants live in homes crowded with mementos. Walls are covered with photos, artwork, plaques and poems, wall hangings, and framed artefacts. Shelves hold photo albums, special books, figurines, and small boxes of buttons, jewellery, or keepsakes. These women are like those described by Redfoot and Back (1988), who "were likely to keep items that had rich biographical meanings, turning their rooms into museums of their lives" (168).

In contrast to this pattern, some women display special objects only in their bedrooms or in another private room, keeping them visible for their own reflection but away from casual observation by others. Still others keep almost no objects at all on display – their special possessions are put away in boxes and brought out only on particular occasions or for specific purposes. Many women spoke of their practice of changing the selection of items they keep in sight. They will put away an object that has been out for a while, supporting a particular purpose, and replace it with another that has greater salience for the current circumstances of their lives. Objects that are put away are almost never discarded, however. They are carefully packed away in the expectation of future need.

We also noticed some commonalities across our participants in how objects are kept. In many instances, smaller items are nested within special containers, which are often keepsakes in themselves but which also contain other valued possessions. A special book, often a family Bible that shows the effects of handling by generations of women, might contain a collection of treasured letters from a friend, a special poem or card, or a needlepoint bookmark painstakingly made by a mother or grandmother. An ancient button box, thought to have originated with a great-great-grandmother, might contain buttons saved by generations of women in the same family. A cedar chest holds quilts, blankets, or handmade clothing, part of a female heritage of fine handicraft work. Objects that have been routinely used by a great-grandparent, a grandparent, a parent, or another special relative are particularly treasured. A piece of jewellery worn by a special aunt is kept wrapped with a photo in which she wore it; a pocket watch that shows signs of constant handling by a grandfather or grandmother might be taken out and gently caressed as the woman recalls what she knows or imagines about its owner. Favourite toys from a woman's childhood are kept, often with collections of her children's toys and art work, or cards they have made for her at school, or articles of baby clothing she and they have worn.

Whichever pattern a particular woman followed in the display and use of these objects, the objects themselves were likely to be of many different kinds, to serve many different purposes and to have many different meanings. Often the meaning of a particular object is completely unrecognizable to anyone but the woman who keeps it and knows the stories it holds. The possessions in a "museum" home, for example, function as a visible diary, but one that is written in a private code. Some objects might appear to have obvious meanings – the photos of children, parents, and grandparents, reflecting the pleasures of family life and a woman's knowledge of the history of her family across generations, for example. But such objects also contain meanings and memories that are invisible to the uninitiated observer. A photo of a much-loved brother, dead at the age of eighteen and indistinguishable from the photos of a woman's adolescent children, might contain a story of grief or inspiration. A small square red rock, placed inconspicuously on a mantelpiece where it can be easily overlooked by a visitor, speaks to a woman of the many pots of stew she made for her two daughters as she struggled, in near poverty, to raise them on her own. Kept visible to her, it provides constant affirmation of her strength and endurance, and of the love between her daughters and herself, created by their shared hardship. She looks at it each day and tells herself, "If I can do that, I can do anything."

One of the central purposes and functions of these women's collections is the preservation of a personal and a family history. Most women showed us artefacts that spanned generations of family. Often these were fragile, delicate things that had been cared for with great skill and patience so that they survived their many relocations and changes of ownership over the years. The fact that such memorabilia of ordinary lives exist at all confirms the time, effort, and care taken by generations of women to preserve them and to pass them on.

Some of the stories we heard were descriptive of what Di Leonardo (1987) calls women's "kinwork." Kinwork, she suggests, includes activities such as

> the conception, maintenance, and ritual celebration of cross-household kin ties, including visits, letters, phone calls, presents, cards to kin; the organization of holiday gatherings; the creation and maintenance of quasi-kin relations; decisions to neglect or to intensify particular ties; the mental work of reflection about all these activities; and the creation and communication of altering images of family and kin vis-à-vis the images of others. A ... conscious strategy, ... crucial to the functioning of kinship systems ... a source of women's autonomous power ... [a] possible primary site of emotional fulfillment and, at times, ... the vehicle for actual survival and/ or political resistance. (442–43)

Such kinship processes are not casual: they are organized, purposeful, and deliberate.

Sandra Martin (1992), writing in *Canadian Living* magazine, tells another wonderful story about an instance of the preservation of one woman's artefacts. Describing the events that occurred when, after her grandmother's death, her aunts and uncles gathered to dispose of the artefacts of their mother's life, she says:

[The] men in the family built a bonfire to burn the trash. While they were hauling out the "rubbish," my aunts were braving the flames to haul it back in again. Now, whenever I visit my aunties on the Island, some little piece of this "trash" gets solemnly passed on to me. This ritual makes me part of a female continuum that is older than Confederation, for some of the family treasures came in chests from the Isle of Skye more than 150 years ago. (124)

She recalls that her father, after her own mother died, sent her a box her mother had kept for her, labelled "Sandra's youth." Opening it, she discovered "among the books and trinkets a kind of umbilical link with my dead mother, a nostalgic message from parent to child." She then went on to sort through pieces of her children's art-work that she had kept "for them," and discovered that

the process was wrenching. My memory bank was clicking like a slide projector: every piece represented a child's stumble toward self-definition. Gradually, it dawned on me that the pictures I put in the keep file were the ones that meant something to *me*, not necessarily to my children. Here I was ... being the archivist of my children's past, the keeper of their memories. (124)

The process of keeping these collections exemplifies women's efforts to remember and value each other as individuals, to connect the generations by treasuring items that reflect the family's life over time, exemplifying the family's continuing values and commitments. Safeguarding these objects honours individual accomplishments; describes the character of the women and, less often, the men whom the items memorialize; and documents important moments in women's own lives and in the lives of the women who came before and will come after them. Taken collectively, these objects contain a women's history, a history of what women have found important. They document a women's ontology, or what Whitbeck (1984) describes as

> a coherent form of cooperative activity ... that not only aims at certain ends but creates certain ways of living and develops certain characteristics (virtues) in those who participate and try to achieve the standards of excellence peculiar to that practice. The ... core practice is that of the (mutual) realization of people. (65)

The history embodied in these objects is not one of global events, wars, politics, or great success or failure on the public stage – though stories of such events may form part of the lore surrounding particular objects. Rather, the history written in them provides the biographies and autobiographies of ordinary women; it is a record of their personal struggles, their "stories to live by." It is a history of emotion as much as a history of events. As important as these objects are for preserving historical, biographical, and autobiographical information, this is only one of the many purposes they serve in the lives of women. They facilitate women's practice of re-experiencing particular events and the emotions attached to them, thus affirming the reality of women's experiences and allowing them to revisit special moments in time.

Many of the objects women keep as reminders of events or persons in their own lives were received from other people. They are especially valued when the gift represents the giver's awareness of the unique needs and character of the child or young woman she once was. A doll, carefully kept for almost eighty years, prompts a story about how it was once damaged by a baby brother and then mended by a father who understood its meaning to his daughter and went to great trouble to be sure it was returned to her "as good as new." A painting chosen for a woman by her close friend confirms the friend's intimate knowledge of her personality and aesthetic preferences.

These objects represent the woman's experience of having been known, loved, understood, and valued, and are used to reinforce a sense of personal worth and to affirm the characteristics most admired by those who have loved her. Holding such an object, she can contemplate the value of those relationships to her, feeling again the support and care of those who have been most important in her life.

Many participants also keep a special item or two that they acquired when they first had money of their own. These items seem to be cherished as celebrations of freedom and independence and as reminders of their developing tastes and interests. They are about the heady experience of beginning to develop a separate life, one based on self-knowledge and relatively free of the influence of others.

A piece of art, purchased at considerable cost relative to a very small income, a small keepsake from a first trip taken without a parent, a decorative object purchased for a first apartment, or even the keys to a woman's first car might serve as this kind of reminder.

The objects women keep are not only those that allow them to revisit happy times. Keepsakes are used to mark progress toward overcoming a difficult experience or to represent personal tragedies and the lessons that have been learned from them. A marriage that ended in divorce might be represented in a ring, melted down and recast to symbolize an aspect of a new life. A special book may have been used to help when, as a child, its owner retreated to her room and tried to drown out the anger of an alcoholic father by burying herself in its pages.

Some objects were of special interest to us since they act as powerful triggers for evoking unresolved grief. They represent and contain psychological "work in progress" and facilitate the expression of feelings that, once evoked, might facilitate the woman's understanding of long-ago events. This kind of memento is kept long after the pain it contains has been worked through, so that its owner can see "how far I have come" and remind herself of new meanings and understandings. Some objects thus become tokens of both failure and growth, of strength and achievement, while others continue to provoke sadness or anger about a life that might have been, a spoiled future, or the loss of an aspect of self that has yet to be reclaimed. The remaining grief or anger can be shut away with the artefact and taken out at times when its owner feels able to work on the issues it embodies.

Still other objects are used to reconstruct a total picture of a place and a time remarkable for its sensory completeness and its power to give comfort. Thus, a small china matchbox evokes recollections of the child helping in the kitchen; the shelf on which the matchbox was always kept; the smells and sounds of her mother's cooking; the music playing; the patterns of bowls, wallpaper or tile; and the conversations overheard. Others conjure up an image of a loved person – a grandparent, father, mother, husband, friend, or child, now lost or absent – or even of the woman herself at another point in time.

Most women also save items from their husbands' or their children's lives – things that they think might one day be important or interesting for their children to have. Their intention is usually to preserve these items so that the child will have a record of her life that will let her, in her turn, revisit special childhood moments, special objects or achievements. Toys and articles of clothing often form part of this record and are kept by the mother long after the child is grown and living elsewhere. When we asked about the appropriate time for giving these items to the child, most women remarked that they would do so when they saw evidence that the items would be cared for or that the child "really valued them." In the case of items that are being kept for sons, this moment is almost always postponed until the son has married and the objects can be entrusted to his wife. Some particularly treasured items cannot be parted with at all and will be accounted for in

a will or by a verbal arrangement with the child: "When
I am gone, you can have this." We often heard about conversations between a grandmother and her granddaughter,
for instance, in which a particular object was discussed, its
meanings shared, and plans made for it to be passed on to
the granddaughter when her grandmother died.

Just as the meanings embedded in their possessions vary,
so do the women's patterns of using these objects. Some
are the focus of a mother-child ritual of story-telling, usually about the child's life; others are used as *aides memoir* or
"gates to memory" that help the woman to revisit an event
or time in her life, to affirm an important value, to take
comfort in a difficult time, or to clarify a current problem. Some act entirely as reminders of heritage, rooting
a woman in the generations of women who might have
contributed to her collection, while others memorialize a
love affair or an extraordinary friendship in her own life.
When we were helped to understand the meanings of the
various displayed objects, when the private code of the
woman's possessions was shared, the sources of meaning in
her life and the stories of the experiences that formed her
were clearly revealed.

In writing this book we have tried to demonstrate, by
telling women's stories about their treasured objects, the
similarities and the diversity in the patterns of what objects
are kept, how they are kept, and the ways in which they
contribute to the woman's sense of self in the past and the
present. We have tried to highlight the diverse uses of the
possessions, but also, by focusing on individual women, to
show how each woman's collection tells about her and

about what is meaningful in her life. We believe that each
woman is the authority on her own life, that if we listen
to and believe in a woman's stories, we will hear her own
version of herself – a version that pulls her life together into
a narrative that sustains her and connects her to others.

Acknowledgements

We first thank the women who shared their time,
their thoughts, and their treasures with us. They gave us
so much, so kindly, and impressed us once again with the
strength and accomplishments of "ordinary" women. Our
families too deserve thanks for their presence, their interest,
and their unremitting support. To each other, a thank you
for colleagueship and friendship, and a sigh of relief!

We are grateful to Joyce Hildebrand, who did a
fabulous job of copy-editing this book, and to John King,
production editor at the University of Calgary Press, who
expedited its publication.

*E*very woman's story is a story of creating herself. The act of keeping a particular thing is always an act of self-definition in which the object represents both an aspect of the self and a way into self-knowledge. Who was I? Who am I now? What is my heritage? What do my experiences tell me about myself? An object anchors its owner in time and place, and positions her as a member of a community or a network of relationships. Possessions tell of friendships that have been central to a woman's developing sense of her self, make connections across generations, allow her to revisit her childhood self, and reassure her by confirming who she is.

Annette clearly demonstrates the role of objects in the development and maintenance of a stable self-definition. Annette described herself as a pack rat who saves many things that represent the important relationships in her life and her own growth and development. At the beginning of our conversation, she told us that she "didn't know what to bring and what to leave behind. There are so many things that are a part of my mother and myself, a part of my daughter and myself. And I had to stop and think about Dad, and my friends. So, I just brought a bunch of different things!" Staying within the suggested five or six items was impossible for Annette. Listening to her, we were easily able to form a picture of her as a child, as a young woman, and as the woman she is now at forty, a divorced mother of an adolescent daughter, a white blue-collar worker, and a resident of a small mountain community. She treats these objects very much as a diary, using them to help her revisit herself at various times in her life, to hold up her image in her mind's eye, to smile, sometimes ruefully, and to move on to follow the continuing thread of her experiences.

We began with a button box that had belonged to Annette's grandmother, and possibly to her great-grandmother.

I love to go through this button box. It's not anything that's much done in today's world, but it was one of my favourite pastimes as a child. My mother and I loved to go and grab Grandma's button box, spread the buttons out all over the table, count them and organize them and so on. We are all very tactile, Grandmother and Mother and me; we love shape and size and texture and colour, just the pleasure of it. We all knit and crochet, and we have clothed our families by going to second-hand shops, bringing something home, washing it, taking it apart and remaking it into something totally different. My mom talks about Grandma going to some store and picking up an old coat in the Dirty Thirties, bringing it home and taking it apart and sending her to school with a brand new coat – it's that sense of value. Use and re-use, and making do with what you have.

Annette described herself through her identification with the values and the strength of her grandmother and her mother. She understands her own ability to make do, a skill she has had to call on often in her life, as their legacy. Her pride in them is clear. From them, she learned her positive self-definition and her sense of readiness to meet whatever life sends.

Unlike many women in our study, Annette also draws on the heritage from her male relations to strengthen her sense of herself as capable, adaptable, and enduring. A knitted baby toque contains the story of the grandfather she loved so deeply:

> My grandfather was a great, tall strapping man, six foot plus, a ramrod straight gentleman, born in England. Through all my childhood, I don't remember seeing him smile. He was that stiff-upper-lip British, strait-laced man. Well, in my teens my grandmother died and we brought Grandpa back to live with our family. We square danced, and we always brought kids home; the house was always full of teenagers and Grandpa didn't have much choice but to bend and loosen up. The last few years I was at home, I'd go to kiss him goodnight and I'd grab a pillow and beat him severely about the head and shoulders. He'd laugh so hard, and it was such a freeing thing for us. Anyway, when I was pregnant with my daughter, we were in Nova Scotia, and Grandpa knit this pink and blue baby toque so that he would have contributed to the baby's warmth and well-

being. He made two, really, but I gave one to my brother when he had his baby a year ago. I had heard that Grandpa knit, but it's one of those things that you kind of only half believe. Apparently he used to knit socks during the Boer War and the First World War, just to keep himself from going bonkers from inactivity. Mom said that, at home, Grandpa would sit in the evening and knit toques and scarves and mittens. To me, it's just wonderful, this straight, straight man doing something as delicate as this. My mother and stepfather gave me a cedar chest when I graduated from high school, and I keep it in there.

A beautiful black-and-white photograph shows Annette's mother as a child, standing beside her own seated mother, Annette's grandmother, each with an arm around the other and both smiling into the camera.

The neat thing is, the child's face is my daughter's; if you look at my daughter, you see Mother as a child. I love to see that, just the genetic carry-through. I like to tease my nieces that we're from Mars and that we were all cloned. The same person standing there at different ages. I have a photo of my daughter in that same dress that Mom was wearing in that picture. It's tucked away in my cedar chest, carefully saved by Grandma, then by my mother, and now by me.

Annette's pride in coming from generations of strong women is clear as she talks of her resemblance to her mother and her grandmother, and of her daughter's continuation of their line. "My grandmother should have lived now," she told us. "She'd have been like Margaret Thatcher. She had that strength and purposefulness of character. Very strong opinions and stubbornness that keeps showing up through these past three generations."

Annette next showed us an intricate Victorian hair wreath, woven with pinecones and flowers and mounted in a large glass-fronted box. The wreath is made from Annette's great-aunts' hair, three different colours and textures. On the back of the frame is a small label saying "Hair of three sisters, Laura, Rose and Kate." She remembers very clearly gazing at the wreath when it hung on her grandmother's bedroom wall. It allows her to revisit her childhood self, to reconstruct and confirm her connection to the skills of generations of women in her family.

From the time I was little, I could look at Grandma's things, but I wasn't allowed to touch. I would be standing with my hands firmly clasped behind my back, looking at all the beautiful things in the china cabinet and saying, "Mustn't touch, mustn't touch." I used to stand on her bed and look at this. It always intrigued me, how delicate it was – I don't think I knew that it was hair then. Later on, Mom says Grandma found it in an attic on Grandpa's farm, pitched in a corner behind a box. She brought it down and asked Grandpa to put it in a frame. He built this box and put this satin in it. So, it hung at Grandma's house. On our visit for their fiftieth wedding anniversary, she asked each of us what we wanted: "Out of everything in the house, what do you want?" I took the gramophone first, which still sits in my dining room, but when my next turn came around, I said that I wanted the hair wreath. I loved it. It is so beautiful and intricate, and it is a shame nobody knows how to do that anymore. I am trying to get my Uncle Bill to bring me out a picture of the three sisters that I can tuck it into an envelope on the back.

Stories about rescuing important objects that had been unthinkingly discarded by the men in their families came up everywhere. It seems that men do not usually understand the importance of these historical items and women's efforts to hold onto the connections they represent. The women themselves were often uncertain whether they should value them and were confused about why they kept them, but they saved them nonetheless. Thinking about why her many things are so important to her, Annette recalled the way her family lived when she was a child.

We always moved a lot, and I think bringing these things tied us all together, kept us from being scattered. We spent one school year in four different schools, so you didn't get to know anybody for very long. Keeping these things is like a security blanket. It doesn't matter where you go, as long as you've got these things. If they are there, then it's home.

Possessions are a portable self that provides security when the world is in flux. When Annette's family finally settled down and stopped moving, their friends got together and had a house-warming party for them. A woman friend made a special cake and decorated it with a tiny log cabin made from dowels, with a shredded pinecone roof, a grove of red wool trees with green trunks, and a bush made of green icing. Some tiny people and a dog were meant to represent Annette's family. "It was finally some place of our own where we didn't have to pack up and move again. So I kept the little house, and the people and the trees, all wrapped up in cloth and tucked in the cedar box. Twenty-eight years later, here they still are."

Annette's cedar box is a treasure trove for herself and her children. Sometimes an object is not taken out for years. When at last she takes it out, it is a surprise for Annette, and an invitation to revisit a part of her life. "Twenty years after you've looked at them last, they can bring that moment back so closely, and you remember every detail: the fence, the farm, even the guys at the party peeing outside and encountering the electric fence! It is like a little gift to myself."

Annette's story then took a sadder turn, reminding us that women's self-definition through relationships requires that we memorialize both happy and unhappy memories. Stories of having been loved and stories of tragedy, deception, and despair both need remembering and retelling. A few years after Annette's family had finally settled into their farm, Annette's father left to be with another woman, her brother's girlfriend at the time.

Previous to that, I had always had long hair, so long that I could braid it and tuck it into my pants. Every night I would take my hair down and Dad would sit down and brush my hair for me – it was our evening ritual. When he left, he left with my brother's girlfriend, which was really heartbreaking and difficult to deal with. I was about fourteen, and I was just sick about it. So, I put my hair into two braids and I chopped it off. This one that is still in the chest, I put away, and the second one I sent to my father. I guess it was pretty much "How dare you leave me?" Just to let him know how much it hurt. I felt so betrayed. I couldn't put it in words to him. The connection we had now was so tenuous, if I said anything it might be broken totally. It would have been like the last thread being cut.

Afterwards, he would come and take the boys for the summer, work with them and do things with them, but he never took me. I always thought that it was because I looked so much like Mom that it made him feel bad. It wasn't until I was in my early twenties and I had a major crisis that Dad and I finally talked. It wasn't that he couldn't stand the sight of me because I hurt him looking like Mom, it was just that he couldn't handle my pain. He didn't want to see it, so he didn't, he couldn't. When he died, he had spent his last six months living with my daughter and me. He had cancer. But I just can't seem to get rid of this braid, I just have to hang onto it. It is almost like a watch, a caution.

Annette's charm bracelet, which we looked at next, was given to her when she was in grade seven and is a history of her life in miniature. Three tiny sets of handcuffs represent Annette's three brothers, one of whom was a foster brother taken in by Annette's mother when he was abused by his father. All three young men joined the military police. Her eldest brother added a Star of David to represent his service on the Golan Heights. Sorting through the charms, we saw a representation of Niagara Falls, a golden "18" charm, and a ski boot and crutch standing for a boyfriend who took her skiing for the first time and abandoned her at the top of the hill. A man in free fall represents a skydiver boyfriend and is followed by a high school diploma, a fleur-de-lis representing a year spent in Quebec, and a golden "21." Each charm has a detailed story attached to it; each is a chapter in the coded diary of Annette's life.

At the end of our interview, Annette showed us the wedding dress she made for herself.

When I was a teenager I started doing things like macramé, tie-dye, anything. I suppose I adopted some of my mom's ways of making things. So I made my own wedding dress. My mom and I made three bridesmaids dresses for my sister, my best friend, and my fiancé's sister. My mom made the cake, someone else iced it for her. When it came to the morning for my wedding, my mom and sister said, "Annette, where's your veil?" I didn't have a veil; I just had a dress, my new white shoes, and a bouquet. They said

I needed a veil. I was getting married in a Catholic church. So my mom went to the bottom drawer of her dresser and found my confirmation veil, the one we all used when we got confirmed. It seemed to be enough, except when we were little girls we wore it with a headband of cotton flowers, and that had faded and died. I didn't know what to do. I grabbed a doily off Mom's dresser, folded it in half, and got married with a doily on my head!

The story is about how much Annette values her resourcefulness and her ingenuity, and about her mother's dresser as the repository of sentimental and historical objects from childhood. Many other women, like Annette, spoke of their connections to the generations of women who preceded them and told us how they modeled themselves after female relatives whose possessions they treasured. An eighty-year-old woman, Dorothy, told us the story of a small gold ring, passed down to her through her great-grandmother, grandmother, and mother. Her grandmother, one of four sisters, was given the ring on the death of her own mother because she had cared for her through a final, protracted illness. Ethel, the original owner of the ring and Dorothy's great-grandmother, worked until her marriage, "not because she needed to, but because she wanted to. Being a schoolteacher was the only option open to her." Once she married, she stopped teaching because, "as my grandmother still says, 'it is not ladylike to work when you are married.'" For Dorothy, the content of this message is not particularly important. Rather, the ring reflects a heritage of principled lives, lives based on adherence to beliefs about "proper" behaviour and the capacity to choose and follow through on commitments. It represents a woman's heritage of competence, care, and commitments.

My mother was going to inherit this china. She always wanted pretty things….

Diane, too, spoke with great pride of her pioneering grandmother, with whom she identifies as an adult.

This beautiful old china – as long as I can remember, when we went to Grandma's house, we'd have dinner on this china. My mother was going to inherit this china. She always wanted pretty things and never had them, and she died about a year before my grandmother did. I use it a lot if we have company, and I had a special china cabinet built for it. I have very, very strong connections with my grandmother. She was a pioneer. When I turned thirteen she took me on my first plane trip. We went to where my mother was born. Grandma always lived with us when I was a little girl. She was a real blessing for my mother. She always lived in the same city, and I visited her a lot.

Janet proudly told us the story of her collection of Dickens novels. When her parents had to stop attending their local Dickens Club, they gave her their whole set of Dickens. Here again is a story that illustrates how a woman's sense of herself was formed by inheriting a prized possession and how receiving the gift gave her an enhanced persona in her own eyes.

Oh, it's beautiful, and I love little hard cover books like this. They also gave me a couple of volumes on Dickens himself. My mom went back to finish her English degree when she was in her sixties. She found out about the Dickens Society through one of the professors there. Mom and Dad both really, really like Dickens, so they went for about fifteen years. The books represent an aspect of them that I really treasure. They passed on this love of reading. There were always books around the house, and reading was as natural as breathing. And when they gave me the books they said, "It is your turn." They meant, my turn to take care of these books and, when I am through with them, to pass them on.

She told us, too, about an aunt who was a special mentor and whose life story fuels her belief in her own capacity to continue growing as she ages.

This photo was a graduation gift from one of my aunts. When I graduated from university, she gave me a hundred dollars and told me, "You go out and get whatever you want, and I don't want it to be practical. No books this time!" I saw this photo, and I thought, "This is it!" My aunt went back to university in her fifties and then went on and got her Master's in philosophy when she was seventy. I come from a family of late bloomers. She's still going strong. She's eighty-four and very involved with the Women's University Club.

Similarly, Paddy keeps a pair of tiny gloves that she wore as a child.

These gloves were purchased for me by my mother, and they symbolize my mother very much to me. I actually wore these as a child. They are a very soft, almost kid-like flannel. They are real grown-up gloves, but for a baby's hand. These just seem to symbolize my mother, not just that she taught me good manners, but to speak well, and that there was a right way of doing things. I must have hated having these put on when I was little. It must have taken ages to get them on and off. So I have a mental picture of my mother very patiently working these gloves on.

Sadly, a daughter sometimes remains unaware of the achievements of her mother or grandmother until after she dies and things are found among her belongings that tell stories the daughter has never heard before. Robin, for example, found many "secret" things in a plastic bag in her mother's dresser drawer at the nursing home where

she died. Looking through them, she felt better able to
understand both her mother and herself.

> They were all inside a big envelope marked "treas-
> ures." There was her diploma from nursing school,
> photos of her class, and three copies of a speech she
> had given when she was valedictorian. And it was
> only looking at this that I discovered that she was a
> brilliant woman with many academic awards. There
> were newspaper clippings about her too. I knew that
> Mother had been a nurse, that she was the public
> health nurse for northern Manitoba, did things like
> take trappers' wives with new babies back to trap-
> pers' cabins by using canoes and Indian paddlers,
> and all this kind of romantic stuff. But I was really
> surprised that she had kept these, that she was still
> so connected with the career that was in fact fairly
> short-lived. It helped to explain to me why, at cer-
> tain times in her life, she was very, very discontented.
> How frustrated she must sometimes have been.

The envelope also contained Robin's mother's nursing
apron and a collection of letters. One of those letters bore
the date 1905 and had been sent by Robin's mother at
age four to her own father when he was in hospital with
typhoid; another contained the announcement of her
engagement to Robin's father. A third letter was written
by Robin's great-aunt Emily, who was in her eighties at
the beginning of the Second World War. In this letter,
she said that she "flatly refused to be evacuated from her

cottage on the cliffs at Dover, that no one was going to
get rid of her and her cottage." Robin's new knowledge of herself as a descendant of strong, wilful women
inspired the confidence that saw her become a brilliant
scholar late in her life.

Charlie keeps a special brass bowl that was left to her
by her great-grandmother and that was a presence in her
own childhood.

> Where we lived, we had a huge breakfast counter.
> There were six kids in my family. And this sat right in
> the middle. It was full of stuff, matches and other bits
> and pieces. But the history of it was that my great-
> grandmother brought it with her from England.
> They pioneered in the Kootenay Mountains. So it
> has a long history of my growing up, plus it connects
> me to the women before me.

She also showed us a tea set that her great-grandmother
won for having the best gladiolas at a rural fair.

> My mother gave me this when my great-grand-
> mother died. I was just so excited, so thrilled to have
> it. I was only a small child, and I wasn't allowed to
> play with it, but my mom told me it was mine and it
> was kept displayed in the cabinet. I would say to her,
> "This is mine, right, Mom?" I felt such a strong
> connection to my great-grandmother.

Many women have keepsakes from the lives of grandmothers or great-grandmothers whom they have never met, and they have woven mythical personalities around these ancestors to provide the missing sense of continuity. These women often invent a character for a female ancestor, using relics from her life to conjure up a complete persona, one that epitomizes some of the characteristics they wish to own for themselves. They are very clear that they have never met the woman in question, have never been told much about her. Yet they talked of the pleasure it gives them to speculate about what she may have been like and then of modeling themselves after her.

Sometimes these fictional ancestors satisfy a nostalgic longing for a romanticized past: a world of gloves, hats, and manners that symbolize elements of a traditional femininity that the women we interviewed longed for. These mythic women represent a missing piece of the self, a romantic femininity common to myths shared by women of different classes, races, and ethnicity. These myths are about being a woman in white, North American culture – they are about the ideal of delicacy, of being looked after and dressed in lace and silk, an ideal that is now, and probably always has been, notably absent from most women's experience. Robin, for example, treasures her mother's trousseau lingerie as an aspect of her mother's femininity. She knows that these things were entirely impractical because the first years of her mother's marriage were spent living in a tent in the bush. "My mother was one of a group of seven white women who were permitted to go to Churchill in the winter of 1930 because they had married men who were working there. But when my mother got pregnant, she had to leave." Still, the lingerie is a poignant reminder of her mother's feminine side and a stark contrast with the realities she lived.

Other mythical grandmothers are developed as models or examples of particular virtues to which women themselves aspire. For Paddy, the re-invented figure was her paternal grandmother. Paddy's father gave her his mother's pocket watch, engraved with the grandmother's initials, after she died. The watch is clearly a much-used object, showing the wear that comes from daily handling. Paddy likes to think of her grandmother holding the watch in her palm and running her thumb repeatedly across its silver finish. Doing so allows her to narrow a gap between herself and her grandmother that could never be closed while she lived.

I didn't have a very close relationship with my grandmother. I always felt that she wasn't that crazy about me. We had a prickly, kind of uneasy relationship. I got the feeling that she liked boys better than girls; she always liked my brother, I think, better than me, but in the long run it doesn't matter. I feel closer to her having this watch that was hers. All these years later, I feel closer to her than I did when she was alive. We have a connection. This is the connection – this beautiful watch.

The watch now suggests the ways in which Paddy may aspire to be similar to her grandmother, whom she has re-created as a woman of great integrity, stern but loving, even if only in her own imagination: a "plain, upright woman, who didn't have much jewellery or fancy things." Paddy is comforted and inspired by defining herself as part of a continuum that includes this grandmother.

Ann showed us a talisman doll she made herself from scraps of things on her own dresser. It represents one she remembers from a fairy tale about a girl whose mother gives her a little doll to put in her pocket so she won't get lost when she is away from home. Whenever the girl puts her hand in the pocket and touches the doll, "she feels her mother's strength and wisdom, and she finds out what is the right thing to do." The doll, Ann said, "reminds me to trust my own intuition, to trust my judgment," and it connects her to a mythical mother she never knew but whom she can imagine is guiding her.

Many women told us about visiting the lives of female ancestors through their possessions. Knowing, or inventing, ancestors helps them know who they themselves are. Sometimes, though, such mementos also tell a woman who she wants not to be. Not all of the memories of women from other generations are positive. Reminiscing over the possessions of female ancestors can also provide an opportunity to draw morals about traps to avoid, to learn lessons about the consequences of dependence, or to reject a particular version of femininity.

Sharon used possessions that belonged to her aunt Vera, her mother, and her grandmother as models for "how not to deal with men." Her mother, in love with one man and pregnant by another, was obliged to marry the father of her child and remained unhappily married to him for the rest of her life. Her aunt Vera, her mother's sister who was always around when Sharon was taken to visit her grandmother and who was an "extra grandmother" to her, was "cheated of her virginity" by a soldier she thought she had married. When she applied for the spouse's allowance after he went overseas, she found that he already had a wife and children. It was a family tragedy, especially since Vera was very beautiful and could have had her choice of many more suitable men. Both Vera and Sharon's grandmother subsequently went "from man to man," usually becoming involved in common-law arrangements that never lasted long. Sharon drew from their stories the lesson that women can waste their lives by being vulnerable to men's duplicity and by centering their lives around their relationships with men.

Sharon showed us a photo of herself from when she was in the Air Force. "I was miserable at home. Mom and Dad lived separate lives and Mom constantly talked against him to us." She resolved not to be a housewife like her mother, but, despite the best of intentions, ended up in an unhappy marriage herself. She next showed us a sewing machine she had bought. "The sewing machine was an admission that I was resigned to being a housekeeper, I think. Until I got that machine I felt like an individual. Once we moved to Sydney and I became a mother, my fate was sealed." In contrast to the sewing machine, Sharon treasures her computer, the symbol of her eventual escape from domesticity.

Many women's treasured possessions also speak of the role of friendships in developing and anchoring a sense of self. Most often, these friendships are with other women. They are long lasting, intense relationships that show what is possible in family life. Tracey showed us a picture of her close friend Tara, her childhood confidante. Tracey's home life was tenuous and difficult. One of the ways she brought stability to herself and developed a sense of her own possibilities was by "practically living at Tara's." She viewed Tara as "my adopted sister." She accepted Tara's values about the importance of doing well in school and being a person of integrity. Tara was unlike her "real" sisters, who disliked school, did poorly, and focused their energies mostly on being popular with boys.

Aimee, a young African-Irish woman, talked about a photograph taken by a man with whom she had a special friendship. He was "one of the first people who helped me dream about things that I wanted, helped me evaluate and push my vision of myself and of what I wanted to do." He took the photo in Thailand. It is a black-and-white image of two children, one carried on the other's back. It hangs in Aimee's living room and reminds her of a special relationship and of the importance of pushing herself to be fully herself.

Childhood possessions are also used as a means of knowing the self. Revisiting one's self as a child soothes women in distress and clarifies decisions they are in the process of making. Tracey showed us the Lego sets she

A best friend's slippers

received as a child and told us how she continues to use them to relax and distract herself. Barbara showed us the drums she has been playing since she was three years old, a set of bongos passed on to her by her father, which she will pass on to her daughter. Playing her drums "has always been a very emotional, feeling thing for me. I've always loved rhythm and dancing. I've been a crazy dancing fool ever since I was little. Rhythm is the basis of all music, and the feelings of vibration behind it puts me in touch with

Remnant from a dress-up box – trying on selves

who I really am inside." Her talent for drumming is part of her sense of herself as essentially musical and acts as a way to focus on herself, to take her talent seriously, and to connect her to her mother, who was also "an absolute wizard on drums."

Eve, now past eighty, showed us a doll with a porcelain face, gold hair, a burgundy dress, and a white crinoline given her by her father on her eighth birthday. She learned to knit so that she could make sweaters, hats, and booties for the doll from her mother's leftover yarn. Her love of knitting has been a life-long source of pleasure, and she keeps the doll and its knitted clothes for the continuity with her childhood self that it offers.

Annette, like many other women, showed us a religious object that represents her capacity for moral strength and a life of principle and self-discipline. Most often, such objects no longer carry a religious connotation. Rather, they connect the adult woman to her childhood self. Annette treasures a rosary, a reminder that she was a very devout young girl growing up in the Catholic church.

> I used this many times. I left the church at the age of eighteen, almost thirty years ago now, and yet I have never thrown it away. I think it defines something about who I was, who I am. When I think about myself now, I haven't really changed at all. I'm still that same young girl, still capable of devotion.

Donna showed us an illustrated Bible she received at about age eight.

For years and years I was so introverted... It was so comforting

I was a very fearful child and very sickly. I had rheumatic fever and allergies and all kinds of chronic problems. I remember once I was really sick and off school for about three weeks, and my mother gave me this Bible and I started reading it. I memorized a lot of Bible verses. This meant a lot to me. For years and years I was so introverted and fearful, I went to this Bible and read it a lot. It was so comforting.

The Bible is signed "Mother," and dated June 16, 1957. Donna also has the old set of Book of Knowledge that she read over and over while she was sick at home and her mother had to be at work. "I learned to read when I was very young – four or five years old – and I read it a lot, because I wasn't allowed to go out and play with other children much. These were my lifeline." Her parents also gave her a set of three books on the history of religion on her fourteenth birthday.

I've always felt that I was a thinker, and I've always felt that there was a place for me in the world, but I didn't know what it was. I felt like a bird in a cage; I just didn't fit in somehow. I didn't fit in my family, didn't fit at school. I just didn't fit. And I always thought there was a connection somewhere between all the religions in the world, and these books helped me to see the connections. It opened a lot of doors in my mind and made me realize that somehow I was on the right track, searching.

Not fitting in, feeling alien was a theme we heard often. Annette also keeps a Mao button from her student days.

I think the retail value is about thirty-nine cents! It's not worth a lot. I picked it up at a student rally when I was eighteen and thought I was quite radical. I suppose I wore this for about a year on my coat and I realize now that, like a lot of teenagers, I wore it like a badge – being a rebel, that I was not quite following the crowd. It reminds me of how I was.

She also showed us her wedding ring, with her ex-husband's blue birthstone in the center and her garnets on either side. She hasn't worn the ring for many, many years, but she keeps it because it symbolizes the nature of the marriage.

The significance of my garnets being around his blue stone was that somehow I was keeping him safe, that I was going to protect him. I had a very maternal relationship with my husband. I mothered him. He needed it, and I was good at it. I'm not going to fight it anymore, or erase the past and say that it was wrong. I stopped wearing it years ago, but it is something I would never give away.

Peg keeps a collection of letters she wrote home while traveling, several old love letters exchanged between her and her husband, and old passports showing the record of their travels.

They make connections about relationships. They are memory keys, not for memory of particular events, but memories of other stages, not relationships with other people so much, but relationships with yourself – about being yourself. It really is a way of sort of reaching into your depths, into the core of who you are, of who you were. Looking back on these kinds of records gives you an opportunity to – I mean forgive yourself is not quite the right word, but almost lets you see yourself as if you were the parent of yourself.

Peg only rarely brings these things out from their box. Her life is busy, and she doesn't like to revisit them unless she has enough time to relive the experiences they describe. "I want to be able to read them sort of in a series, so that I get the feeling of them. Start at the beginning and read through. It's something I don't want to do for five minutes or ten minutes or whatever. I want to sort of wallow in them."

Nancy's childhood diaries serve a similar function:

A symbol of Peg's connection to her husband who sculpted the giraffe for her.

I kept diaries in earnest since I was very young. Most of what is in it is about my relationships – who likes me, who I like, does he like me? The agonies of adolescence and romance. I have to chuckle when I read these and remember. I used the diary, not just to keep track of things that happened, but also to sort things out. To define myself, because I find that a challenge. Like, "What am I like? What's important to me?" So it's not just what was happening, but what I was like, the types of things I was struggling with, the things I was excited about.

She also keeps old letters. One important letter was written to her fiancé by Nancy's best girlfriend, telling him about her friend. "I love this one in particular. It is beautifully written, and it really reminds me of who I am. It is sort of flattering, but I need to keep that. I need to be reminded of my positive qualities."

Holly showed us a small pair of leather booties that she wore as a child. They recall the reality of her own childhood and explain both her commitment to mothering her own

child and the depression she struggles with in her adult life.
Holly recalls that her mother always kept the shoes in her
dresser drawer – a drawer that fascinated Holly as a child
and that she went through frequently. For Holly, the shoes

> represent my infancy, which wasn't a real happy
> infancy, starting with a very traumatic birth. My
> mom and I were apart for twenty-four hours, and I
> think that because of that and because of the health
> problem I had – I was about eighteen months old and
> I was back in hospital. It was at that time when they
> didn't let parents stay with the child, and I have this
> image in my mind – I don't know if it's an actual
> memory, but an image of me in a white crib in this
> white, sterile room, and my mom looking in the
> window in the door and not being able to come in. I
> just – it makes me wild.

Holly understands her own adult problems and depression as originating in this traumatic separation from her
mother. Revisiting that time through contemplation of
the shoes reassures her that there are substantial reasons
for her depression. She can feel empathy for the child she
was, avoid judging herself or her mother in the present,
and be patient as she struggles to recover positive connections to her family.

Charlie told us about the elementary school report cards
she keeps and what they mean to her:

My grade one report card said — oh it is just scary to look back at what was done to us as women, because it said that I was over-confident, too self-assertive and stuff like that. And I can remember myself at that age — I was a bit talkative, but I did the work and I was very influenced by wanting people to approve of me. I was a bit of a slow reader — always good at comprehension, but it took me time to read. It's interesting that I still constantly feel insecure, sort of paranoid about time because I constantly feel that I don't have enough time to do it my way, the time that I need to be thorough.

She spoke, too, about a kachina doll that represents

a little bit the native blood part of me, but it also rep-resents a couple of things to do with my mom and to do with me as a ten- to twelve-year-old. I used to love needlework — I did this huge big needlework of a kachina, and I loved it. I had it in my room all through my teenage years, and I was really proud of it because it was a big piece for a young person to do. But it got lost — I don't know what happened to it. So about four years ago at the Native Arts Festival I went and they had this kachina silent auction. So I put a bid in and I got it, and that's where it came from.

Laurie keeps "the first thing I ever made — a pin cush-ion." It was made in grade two in England, when little girls were taught embroidery, knitting, and household skills from a very early age. "The next thing we made was an apron, which I had to embroider in writing. I would have made someone a good little wife if I had stayed in England a little longer!" Laurie also has a small book of sequential versions of an essay that she wrote in grade eight.

> I get such a kick out of reading these, and also the teacher's editorial comments. I had a wonderful teacher in grade eight, but for the most part I disregarded her suggestions and wrote the way I preferred. I think it is very representative of my personality. I really enjoy feeling the growth there. What a terrible writer and speller I was at the beginning of the year and the change by the end of the year.

This vision of herself as learning and growing, but also as resisting efforts to shape her in a particular way, especially efforts to clip her wings, is central to Laurie's definition of herself. "It makes me real to myself. An indomitable little person who made it."

Annette returns to her childhood, too, through an elaborate diary she began to keep when she was seven. In it, she kept a record of

> every concert I went to, every date I went on, every movie I saw – I can prove to my children exactly when I saw Jim Morrison and the Doors. I had this

sense when I was young, I suppose because we had so little, that whenever something did happen to me it was precious. I still have the ticket from when I went roller-skating. That may not be so significant to anyone else, but I only got to do that once in my life; I cherished my chances in life. And it provokes, reminds me of things. I keep a list of all the books I have read, and when I look at it, it serves as a reminder of everything else that was happening. As soon as I know what book I was reading, I know everything else.

Robin, too, keeps her "dolly trunk" from childhood. It contains all the things that were special to her as a child. It is a record of her life in small objects. A piece of chalk with classmates' names from high school, a letter from an uncle in Europe from just before the war, a Governor-General's Medal for achievement at school, photos of herself at different ages, an outfit her grandmother knit for one of the dolls Robin had as a child, her baby boots, childhood clothes that her mother kept for her and that Robin's own children later wore, and gloves her father gave her at her first daughter's birth – all are preserved together in this special trunk.

Alex showed us her travel journal from "the trip of a lifetime" when she was twenty-two. The diary is filled with her thoughts and feelings about the experiences she had with her friends, with scraps of paper she wrote on, and with postcards and other mementos of the trip.

There is lots of stuff in here – stuff that I really don't even want to read at times. Just because I can feel it in my gut when I'm reading it, you know? At first I was really, really homesick and I was like, "Why do I want to do this? This is crazy. I don't have any money, I'm starving, I miss my family, I miss my dad. I want to be home." And I hated the friend I was with most of the time, because, you know, you learn a lot about someone when you travel with them … so then I went through a real thing of, "What's wrong with me? Why can't I make friends? Why do I not like anybody?"

As painful as looking at these objects may be, Alex would never consider throwing them away. She will keep them and, with increasing age, will perhaps learn to see these events differently, to retain her pride in having endured very difficult times but to think differently about her fears and the ungenerous judgments she made about herself. Like the older women we spoke with, she will no doubt come to see these experiences as building blocks and look back on her unhappiness with a rueful smile and fond understanding.

Some women keep objects to commemorate these lessons learned about themselves or about living. Kate's grandfather's letters, one of which will appear later in this book, are lessons in living, in being a principled person, and in making the most of your abilities.

My grandpa's dealing with me was always a mixture of caring and making sure there was a lesson in there. Just a tone of caring, and always the message. It was guidance about him always expecting me to do my best. He expected a lot but the caring came through in his words too. He probably was sort of a woman's libber. He really did support women. He expected them to get busy and take care of themselves and design for themselves a good life, live it well, get to school, get an education, a career. I should be good, I should be applying myself.

Alex keeps a photo of a family friend who was killed by a plane propeller when Alex was about fourteen, and a copy of the poem she was asked to read at his funeral.

It was so hard, one of the hardest things I've ever done. But I had been like a daughter to him, and the rest of his family couldn't do it – it was just too much for them. For me, it is not only a memory of him. It is a memory of doing something that was so hard for me. Just not wanting to do it, not thinking I could do it, but getting through it, doing it. It was an obstacle that I had to face that I got through.

With the photo and the poem is a photo from a newspaper. "It's like pieces of a puzzle. Memories of him, our relationship, the kind of person he was, and the strength I needed to get through it." The collection reminds her, too, of her own strength.

Carole's scrapbook commemorates her years of work at a women's shelter. It includes photos of staff, their messages and cartoons; they assembled the memorial on the occasion of her retirement. She said, "It really encapsulates me." It also marks an important achievement that defines her – her lifelong work on behalf of abused women and their children, her skill at fundraising, the eventual building of a new shelter, and her commitment to improving women's lives by valorizing their strength and heroism.

Micheline looks at a brass sculpture of a mother and child, the mother swinging the child, leaning backward, her hair flying out.

[It was] the first piece of art that I really fell in love with. I'm sure that the reason I love it so much has to do with the maternal aspect of it, which is what my life has revolved around I think. For me, having children, being a mother was the only thing I was sure that I wanted to do. It just came from within, you know, from when I was very, very young. That was a gift I was going to give myself. I was going to have children when I grew up, but I wasn't going to get married. There were problems in my family with my father, who was an alcoholic. So men were not prominent in my life. To have a man in my life was not something I aspired to. In my mind, having children and getting married didn't go together at all.

The sculpture reminds her that she has learned very well the lessons that can be taught by mothering and the importance of following one's childhood sense of what will be central to one's later life. Micheline has remained true to her earliest knowledge of herself.

Other possessions demonstrate dramatic and self-conscious personal change. Some women knowingly undertook to re-create themselves. Sometimes they surpassed their own dreams. Dorothy showed us a plaque, awarded by the City of Calgary, honouring her as Volunteer of the Year. She won this award twice late in her life. Dorothy spent most of her middle years working, raising her children, and caring for her mother. After her mother died, she began volunteering as a foster-grandmother at a daycare and as a visitor at an elder care center. The plaque represents her achievement, certainly, but also serves as an emblem of activity. "[Being active] has kept me young," she said at eighty-two. "It's better than sitting in the house all day getting old." Women who don't get out, she said, "have no idea what the world is about now. They can't identify with the problems facing their children and grandchildren, because they are caught up in the past."

Charlie told of a crystal glass that she keeps as a reminder of a life she consciously gave up and of the passage of time that has allowed her to recover, and even to accept it.

Partly it is that I think it is totally beautiful, and it feels good. For a long time I didn't use this glass because it was connected to that whole past that I rebelled against. It was a wedding present. I think I

A crystal glass, "a reminder of a life she consciously gave up..."

had eight of them and now I have maybe two. This glass allows me to come back full circle and not be so rejecting and rebellious of what I grew up with. I went through lots and lots of abuse and struggles as a child – that was connected to a group of old, wealthy, abusive men. And so it was essential for me to leave that for a long, long time, and it took a long time for me to genuinely come back to myself. I always loved this glass for what it was, for how beautiful it was, but it was almost too painful to even think about the part of my life that it represents.

She now feels able, with the distance she has achieved, to come back to her pleasure in beautiful objects and in the kind of life she could not allow herself to experience for many years.

Charlie's re-creation of herself did not come easily. Nor did Donna's. She had earlier described herself as having been a very timid child, fragile, often ill and very obedient, but she also described a reinvention of herself that began in her mid-forties. She became determined to live more fully, to do things that the "timid child" would never have done, to open up her life to new possibilities. A symbol of her blossoming is a multi-coloured, tasselled cushion she received when she attended the International Women's Conference in Beijing.

It reminds me of the most wonderful experience in my life so far, aside from my children. I think I passed a lot of milestones. I had always been afraid of being in a large space with a lot of people – I'm afraid of airports – but a friend asked me to go. I wanted to go. My husband did not support the idea, and he is not a traveler at all. So I took the opportunity and went with her. I managed to survive the fifteen-hour flight, and the conference had thirty or forty thousand people at it, in a town about two hours drive from Beijing. I actually found my way there myself – I was forced into that because my friend was hurt, she had banged her head and had a concussion and had to stay in the room. But I wasn't going to miss anything.

And I feel that it was one of the big accomplishments of my life. And I went to a college there – my friend teaches at a college and this one was its sister college – and I talked to three hundred students without any warning that I was going to be on stage. I couldn't believe that I had done this. And I was just so enchanted with China. The people who were taking my friend and I around one night took us to a new restaurant where there was dancing.

They asked us to get up and dance. We were the only foreigners there, and they gave us each one of these cushions to put around our necks. When we got home, we gave talks in the community – I did it on my own for about sixteen different groups. Gave this talk on China – and this was the little girl who couldn't talk to anybody!

Maria has a "freedom necklace" that symbolizes her divorce and her subsequent new life. Her daughter made it for her to encourage her to re-create herself by using her new freedom in a positive way. She succeeded, though "it was a very hard thing. It wasn't as common to break up a marriage then, and I had tried to be the good girl all my life. It was very difficult to do, but I've never regretted it." Gerry keeps a journal that goes back only about ten years.

I write for nobody to read, but at the same time it's not just a journal where I enter what I did that day. It's more a response journal – my reactions to things that happened, feelings. It helps me to recognize the way things have changed; I look back and I am a different woman. I have been changed. Because of reading my journals, I can see where I've come from. It gives me a vantage point.

Barbara told of receiving a piece of art, a birthday gift from her mother for her fortieth birthday that symbolized her mother's acceptance of Barbara's decision to live openly

as a lesbian and her understanding of her daughter's love
of beauty. It marked a change in their relationship and a
confirmation of Barbara's desire to live more fully.

> Now, it is symbolic of the first time my mother had
> been to see me in over ten years. And of her accepting
> the fact that I am with Janet. We were at an art show
> together and we both admired this piece of work.
> And she looked at me and she said, "I'm buying you
> it for your birthday. I am not going to buy you a
> shovel. I know you always want practical things. But
> I'm going to buy you something you would never
> buy for yourself." Artwork is one of those things I
> love but could never afford. So it means a lot to me
> for all the underlying reasons.

Women's collections are an active part of their struggle
to acknowledge and maintain a strong sense of a separate
self. They do not just record events. By keeping and
interacting with these possessions, women confirm that
they are more than the sum of their various roles and
experiences. They look for themselves in the artefacts of
their own childhoods and their female ancestors' lives,
seeking to experience empathy with their early selves.
Achieving it, they go on to later items, using them to
continue an active process of life review. These objects
support women's consideration of critical relationships
and what can be learned from them. They help women
reconsider lifelong patterns and values, and add to their
knowledge of their own growth and development.

Women build, more or less successfully, on these understandings, marking moments of fragmentation, returning when necessary to particular items, seeking resolution of the problems they represent. Far from being mere hoarders or sentimental collectors, they are engaged in a process of creating, supporting, and renewing themselves through the stories they tell.

*T*he possessions that women showed us — well over a thousand of them, enough for a large museum exhibition — are unlikely to be displayed in any public place. They remain private, the possessions of women who share in the larger culture but are also marginal to it. They sometimes serve a public function among women, as a form of intergenerational conversation. Women who save things — and as far as we can tell that is every woman, since none of the many women we asked ever said that she had nothing to show us — become the archivists of their own and other people's lives. They create a women's history which, while it may not appear in textbooks or museums, informs how women live their lives; how they earn their livings; how they think; how they relate to their foremothers, their daughters, their friends and lovers. Women save possessions from their own lives and the lives of others to create both a personal and a collective narrative. As one of our participants, Paddy, put it, "This is who I am, and this is where I come from, and these are my people." The keepsakes comprise a story she tells herself and sometimes tells others. These stories create meaning for individual women, sustain the private culture of women, and encourage women to enter the public realm.

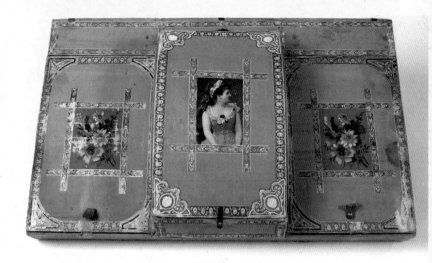

Inside my memory box

The artefacts, possessions, and treasures that women showed us were not lifted out of their environment as happens in museums. Rather, they are ongoing parts of our participants' lives, sometimes seamlessly blended into everyday life; sometimes serving almost ceremonial functions; often removed from their resting places to help women revisit the past, celebrate or mourn the present, or contemplate the future.

We have come to think of these collections less as discrete objects and more as emblems of women's realities. Initially, we thought that we would organize this book by type of object – family Bibles, journals, jewellery, and so on. But we soon understood that the possessions themselves are meaningful, not for what they are but for the stories they contain. Each object represents and helps define the whole. Women's collections of meaningful objects are like libraries in which stories are told, each book contained in its covers and yet each part of a totality of personal knowledge and collective history.

Many of the women we interviewed said it was a great pleasure to sit down with an interested listener and tell the stories hidden in their cherished possessions. In their experience, there have been few occasions when anyone has cared about the details of their lives. Some told us later how their participation resulted in sharing stories with their adult children and about the unusual closeness this engendered. Others fantasized about the possibility of getting together with a small group of their close women friends and hearing each other's stories. As Liz put it,

> I mean, think of it. It is really rare. Wouldn't it be nice if a group of friends stood around and said, "Tonight let's get together and bring six things from our memory box and let's share our stories with each other tonight. We don't have to go home until four o'clock in the morning. And if we don't get through, we will meet again." It's a wonderful thing to be known, for people to actually know you.

The chance to talk about oneself for "a whole hour" struck many women as a marvellous indulgence. As Paddy said, "It is always a pleasure to talk about these things, but I rarely do, to anyone. No one has ever asked! And it's been such fun." Reviewing the stories of their special possessions with another woman was intensely personal and emotional. Yet as gratifying as it was to be taken seriously and seen distinctly, there were risks involved. Betrayal was possible.

Part way through the project, as it became evident to us that these reviews were intensely emotional experiences, we each took the most precious artefacts out of our own personal "libraries" and interviewed ourselves and each other about them. Our own interviews could not, of course, be identical to those we conducted with other women. Our attention was already drawn to the significance of the process. This awareness no doubt influenced us to focus more specifically on the meanings of our artefacts rather than on a detailed recounting of specific stories. It seemed important to us, though, to complete these interviews so that readers of the book could understand the stories we would later tell about other women's experiences as being filtered through our own perceptions. Inevitably, at times consciously and at other times without full awareness, we have allowed our own biases to colour these accounts. Best that the reader should be able to discern them. Best, too, that we should share in the experience that we were asking other women to undertake, that we should discover for ourselves how intensely personal such an interview is.

In our own interviews, we shared the same feelings women told us about — enjoyment of the opportunity to deepen a relationship, pleasure in telling the stories to an interested listener, anxiety about the risk we were taking, doubts about resurrecting old ghosts. Although we knew each other as colleagues, enjoyed each other's company, and often talked together about our present lives and our work, we had never shared much about our pasts. There was a lot of uncharted territory that we could only present uncertainly, with apprehension and fully aware of an opportunity to deepen our friendship. The excerpts below are taken from our interviews with each other and from notes we wrote to ourselves as the project progressed. Elly interviewed Kathy first. Kathy's written reflections on the interview and the meanings of her treasures follow here.

When I first sat down to write about my own process of keeping special things, I focused on the process itself and on what I could discern about its meaning. Rather than telling the stories of particular objects, I thought about what the collection as a whole had to tell me about myself and about how and why I kept these "reminders." The resulting essay suggested very mixed motivations and reactions and showed pretty clearly, I thought, that there were two separate processes involved. I keep many things that will remind my children of their own lives – mementos that record their growth and development, their accomplishments, and the important events in their lives. But I also keep a similar set of things that form a personal, private diary encoded in objects. These things remind me of people and events in my own life, but in a much more subtle and comprehensive way than what I keep for my children tells about them. There were, of course, the photos, symbols of achievement, and so on – many of them saved by my mother and later passed on to me – but there were

Old letters, old valentines

also keepsakes from important friendships with other women, from lovers, and from particular events. The stories contained in them were complex and were certainly not uniformly positive, as my collections on behalf of my children tended to be.

I keep two large boxes, trunks really, filled with old pictures of long-dead relatives; newer pictures of babies born, growing up and gone; old report cards from school with their smug H's and A's, and their miserable F's; old letters and Valentines – my life and the lives of my husbands and children. I think of them as my memory boxes. My children called them that when they were growing up; when it snowed or was cold we would make hot chocolate with marshmallows and sit on the living room floor and review everything in the boxes. It was a family ritual, a ceremony introducing them to sentimentality, I suppose, and to a more positive lesson: that their lives are worth remembering, that their everyday struggles and achievements and their simple being are worth remembering.

When I try to talk about what is in these boxes, especially to the children, what I say about my own life rapidly merges into the stories of other people's lives – the stories of my children's lives, my sisters and brothers, mother and father, or stories of my husbands' childhoods and accomplishments. It is easy, too, to talk about my own accomplishments – the high school academic letter, the valedictory pictures, the pictures of graduations, culminating in the Ph.D. On the surface of it, these photos and relics tell the story of a happy, accomplished life. But much of what I tell my children about these events is not about the me they know – not about the me who collected and preserves these things and their stories.

I suppose the "new" psychology of women would say that it is about me – about the relationships in which I have defined myself and lived my life; about the mixture of self and other; about self shading into other until there is really no way to know what is me and what is them. But this perspective gives only a glimpse of the meanings of these things and of their associated rituals. I can tell many versions of the stories in this memory box. I know what is me in each version, and what is not me. I know when I digress into describing the experiences of other people under the guise of telling about my own life. It is so much easier that way. I know how pointless it can feel to try to tell people about my real life. But I preserve it here in the secret code of these objects.

A poignant reminder of my first son

There are many true and acceptably romantic or sentimental stories of my life that I can, and do, tell based on the objects I keep in my memory box. But these things tell stories at more than one level. The little booties are easily a poignant reminder of my first son as a baby – how small he was, how beautiful in my eyes. Or they are a reminder of the woman who made them – a woman I never really knew but who made them for me and for my son with painful exertion, overcoming handicaps that ought to have prevented such fine work, such delicate embroidery, from being done at all. Her stoicism, hidden in these booties, is sometimes a metaphor for the silent, uncomplaining struggle of women in my family to survive and even to triumph over their pain – that struggle that was a constant refrain in my mother's life and is now often repeated in my own.

These booties are about pain, too. Like so many things in my memory box, they are a secret repository of suffering that I could not (should not?) acknowledge to others, or even to myself, lest it be seen as self-pity, as weakness, as a display of poor self-control and bad taste rather than as real suffering. Silence has been and still is often essential in the lives of women. These booties are reminders of my exile from my family, of the pain of childbirth suffered alone while still a child myself. They remind me of how closely related love and pain are. If I allow myself to "indulge" in my own past, these booties will show me the nightmares, the loneliness, the despair that closed in when I left home disgraced and ashamed.

Do all women keep such secrets? Are we all afraid to tell our stories? To be seen as "crying over spilt milk," as wallowing in our misery? Failing to "get over it"? A lifetime of denying the importance of our own lived experience, imposed as partial retribution for the sin of being female? We are supposed to be the more emotional sex – finding it easy to express our feelings, to tell each other about our pain. About some kinds of pain, I suppose. But there seem to be so many difficult experiences in my own life – many of them locked up in these objects – that no one knows. This box is full of my joy that can be shared with other people, but also of pain that is kept to myself.

It isn't that I haven't sometimes told these stories. But I have never told them fully. I know that they have never been understood and that I wish they could be. But they are, I suppose, the female equivalent of old war stories, and they are as likely to impress most listeners with their tediousness as with their tragedy. I am no different from the average person in the street – keeping my tragedies to myself, living alone as we all must. So, they are kept hidden in the box and in my heart, waiting for a rainy day when it is safe to take them out and remind myself again that these things happened. That I didn't dream them. They are, I think, the symbols of my survival.

Elly's interview of Kathy added details about particular stories behind the objects Kathy chose to discuss. Many of the stories were about generations of strong women in her family, those female ancestors about whom her grandmother used to say, "Ha! They couldn't kill us with a tack hammer!" There were generational pictures, from great-great-grandmother on down to her own mother; photos of her with her four sisters that recalled their continuing relationships and the troubles they got into growing up. Her grandmother gave her a special Bible for her high school graduation. An amethyst ring came from the same grandma. A hospital bracelet and booties were worn by her first son. There were also many photo

Four sisters, still close

albums, only one of which contained her own childhood and adolescent photos. Many of these were taken on fancy dress occasions like graduations. Talking about these, she said,

These photos are reminders of my ambivalence about femininity, my interest in the contradictions between what the world said a woman should be, and what my own life, my grandmothers' lives, my mother's and sisters' lives required. Something about being feminine. Because I never had the luxury, quite honestly, of being feminine. Most women don't, I guess. One was always told that one should be this feminine person, what my mother called "being carried around on a silk cushion." She used to say to us, ironically, "I don't know why I work so hard. I should have married some rich man and been carried around on a silk cushion." But she had contempt for women who did that. You could hear it in her voice when she said this. Certainly it was never my experience that I could be feminine – live out the social script of femininity. I worked from the time I was twelve at various jobs, and mostly gave the money to my mother to help provide for my eight brothers and sisters. I was a night janitor in high school – grubby, miserable work that I hated. You were dirty and tired, and you were certainly not feminine. During the day, at school, you were masquerading as a feminine person. You wore starched crinolines. It was like living in some kind of split reality and yet, there was this dream, this dream of being this feminine person, the one dressed up in a white gown for graduation. And she didn't really exist, never really existed, except as a fairy tale or an ideal. Here is my real life, and way over here is what I am actually expected to do, what the world says my life should be. And the two are completely different.

Being interviewed by, and interviewing Elly, listening to what we had to say about our lives, I was struck again and again by how little we really knew of each other and by how few of our central stories, the stories that made us who we are, had ever been shared – with each other or with anyone else. As a psychologist, I was fascinated by the congruence between the objects we showed one another, the stories they encapsulated, and the central narratives of my own life and of Elly's. It seemed to me that reviewing such objects with a woman was surely as effective a psychological assessment tool as any I had ever studied. I continue to believe that such a review can be a most effective way of understanding the central beliefs, values, and events that have shaped an individual woman's life.

We continued the process of self-examination by interviewing Elly. She said that it was not an easy experience and that the self-consciousness it evoked caused her to think about issues of privacy – this was an interesting revelation from someone who has lived a rather public life as a teacher and a political activist. Her reflections on the possessions she has saved over the years follow.

At about forty, I promised myself that my inner and my outer lives would be as close to one another as I could make them, and still be polite! I have no need to reveal all I am in all circumstances, certainly; but I no longer suppress or ignore what I know and feel. I have learned to listen carefully to myself and act in fidelity to myself, knowing too that I have been constructed by very particular moments, places, and events of the twentieth century.

My possessions indicate to me the tension among the layers I see in myself and all around me. Each contains many meanings; I have known about levels my whole life, about keeping many meanings hidden. As a child, I kept that knowledge to myself. I had an inner life and an outer life. One of my possessions, my favourite book, reflects my inner life, in contrast to the girl in American culture. The fifties demanded passivity and good behaviour; I conformed nicely on the outside, but truly I was the main character in *Understood Betsy* by Dorothy Canfield Fisher, the story of a little Vermont girl who learns to be independent, decisive, and competent. I learned from Betsy and was fortunately able in my New England summers to act on that knowledge – to be bold, resourceful, and reliable. Those summers shaped my present life; I recently bought a country house on the west coast.

When I first laid eyes on it, I gasped and knew that was the house that represented all the outdoor things I am and where I could be alone, and that we would need to buy it. It is quiet, quiet there, but you can hear the wind at the top of the trees, and distant sounds – hear the ferry's whistle at night, like the distant railroad of my summer childhood, very very far away, sparkling like the billions of stars in the black sky of the island. When I am there I feel like I am my whole self, the way one is a whole self as a child without knowing that you are this self, but just being it.

Outdoors all summer, with just my sister, our pets, and our bicycles for company, I knew how to be

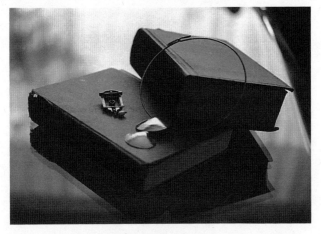

Books and talismans – beautiful luxuries

true to myself. And then, in September, shorts were replaced by skirts that brushed at your legs, sandals by closed shoes (I've always loved new shoes!) and I became a good girl again, a really good girl.

Not so good though as not to be cerebral and smart. Another book among my treasures, *The Oxford Book of English Verse*, I won as the English essay prize in grade ten. It reflects my inner life again – I, a child of European intellectual parents, refugees all of us, who spoke French at home. We hiked and read and I played the piano seriously – at home only. By high school I knew that those were odd activities that must remain private. Here is a lovely photograph of my parents, exuberant at twenty and a little bit shy, but outdoors in the Europe of poor students. Perhaps

Parents

in order to protect my parents from the knowledge
of who I needed to be to fit into this other world
– cute, sweet, not too smart – I also learned not to
tell them: my outer life was also a secret. My double
life was complex, but I took it as normal.

But my next possession, a jar of eye cream,
represents another way I know myself. I am happy to
pay attention to how I look, because it seems another
way of being mindful, of attending to myself. I used
to be very stylish; I am less so now, and probably less
vain, and my caring about my appearance reflects

the respect I have gained for listening to myself. In my heart, I hope that people think I look OK; but in the end I am the judge of that.

A vial of aromatic oil connects so many of these other things: the sense of smell that is so important to me but also symbolizes a new departure for me in the last few years, letting alternative health care into my life. It started with an auto accident and a chiropractor. I feel very good about having discovered a new way of minding my body. I love that new ways of attending to myself are my own discovery; they are a continuation of my capacity to find out what matters to me and, I think, incorporating it into my life.

The scented eye cream and the oil connect also to my outdoor life, my need for the smells of forest and fresh air. I feel clean inside and out when my feet are on the earth. When I do that, I like myself best; I am most whole, with a mind and with my senses, strong and alone and at the same time connected to the people I love.

Feeling resourceful and powerful seems, my objects tell me, to be very important to me: they include luxuries like the silver clamshell necklace I bought with particularly meaningful paycheques of my own. I can say to myself, "I picked this, I chose it, I bought it, without feeling obligated to anyone." Clearly I have always had a need for that kind of independence, which, when I can buy something beautiful, translates itself into euphoria. I can't

58

An adventurous father

get over the wonderful feeling it gives me, to buy something completely on my own with money I've earned.

This is the pink slip, the ownership to my car. I bought it in 1985,- after getting divorced. I did the research on the car; I paid for it myself; I bought the license plates and the insurance all by myself. It was my real coming of age, American style. I married very young, so I never had the chance to do such things. I went from being someone's wife to being myself. Shortly thereafter I got a parking ticket. At first I thought, "Oh, no!" But then I realized: that's my own parking ticket and my own money to throw out! I never relished a parking ticket so much!

My independence is only one layer; my connections are another. It interests me, though, that a beautiful Japanese doll in a red silk kimono who turns slowly on her lacquered music box is my happiest reminder of my mother as her own person, a separate person and not just my mother. It symbolizes her success in her mid-fifties at going in her own direction, in this instance literally around the world by herself. At this period she made her own decisions, doing things her own way.

She was my father's wife first, and our mother, and even though she had worked for pay for so long, I suddenly saw her – going off to Japan in white gloves and an elegant knit suit and her pretty suitcase – as striding, despite being not even five feet tall, on her own into the world, completely different from the person I related to as my mother. Both my sister and I wanted one of the Japanese dolls when my parents had to move out of their house, even though we had never talked to each other about them. The sad thing is that Mother didn't know and didn't care anymore that they meant so much to us.

And interesting, too, that in my favourite photograph of my father he is sitting on a mule, fifty years ago in the interior of Ethiopia, far from his family. I like that he was bold and adventurous.

I am a mother too; the treasured objects from my daughters represent my life story as much as any

She turns slowly on her lacquered music box

possessions could. I have a beautiful taupe silk blouse that my older daughter Lisa gave me for a birthday, going to get it after a very dangerous time for her when she was nineteen, showing her usual tenacity by walking a very long way and showing her usual consideration. The blouse sadly no longer fits me, but it will be in my closet forever as a sign of how I treasure her strength. From that terrible episode in her life, I learned total fear; my life was never the same after that. Even if our relationship is sometimes opaque, needing us to step delicately around each other, she is my deep reality. To say that I am a mother seems a meagre way to put it. That expresses my connection with my daughters on the surface; the inner reality is that they are the sun and moon to me.

Young artist's elephant

And from my younger daughter, Monique, I have brought to the interview a grey cardboard elephant she made out of a juice can when she was probably four or five. She is an artist who has created her own sphere, in and outside the family, as a photographer, using her capacity for self-knowledge and inner calm, her big eyes turned on the world as peacefully as she turned to me when she was born. I am happy that I allowed her to go all the ways she needed to go, even when she was very young, and that I recently received a note from her that thanked me "for making me feel better at every level." My daughters and I have shared our crises, but we have also shared our creativity, reinforced our connections when necessary, and built a shelter in our relationship. Here there is no inner and outer truth. A foreigner in many settings, I am truly at home with Lisa and Monique.

And now there is a grandchild, Jeremiah, whom I don't know well enough yet. We will come to know each other as he grows and as I respond and he influences me, and as he responds and I influence him. We will certainly change each other. I don't know much about this connection yet, but I'll soon find out. It is a relationship filled with mystery and anticipation. No doubt, our love will be straightforward and clear: no double meanings here.

And my final beautiful object is the pin I think of as my talisman. It comes out of a relationship that never requires of me to be untrue to any part of myself. I am whole in it. I touch the pin and I feel safe.

Having experienced this personal review of our own collections, we felt better able to understand the thoughts and feelings of the women who engaged in these conversations with us. Their stories vary; the common thread is the way they treasure their possessions and the stories they contain.

Some of the women we interviewed have so many treasures that their homes resemble private museums in which the day-to-day presence of memories is enormously strong. Gloria's home is like that. She uses her collections in all the various ways we heard about from other women. She provides a glimpse into the process we will examine in more detail throughout this book.

Gloria is an enormously generous woman who has maintained a basic optimism and hopefulness about life through many difficult times. Her possessions are central to her sense of who she is and to her continuing development. They commemorate her childhood, showing the continuity of the child she was with the adult she has become. They tell the story of her important relationships, of the roles and commitments she has undertaken; they symbolize the sources of meaning in her life and embody her future hopes for herself and her children.

Like most women, Gloria has had her share of tragedy, loss, and disappointed hopes, and these too are recorded in the museum of her life. We can't begin to tell the stories of all of the objects Gloria shared with us; a whole book would scarcely do them justice. We include several of them here because they show that treasuring these things is central to Gloria's sense of who she is. They support her ability to review her life, anchoring herself in a personal and cultural past. She builds a hopeful future on the foundation they provide.

At the beginning of our interview, Gloria described herself as a selective collector and told us how her collections are part of her effort to understand herself and the world around her.

Everything I keep is of value to me. I collect crystals and fridge magnets, and I've begun a seashell collection in the last five years. I collect my crystals mostly for their beauty and their energy. I can feel their energy. My dad used to say that a thing of beauty is a joy forever, so I like things that are beautiful. The seashells are also beautiful and I feel very drawn to the ocean these days. It is increasingly mysterious to me. I am learning about what its energy means, how it's changed and stored, and what that means for healing the planet or individuals. There are deep meanings for me in the seashells and the crystals. The fridge magnets – I collect them because they are artistically funny. I like miniature things and I do a fair bit of painting. I originally started getting them when I traveled. I could never afford to buy a souvenir, anything really nice, but I always had two bucks for a magnet. Then I had quite a collection of them, and people started giving them to me as gifts. So, seashells, crystals, and magnets – those are the three biggies for me right now.

Sometimes, as my life changes, I will stop collecting something, or start something new. Crystals, though, I have been collecting for fifteen years now and I can't ever see myself not collecting them. I find that I am quite drawn to nature; I love to be outdoors now. My crystals remind me that energy is always flowing, always moving, always changing. That we never really know what the future is going to hold. They give me hope.

I used to collect teddy bears, but I don't do that anymore. All sizes and shapes. They had to be squishy, soft, and they had to be aesthetically pleasing and have a cute expression or somehow be cuddly. I have twenty still, which isn't a lot, but as I have become more confident in myself and have a lot of healing in my life, I find I need less of the tactile comfort of having them. I suppose other people keep them for different reasons, but for me it was that comfort. I still keep a couple of them around, but I don't spend a lot of time fondling them. I just like to see a few up there, sort of haphazardly. People used to come and want to hold my teddy bears, and that would please me – to see their pleasure in being able to have a good cuddle or whatever. But that was just a period of time. They were a need I had for many years. I have given a few away now.

I have some childhood things that I keep in my cedar chest, primarily because when I die, those are the things that I'll pass on. I've even labelled them. When my mom died, nothing was labelled. We didn't know if things were three or four generations back, or were her sister's. So I have labelled all my kids' baby clothes and things, "favourite toy of Todd's" or whatever.

At this point, Gloria moved on to tell us the stories of some of her own childhood objects, things she has kept for several decades because they make her child self real to the adult she has become.

I have this baby rattle, because it's something I remember playing with as a youngster. It's a plastic, beaded little black person, and I remember a loop on his head to hold him up by. I remember my mom dangling this over me, and me grasping. It sounds crazy, but I remember – I have some strong memories as an infant, and I know they say you can't do that, but I do and they are very vivid. For some reason this rattle brought me a lot of happiness as an infant. I don't know if it was the noise or the colours, but I remember it was put away and I hadn't seen it for a long time, from when I was ten until about four years ago when my mom died, and I was going through her stuff. It was in her cedar chest as well. Obviously, she knew it was important to me. I was so delighted to see it again. It was like a long lost friend. I was so pleased that she had kept it.

Something else that was in my mom's cedar chest was this little recording. In the Mormon church, they have many wards, and the wards make up a stake. Sometimes they have a stake conference, with speakers and so on. There is a primary association in each church for the children twelve years and younger. I remember that there was one of these gatherings at Christmas time, and the children were presenting a program, and I had been asked to say the opening prayer. What I didn't know was that they had made a recording of it. So I have this record and when I found it, it said, "Daddy's present, Gloria's prayer, December 1952." It's a little 45-rpm record. I

remember saying the prayer, and everybody making
such a big deal of it, and my mom being moved to
tears. It's very close to my heart.

Gloria played the prayer for us on a small record player
that is also a childhood memento. It is a very old pho-
noplayer, similar to a small television set, with a record
player on top. Coloured red and cream, and originally
equipped with two viewing lenses and a set of different record stories that could be played, listened to, and
looked at, it seemed rather like an animated View Master.
We sat and listened together to Gloria's four-year-old
voice saying the prayer. She recalled that her mother had
helped her decide what to say.

> My mother was really, she probably was the most
> creative person I've known, and also a wonderful
> teacher. I remember her saying, "Now Gloria, you
> have to give a wonderful prayer, because this is for
> the baby Jesus." She was so ill, and I never knew
> what was wrong, and it wasn't until just a few years
> ago that I understood that her problems were not
> because of me. I certainly gave her problems. I was
> a rebellious teenager. But she was mentally ill, and
> now I know that there are a few labels I could ascribe
> to her condition. But she was very loving and kind
> and gentle at some times, and quite crazy at others.
> I loved her to pieces, and I made my peace with her
> before she died. I finally got to the point where I saw
> that this woman was so ill mentally and physically,

and that I loved her and she had given me life and I owed her that love. Everything else got stripped away and I saw this human being who was basically a lot like me, wanting the same kinds of things, and I was able to fill some of those needs. So that little record triggers all these memories. I can see myself as a little girl, giving that prayer, and I can understand what that meant to my mother. I remember not being afraid.

Gloria also has a lunch kit that she used as a child. It encapsulates many memories of special times, childhood moments, and reminds her about the aspects of herself that have remained constant since those times.

I was raised out in the country. My dad was an educator, but he got his original degree in horticulture and he loved to work on the land. My best memories of happiness were during the summer time, having my lunch packed in my barn-shaped lunch kit with the black roof. It's tin, and it has chickens on the outside, standing on some hay. My mom would pack the lunch and it was only at these times that I could have pop – normally pop was not allowed. So pop called Nehi was poured into my thermos, and I would ride on my dad's tractor out to the fruit trees. And I would pick fruit, and we would have lunch, and I was very, very happy. I don't remember my dad so much, but more the enjoyment I had because I loved to be outdoors, to climb trees. I was never one to play with dolls; I never wanted to baby-sit. It was a carefree time. Idyllic moments in a difficult childhood, because on those days I was in another world.

Next, Gloria showed us the remaining pieces from a doctor's kit she had loved to play with. The story was one of childhood pleasure, the development of a dream for her future, and the loss of that dream.

I remember that I was going to be a doctor when I grew up. I wanted that in the worst way. I had a little doctor's kit, but these pieces of it, this little red thing for looking in people's ears, a little metal container that says "soap" on it, and a little brown pill bottle, are all I have left. I spayed all the cats in the neighbourhood, and took out a lot of tonsils. I had cotton balls that I smeared with red lipstick, and I found that when I dropped them in water they would expand and look like veins. I drew pictures of bones and all the different parts of the body, and I had a sign on construction paper hung over some branches of an old tree, and that was my office. A red wagon was my ambulance. When people came into my office, I had them lie down because I had to take x-rays. I'd pull a branch down, and with it these pictures that I had pre-drawn and put in a manila folder, and I would hold it down and make the x-ray sound, and then pull out the x-ray picture. They were always so amazed by it.

I'm still disappointed that I didn't go into medicine. But my mom, my dad, my sister, and my grandparents had all gone to the state university, and it didn't have a medical school. It was like I had to choose, and I don't know why I chose to go to the state university. It was a dream that I had to give up.

Gloria said that her mother had kept all these things safe for her in her cedar box, and she spoke about the importance of discovering them there after her mother's death.

She kept these things for forty years and more. I don't know whether she got them out and looked at them. She never shared that with me. But when she died there were little aisles of boxes in the basement. My mom did the very best she could at the time. I only wish she had been able to have more help. She managed to be an exciting and inspiring teacher. There are still people who tell me that my mom was the best teacher they had, and she changed their lives. But at home, our house was not working. There was a lot of turmoil. Sometimes I wonder how things might have been if she had received the help she needed.

The next thing Gloria talked about was a group of rocks from a piece of land that was originally meant to be a part of her inheritance. The rocks remind her of her child-hood ambition to have horses. She joined and became president of a horse club and drew pictures of horses. When she was twelve, she was given her first horse, named Ginger. She took Ginger on many rides through the land she was to inherit, riding up and down the corn rows, and asking the pony,

"What do you think?" It was a gorgeous area. I would ride until I found the spot with the prettiest view, and I told my dad that that was where I wanted to build my house and raise my children. It never happened. These rocks are a memento of broken dreams. A lot of the decisions I made in my life were based on being on that land. I just knew it was going to happen. I would have my land and raise my kids there. But it just couldn't be.

Gloria also told us the stories contained in a lovely, flowered blue plate, one of two surviving pieces from a set that belonged to her great-great-grandmother. Gloria received one, her sister the other.

It meant so much to me, even though I never knew my great-great-grandma. For its antique value, and also because my mom put such emphasis on it. But what made it even more special to me is that after my husband and I separated, I was thrown into starting all over in my late forties. I had never worked full time. I had gotten my degree when I was pregnant, then graduated and proceeded to have my children. And I was scared spitless, and I didn't have any money, and I started looking at what I had and I knew this plate was worth something. So I took it to an antique dealer, asked him how much he could give me for it, and sold it. I had to feed my kids. When we split up I didn't get much money, and he insisted that we had to split the bills too, even though he was making about four times what I could. So I had to sell it. I knew at that moment, when I needed to find out who I was and who I am, if that meant being poor for the rest of my life, having no one to love, so be it. I let go of a lot of things that were valuable to me – things that I swore I would never sell. I took a big breath before each one of them, and I thought, "It's just a thing, it's not about who I am as a person."

But my friend Liz went and bought the plate back. I didn't know for several months, but at Christmas I opened the package and of course I cried. I don't know what she paid for it, but it means a great deal to me. I was able to let go of a lot of things, and there is no remorse, just nostalgia. I know now that when I go I take with me my relationships, my knowledge, whatever talents I've got, but that's it. But this one thing that came back to me, this one is so special to me now. It's interesting to me because I've felt, at least in the church, that women haven't had a lot of power. They sometimes say they do, but it is always secondary to what the men want. And yet I've done a lot of research on the history of the church, and the women were the healers. They blessed each other

and had a lot more power than they do now. That's
important to me, to have this plate to remind me
that I had a great-great-grandmother who was a
midwife, that another was a talented musician.

Gloria also keeps a set of scrapbooks. Each book is about
two feet wide and a foot high, and contains several years
of Gloria's personal history. She occasionally adds sections to it. Her own drawings illustrate the memories
in the books: one, for example, shows a train with each
window filled with a photo of a child who attended
Gloria's eighth birthday party. There are programs from
church conferences, sports awards from her athletic years,
samples of all the embroidery stitches she learned as a
child, and mottos and morals to live by: "Greet the day
with song. Make others happy. Serve God."

I've got it in sections, so it goes from younger to
older. I have kept it up. I even made a scrapbook of
Jim's and my courtship – the places we went, our
first grocery bill together, the cards he gave me,
pictures of us, how he proposed, the card he gave
me with our rings taped inside. I made up my own
scripture about our love, and people asked where
that was found. I can't bring myself to throw it away.
I put it downstairs and some day the kids will see
it. There are many things in here about my friendships over the years. My friends are important to me,
and always have been. Each friend has her own page
because growing up they were a very important part

of my life, even the ones I don't keep in touch with anymore. I was looking for ways that brought stability to me, and I think that these scrapbooks had a way of doing that for me.

Her scrapbooks helped Gloria through a very tumultuous childhood. They created a sense of life's being organized. Now they show her the person she was and is, and how she has changed over the years. From the vantage point of her fifty years, she no longer needs the scrapbooks in the intense way she remembers needing them as a child and a young mother, but she enjoys them, treasures them, and hopes that they might one day help her children and grandchildren understand her.

Gloria hints at the pain caused by the loss of her great-great-grandmother's china plate, and at her joy in having it returned to her. Her experiences echo the stories of so many women we interviewed who had suffered the loss of treasured possessions. Some lost one or two things they still grieve for; others lost virtually their entire collection, usually while moving across long distances. Still others think longingly of things they never had but which had great meaning for them – often things thoughtlessly discarded by men in the family.

Moving to Canada from Australia, Jill lost most of her archival objects when the cargo vessel containing them sank; several women suffered losses when they were forced to flee their homes as refugees. All of these women have grieved their losses intensely. Without the anchor provided by their treasures, their memories are fragile. The few things salvaged or sent on by relatives have become particularly precious and are carefully guarded. Donna told us about her experience with the loss of treasured things.

I've always kept things, since I was a small child. I had a memory box for many, many years, until about twenty years ago when we moved, and it was lost in the move. I had all kinds of little things in there – jewellery, rocks, an old Indian arrowhead that we found in our yard as children. It is a terrible feeling of loss. I still haven't really gotten over it. I had letters in there from my childhood. When I realized I had lost the box, it was like losing a piece of myself. I kept on looking. I think I got a glimpse of what it's like when a person's house burns down and they have nothing. Even talking about it still upsets me. I have tried to find it for years. My husband is not a keeper of things like that, and I suspect he just chucked it out when he was packing, not thinking about it, not doing it on purpose. I was always a very fearful child and I didn't really have much sense of self and I think I saved those things to try to create a bit of identity.

Donna still has many things from her later life, of course, but the loss of her childhood possessions still haunts her. Another loss also brings her grief.

I have this big Bible, very, very old, handed down to me from my father's father. It is at least a hundred years old. It has a history of my father's side of the family in it, birth dates and names. But I also found another one, in my grandfather's basement, that was in Gaelic, and I asked if I could have it but Grandpa said no. It was very musty smelling and we were traveling across Canada in a car, so I wasn't allowed to take it home. Later, when I wrote to him and asked again, he told me that he had buried it in their back yard because you didn't burn Bibles, and he thought there was no value in it. That was another devastating loss, and I still think about it. Every time I look at this other Bible, I think about the Gaelic one. It also had birth dates and things, much further back. I was just devastated and furious with him. I don't think I have ever forgiven him, actually. He's dead now, and every time I look at his picture I think of that Bible that he buried.

Many women, whether or not they had ever lost any objects, insisted that if they moved, the boxes containing their treasures could not be entrusted to anyone else. Men's unreliability in preserving personal and family history was a common refrain. Women cannot consign their collections to the care of movers, well-intentioned relatives, or friends. Nancy, for example, told us,

We moved a year ago, and I kept these things in a box with me – things that I didn't want to trust the movers with. I sort of, in my mind ... if our truck were to be lost.... And in that box are all my treasures, so they are easy to find. If I had to get them in a hurry, I could pick up the box, lay the photo albums on top and head for the hills, right? But so easy to lose.

Occasionally, when it is absolutely necessary, women might arrange to store some treasured things, usually in a mother's basement. But if at all possible, they take everything with them. Even mothers are sometimes unreliable. Laurie is one of the very few women whose losses are associated with her mother's lack of care for them.

> I left some things with my mother, but I'm afraid they're gone. I know a few things aren't, but some things aren't there, and no one else would have them. Two things that were really important were my children's hospital bracelets from when they were born. I know I had those and they have disappeared. It would be really nice to still have those. And the dress I brought my daughter home from the hospital in – I'd like to have that, and I thought I did.

We also heard other stories like Gloria's, about the temporary loss of a special possession and the profound relief on its recovery. Margaret, for example, had a special sixteenth birthday ring that her mother had made for her from a baby spoon. The baby spoon, a gift from her father on her sixteenth birthday, included a Yukon gold nugget, which was also incorporated as part of the ring. She was very attached to it, partly because her father died not long after she received the ring and partly because it reminded her of her childhood in the Yukon.

> And then I wore it all the time as a teenager, until one day I lost it. And I was working in a store, we were doing an inventory of the jeans, and I didn't realize that that was when I lost it. When I lost it, it was very traumatic. We went through everything in the house and, because it was right after Dad died that I lost it…. We just searched everywhere. Finally, I thought, "Well, it is just gone." A year later, after I wasn't working there, they were doing inventory again and they found my ring. Wow! And someone remembered that I had this ring so it came back to me, and I thought, "That's really … isn't that amazing!" So that is one of my favourite things.

We asked women about their plans for disposing of their possessions. Would they give them away? Under what circumstances? To whom? The most striking pattern in their answers was the almost universal intention to pass special things on to a daughter or a niece when she was old enough to understand the gift's importance, or to a female friend. The particular woman chosen to receive the object was one who had a liking for "these kinds of things" or had expressed a strong wish to have one object in particular. Women who have no daughters of their own often pass things on to their daughters-in-law or skip a generation and give things to granddaughters.

Some women do pass things along to men, just as they receive some things from men, but that is rare. Many women believe that men are not appropriate or "safe" recipients of women's treasures because they have little understanding of an object's importance or of the reason for keeping such things. As Paddy told us,

I have my great-aunt's wedding jacket. But my brother would just feel silly to have his great-uncle's wedding jacket, and he would feel even sillier giving that to his son and telling him that this was a family heirloom. I can just imagine that! And I have my grandmother's whole wedding dress, which is an astonishing creation, and it catches my heart to think that my daughter might someday wear it. The idea is there, and the idea pleases me. I don't think that's a male thing at all. Even though my husband and I have split up, I still keep some things from his family to give to our daughter. I'm not sure how important he thinks they are, or if he even remembers what they are. I have his christening dress, but I have this feeling that if I gave it to him, it would be stuck in a trunk somewhere and years from now someone would pull it out and say, "What's this old thing?" And that would be that. Maybe not. Maybe I am underestimating the species!

Sometimes a woman who has no daughters passes objects along to a son but later takes them back because they are not being properly cared for or are in danger of being lost. Usually, she then resolves to wait until the son marries and to pass the objects to her daughter-in-law instead. Deciding who can be expected to take care of the objects is a conscious act. As Mary said,

> It's because these things represent important parts of who I am, who I have been. They have to be given to someone who will respect them because if they abuse them or lose them or something, it is like a failure of respect, a failure to understand their meaning. For them not to be kept carefully is like a denial of my experiences, my life. It would show me that [they] don't understand my life, don't value it.

Holly, speaking about how she would select someone to receive her things, said,

> I'd probably give them to my niece Joanna. She's the kind of kid who gets fascinated by stories, and I think she would appreciate the memories that go with these. My stepchildren love them and think they are really cool, but I don't think they have the same connection.

Leila expressed a similar intention:

> My one daughter is jewellery nuts, but none of it seems to mean too much to her. But the older girl is different; she doesn't care for a lot, but what she has, she has an attachment there. And I know

that she would be attached to this ring. And she has a daughter too, that every time she comes just looks at this ring. She understands the love that is contained in there. The one daughter would look at it and think, "Well, why wasn't it gold plated?" or something like that. She just sees things differently.

Another woman has many treasures of her own and recently received others from an older relative who has begun to give things away.

All it takes is a mention that you admire something, and she will give it to you. As long as she trusts that the item is going to someone who genuinely appreciates it, she is prepared to give it away. She recently gave a hundred-year-old family rocker to her youngest son's wife, and a glass clock that had been given to her by her Bonne Maman was given to her sister-in-law when Bonne Maman died.

Others, like Kathleen, think passing down such objects is a way of emphasizing shared strengths across the generations of women in families: "I like the idea of continuity. I really think that we have to be strong women and get this across to our grandchildren, too." Peg's reasons for passing things along are similar:

I will pass them on so that my children will be able to make connections between what was going on for them personally and what was going on in their family, in their bigger family, and in the communities they were living in. To help them feel sort of grounded in the world. It's not so important for them now, but it will be when they have kids of their own.

Women whose daughters or other female relatives have expressed an interest in having one of their treasures sometimes have mixed reactions to these requests. Some, like Joyce, are pleased and make note of the request for the future:

> I was laying out that cloth the other day, and one of my daughters saw it. She said, 'Oh, where did you get that, Mom? That's lovely!' I just thought, I'm glad to know that she likes that. I'm at that age and stage where I want to make those decisions.

Others are more protective about their things and have no intention of ever giving them away. They were are very clear that the objects belong to them as individuals, and they believe that their relatives, as Betty put it, "can fight over them when I die. If they asked me for them, I would say no." Laurie has similar feelings: "Well, I have to keep it still because I might need it. I might need to go back and study that, or remember that." Donna's response also contains this ambivalence about the process of passing things along:

My daughter saves things and is attached to some of these things, but my son isn't at all. I'm actually rather pleased that my children didn't become that attached to them, because they would want them, especially my daughter, but I don't want to give them away to anyone. I want to keep them until I am not here anymore and then they can decide what to do with them.

Some women consider eventually returning the objects to the people from whom they were received. Anna said,

If I die before my mother does, I will give this bear back to her because anyone else would just look at him as an ugly bear that is falling apart. Then, if she died, and I don't have any children, then he will go to a friend of mine who also has a bear that is pretty much in the same shape. Hers is a bit better because she still sleeps with hers and I can't because he would be dead in a few days!

When loved objects were imbued with human characteristics, their future has to be especially carefully planned. These objects, especially dolls and stuffed animals, need to be provided for, need a good home. Most women want to think of their treasures being valued by women of the next generations as remembrances of their owners' lives and as symbols of the continuity of family. Paddy told us, "I guess I like to think of them being valued, always, in some form. I hope that some day my daughter will enjoy having them, or my brother's daughter. I like to think that she will pass them on as well. I would like them to stay in the family and be part of the continuum of the family." Continuity is itself a treasure, and is symbolized by the objects as talismans that give reality to the lives of female ancestors who cannot be known in any other way.

The layers upon layers of meaning contained in objects make them useful to women for many different purposes. Primary among these purposes is the sense of stability and proportion they provide by representing experience, whether a woman's own or a treasured friend's or ancestor's. Over and over we were told that these objects make a woman real to herself, validate her experiences, make her part of a history. They provide stability, connection to something more permanent than one brief and ephemeral female life. These objects anchor women in place and time, past and future, and give them what their cultural context often does not: a sense of a shared history, of women's personal and collective significance. Holding or wearing such objects is reassuring and supportive. As Leah told us, "I always put this jewellery of my mother's and daughters' on when I am going to a special occasion, or an interview, because it feels like having the people I love around me."

Strong emotions accompany experiences like these. In fact, some objects are used precisely for their power to evoke a feeling about a current problem or a remembered happiness. They might facilitate or intensify emotional expression, allowing a woman to break through to a better understanding of herself, of a challenging situation, or of a relationship. Another object might assist a woman to calm herself, to restore perspective during an emotionally stormy period. Women seek out particular objects from their collections at particular times. Laurel, in despair, retreats to the attic room where she keeps her treasures hidden away: "The stuff I have in my cardboard boxes is more consoling to me than anything. I would just sit and look at that stuff."

Younger women, especially, are likely to display objects, most often in their bedrooms. This kind of display defines and symbolizes their current understanding of self or identity. Tania, for example, keeps certain things out and puts others away depending on how she feels: "I'll scan my room, and I'll say, 'Hmm, okay, that one can go' and I'll put it away, back in its little place, and a new one will take its place." As she experiences personal change, encounters difficulties or enters a particularly intense mood, she changes the assortment of items on display to reflect and support her changing identity.

Most women have at least one small box that is itself a treasure and that serves as a container for other items. Tania's special box came from her mother and is an important part of her frequent review of objects.

My mom, when she signed up for something at the bank, received this blue box with a combination on it. So she gave it to me. I was so excited that I could lock away stuff. I used to take all the stuff I didn't want my parents to know about and put it in this box.

My secret life – letters from boyfriends, that kind of thing. I was the only one who knew the combination, so I'd get it all out and sort it in piles and read over everything. When I cleaned my room I would go through it all too, and other times depending on my mood, sort of in a thinking mood.

Treasured objects have the power to arouse emotion by evoking whole scenes – a short story or a play – sensory pictures that capture who one was at the time, what the world was like, and the emotions that accompanied the moment, keeping the past real in the present. Gerry told us about a pin her father sent her when he was away at the war.

So actually, he was gone so long – we knew we had a father, but I didn't know what he looked like. I remember he was coming home on a certain night and the next morning we were getting up and we were peeking into his – into Mom and Dad's bedroom, and we didn't know who that man was. See, we had forgotten what he looked like. He was gone almost five years and mom lived alone with us two girls. The pin brings back all the memories of what our life was like while he was over there ... that we couldn't have any icing on the birthday cake because you couldn't get icing sugar, how the blinds were down every night and the lights had to be off because we were right by the coast. Mom would wash this pin in with the wools – there was no dry-cleaning then – and she would keep it for me sometimes in her bureau drawer, all wrapped up. But finally she said, "Now it's time for you to take some of this," and I took it and always kept it in a special spot in the bottom drawer of my dresser.

Now my daughter wants the pin. She thinks it's lovely. When my daughter and I talk about the pin, we talk about the war a lot. I tell her how you couldn't get different things to eat, when butter came in, how we ran up to the store really quick. Mom would holler at us "Come in quick, there's butter!" and we'd go running to see if we could get in line to get a half-pound of butter. And the coupons to buy certain things, how there was no oil, how mom used to boil up the old flour bags and bleach them to get out the Robin Hood on the front. It took three days to bleach them, but it was good cotton and Mom could make our bloomers from it. How we had stockings with garters to hold them up, and there was a space there – that space of leg. You wore bloomers in winter to keep warm. Mom could get two and a half pairs of bloomers out of a good Robin Hood sack. So, you see, there are a lot of memories there. This pin brings back those years when we were there without him, and how we were scared of him when he came back. He was a strange man in our house. My father knows I still have this pin. He was quite surprised when he found out.

Some women are concerned or ambivalent about the function of their possessions as emotional lightning rods. They wonder if such emotionality, such a need to revisit the past, is healthy. They criticize themselves for succumbing to the need to revisit objects that they know will elicit profound emotion. As Susan told us:

> I wondered, when I started crying over my grand-mother's things, "Does this mean I have a lot of unfinished issues that I need to deal with? Or is it just okay?" It's not like I have to be done with it all, have nothing that makes me cry. Some things are very close to my heart – especially the ones that are tokens of love or that stand for a person I experienced as loving and kind – even if I didn't know her well.

Lorraine agreed, saying,

> The emotion is still there, just as poignant as ever. Some are sad and some are good memories. If a relationship turns out badly or something, you still keep the treasures to remind you. A treasure becomes a treasure when it evokes a certain feeling in you. I change my collections as my life changes. But everything was, at some point in my life, a very important treasure and that's why I've still got it.

Paddy told us about how she sees certain objects as sym-bolizing particular relationships. Speaking about an ornate, carefully preserved pair of baby slippers her father sent her from Italy when he was in the war, she said:

In many ways, they do symbolize the ambivalent relationship I have to this day with my dad, who is a wonderfully warm, exasperating man. And I will never forget this image of my father when I was in hospital – right after I had brain surgery and I was unable to say anything. Dad would always ask if I needed anything. It was like if there was something he could buy that would fix everything, he would feel so much better. And my mother would say "Oh, for God's sake, just sit down and visit!" And he simply didn't know how to do it. So these slippers are like having that relationship set out before me. You could say they represent a great part of where I come from, where I belong, and how I see myself.

Leila told us about the meaning of a particular ring in her collection.

That is a ring my husband gave me. The stone from it was lost long ago. I keep it in this little case on my dresser, and no one touches it. They know that that's special to me. In there is an awful lot of love, and that's something you can't buy. If I get feeling down, I can glance over and look at that and I can almost feel warmer. And you can't buy the feeling of love, you can't put a dollar value on it. It's priceless.

Deborah spoke of this same process, holding a jewellery box full of many small things handed down from her mother and grandmother. "I keep a few things that I use in it as well. Then, when I open the box to get something, I can sort of emotionally touch base with these other things." It is important to Paddy, and to many other women, that we understand that the emotional connection they feel to these objects is not mere sentimentality.

> I don't think it is a sentimental thing at all. They trigger images. Some are very, very funny, and some are very sad. What goes through my mind, no one could label sentimentality, which I have a horror of. As my daughter says when we watch television together, "Oh, close your eyes, Mom, here comes heartwarming." But each thing – like my grandmother's watch – it's not just about my grandmother, it's also about my father giving it to me.

Some women, particularly those who come from abusive backgrounds, find it difficult to keep objects from their childhoods because of the emotions they evoke. Still, they keep them or pass them on. Marie, for example, said:

> A few things that I have from my mother just don't mean a lot to me. I found a plate from my mother's wedding china in a second hand store and I thought that would be neat to have. But I just couldn't look

at it – it made me feel ill. I ended up giving it to
my sister; otherwise I was going to throw it away.
I do have an afghan my mother made not long ago.
She's eighty-six now. I do treasure that, because it's
from a different time, a time when she felt more able
to love us and even say that she loved us. I left my
marriage after twenty-two years, and I find that
things I thought were treasures back then have the
same effect on me. I can't relate to them with any
affection.

Others, like Micheline, told us about objects they wish
they could throw away but feel impelled to preserve for
their daughters:

I have two very good rings, one a wedding ring.
I like them, but to me they don't have too much
meaning. I keep them to pass on to my daughters.
I have my mother's fur coat in my closet, and that
I hate! I hate that coat. But my daughter wants it
when I die. My mother died seven years ago and I've
never worn that coat. It's not me. I feel burdened by
it. I'd like to unload it. But I could never have told
my mother, "Mom, please don't give me your coat,
please give it to someone else," because she was so
proud to be able to leave this coat to me. I have my
mother's wedding band too. I own it, but again I
wish I didn't have it. Part of the reason is that she
had it on her finger in her coffin, and to me it's not
a good reminder.

Other women keep objects that function very specifically as talismans. Patsy told us the story of her porcelain Buddha: "When I came from Shanghai in 1968, my mother gave this to me to protect me wherever I go. It is my guardian angel and a treasure from home." She also showed us a painting done for her by her niece: "It is a lucky star. It's supposed to make me lucky all the time. It brings good fortune. My life has been smooth sailing, I would say, and I stay healthy, I don't get sick." Another woman keeps a seedpod she was given while traveling in New Mexico with a woman friend.

> The family that made it told me how the design of interconnecting lines has to do with family, friends, relationships, and longevity. I really wanted to buy it, but I had run out of money, and my friend bought it for me. One of my fears was always dying young. In a way, it comes from my fear, wanting this thing, but it's been such an inspirational object. It's so interesting to me, it says so much about the paradox of life. It is a seedpod. The family that made it would have usually put a seed in it and, in the spring, smash it and re-grind the clay. One of my fears is that I might break it, and yet it's a beautiful thing, made to be broken.

Such talismans are not always connected to cultural beliefs, however. Some are created by the woman herself to serve a protective function. Diane, for example, keeps a special object whose function is entirely to reassure her and make her feel safe:

> I keep this white stool by my bed. I picked it up one year when I was camping. Whenever I left my tent, I would put it in front, and that meant that everything would be safe while I was gone. I've always kept it by my bed – it still symbolizes for me that I'll be safe.

Some of the young women we spoke to have not yet reached a point where they feel comfortable with their emotional attachment to objects. Uncertain about which things to keep, they avoid throwing anything away until they can be sure of its possible future importance to them. They keep their old school work, favourite toys and books, and every card they have ever been given. Occasionally they become exasperated with themselves and pull everything out to try to throw some of it away. What usually results is a long process of reminiscence as each item is reviewed and, finally, the realization that nothing can be discarded. As Tania said, "In a way, it is all the same thing. It is all about relationships. It's all pieces of a big puzzle that makes a whole picture of my life."

Many younger women want to keep and display things, but don't understand why they want them. They worry that keeping them might be a sign of insecurity, that others will see them as immature for keeping such things. Angelina told us:

Well, I don't really want to display a bunch of old stuffed animals. I have a box full, but I have a really hard time parting with them and I don't know why. I have given a few away to friends' children, but there are a few I just can't part with – they have a story behind them or something. I can't display them in my house. They'd say, "What's wrong with her? She still keeps her teddy bears?"

The developmental sequence involved in building these collections varies with cultural influences and with personal circumstances. The extent of a woman's collection depends in part on her access to material things and to private spaces in which to keep them safe. Where these conditions are present at least to some extent, the process seems to begin during adolescence and young adulthood with ambivalent but inclusive collecting as a sense of self is being developed. This phase gives way to a more selective one, especially if the woman marries, has children, and begins to save items for them and on behalf of her partner. The same is true of lesbian women, their partners, and their children. Sometime in this middle period, a woman may receive items her mother has saved for her and, a little later, things from her grandmothers and from her mother, passed on as these women die.

In this middle period, women continue to keep important items, but they may also begin to discard things that have become less important. Often these are items that no longer seem to define who they were, who they are, or who they anticipate becoming. Some items, particularly those associated with difficult childhood events, are not thrown out but are put away for years at a time and visited only in response to major changes or disjunctions in their owners' lives. At the beginning of the final phase, women begin to give away items – first to their daughters as they become mothers themselves, or to their nieces or their sons' wives if there are no daughters. These initial gifts are generally items from the son's or daughter's infancy and may be taken back if the woman believes that she has misjudged the recipient's readiness to care for them. Much later, women begin to give away some of the relics of their own lives and the lives of their female ancestors. But the most central, most self-defining objects are kept until death. They may then be thrown out by surviving children or other relatives who mistakenly see them as merely a lifetime's accretion of junk. They may ask themselves, "Why would she want to keep this old thing?" and, having never heard her stories, be unable to discern gold from dross. Perhaps, if the provenance of the item is known to a daughter, a surviving sister, a niece, it may be kept and added to her own collection. There it will remain as a marker of relationship and of family history, continuing the cycle of remembering and recording women's lives.

A malia had a complex story to tell, one filled with emotions and events. Hers has been a particularly complicated life, and yet she described it in a calm, almost ethereal way that belied the turmoil. Amalia lives on an island off the west coast of Canada in a small house packed full of books, children's things, light, and colour, yet everything is tidy and serene. The room, like its beautiful natural setting, was bursting with signs of life – copper-bottomed pots, cooking utensils, photographs, a vase with flowers, children's drawings and paintings. A fragrant, recently baked pound cake awaited us on the table, the kettle boiled. Activity and tranquility prevailed.

On reading the transcript of the interview, we knew that rather than excerpts, the whole story needed to be told. It is a rich and varied story, capturing the fluidity of women's stories, the variety of emotions and events in women's lives, and the capacity to maintain a sense or core of self even while responding to, and being available for, complications. The word "fluidity" kept coming to our minds. We did not know which chapter Amalia's story could fit into.

We later began to understand Amalia's narrative as a story of women's connections – to parents, children, lovers, friends, and the myriad people in their lives. Feminist psychologists have been writing for almost twenty years about women's capacity to define themselves as part of a web of relationships. Writers have suggested that rather than growing into individuality and defining themselves as persons separated from others, girls learn to connect with others, developing a sense of self from those connections. Through mutually empathic relationships, we understand ourselves both as separate persons and as part of an interconnected, caring community.

Clearly, this pattern of connections makes for a complicated story. As relationships change and grow, flower and fade, a woman's understanding of self changes as well. Amalia's complex story found a place in this chapter on connections. Her rich inner life, fluid and ever changing, is fed by her connections with other people in her life. The possessions of which she speaks prompt her to recall the web of relationships she has spun around herself, with her own aesthetic of calm and her strong sense of herself maintaining a center of tranquility.

She began with a poster by Matisse, establishing from the beginning of our interview that she is connected to the beauty around her, perhaps even dependent on it.

Even if I live in one room, like when I was at university and I had one little tiny room, this poster with the dancing figures is necessary to me. First of all it is the grace, the figures, and then the colours, its sensuality; it breathes texture, even though it is a flat surface. The colours are soothing to me, the blues and pinks, greens and peaches. No matter where I was it was a big piece of colour.

She bought the poster at sixteen, when she first went to university, at a "cheap little poster store," to ensure that "I could have colour in my world." Next she gestured to a framed photograph from the same period, if from a different place. She described it and began to evoke the people in her life.

My brother gave me this photograph. He said it was like my recurring dream from childhood. I used to have a recurring dream when I was a little girl of living on a cliff and walking down stone stairs that were cut into the bank of this cliff to a little tiny beach. I was with my dog. It's a dog that I haven't had yet, a border collie kind of dog, and I would just play with him, throwing sticks into the water and he would swim back with them. It was all misty, and then I would walk back up and I was an old, old woman with a scarf around my hair. I have put this photo up everywhere I have been since I received it.

I have always felt drawn to water, even though I was raised in the prairies. Even there, I remember being out on the farm in the spring, and there was a culvert, just a trickle of water from the run-off, that made a slough or a little pond. That was my special spot to go and sit by. I have always felt drawn to the water, especially the ocean, and I love rocky cliffs, like the Oregon coast, or Cornwall in England. The water: to me it is fluidity, outwardly too but it creates an inner fluidity.

Amalia moved from fluidity to freedom. For her, childhood freedom is associated with the presence of her brother, who was a year younger than she. They lived on top of a cliff, and

> Gary and I went on our explorer trips in the park below. One day we came across a box down the cliff. We had found another of what we called treasures! We were in our fantasy world, and pretended the box was a pirate's who had dumped it. This little dish shaped like a clown was in the box. It is lying on its back, with a white painted face and a green round cap on his head, a ruff around his neck. This clown went everywhere with me, and served a variety of purposes. It has really endured. I've put wax in it, scraped it out. Kept a candle in it by the bathtub. It's been a child's treasure as well as an adult's. Now I put these little rocks in it, and it's on a shelf with other special little things that are meaningful to this family.

Amalia's children began to enter her narrative of relationships almost imperceptibly, adding more texture, more colours.

> Sometimes the children fill it up with different treasures for themselves, like beads. So I am sharing it

now. I told them the story of it. I told them about me
and my brother, and how this signifies a time when
we were little. Gary and I did everything together.
We were very poor, and the cliff was our refuge. It
was our magical place. And, you see, the clown is
receptive to being filled with whatever I choose to
put in it, whether that is wax or beautiful jewellery
or beautiful rocks.

Next, prompted by a large saucer, Amalia evoked yet
another connection as she unfolded her story of relationships.

This was the saucer of a cup that has always been
a very important part of me. If I had one suitcase
to take someplace, like when I went to London for
two months, I would take·this. And a plunge pot for
coffee, and the cup that went with this. It was a big
cup. My very good friend Lynn got me this when
she lived in Switzerland, at a second-hand store. I
always had my morning cappuccino in it. It never
broke until I was living in California. The people I
was living with broke it when drying dishes. It took
me half a day or a day to be able to look at the person
who did it because they were sort of uncaring about
it.

It's not a flat saucer, but almost a bowl, Wedgwood
blue lacy leaf and flower pattern. See the potpourri
in it; all these flowers were in our garden last
summer, and they have held their colour. Sometimes

the twins play with it and get potpourri all over the
floor, and it doesn't matter because they're sharing
the beauty of it. Then, sometimes I use it for olive oil
and balsamic vinegar, to dip bread into, because then
you see the little peacocks shining through the rich
green-yellow olive oil.

Her house is filled with rich images of Amalia's life,
crowded with memories of people. She showed us a
photo album.

My ex-husband did this for me. It's not that he did it
for me, but it's that it's all the pictures of my brother.
It's pictures of my brother Donald. I take this
everywhere. [My ex-husband] collected the pictures
I had, but they were kind of in an envelope. The
turning point in his and my relationship was when
Donald died. He couldn't handle my grief; he went
off on a seminar that he didn't really have to go on.
He went the day before Donald's funeral.

That particular time was very difficult. My parents
weren't speaking to each other and I had to go to the
funeral parlour to pick out a – to help my parents
pick out a casket. I had to be the mediator. And I
was being a support for them because they were in
incredible grief. Totally, totally grief stricken. Donald
was incredibly sweet, very loving, very sweet, and
always the one who was more demonstrative of his
love with my parents. I was holding myself up for
them. I was also just beginning graduate studies that

year. And then Sam took off because he couldn't handle this. I thought, if he can't handle this, what is there? And this is just the beginning. If I had a child, and the child died, would he just take off? So this album means a lot to me. He did it for me, to take pictures with me of people who mattered to me. He put himself at the end. We parted as amicably as anybody I know. So it means a lot, for the actual pictures, and also that he did it.

The couple was separating when he created the book. He put pictures of Donald and of Amalia's living brother in it, along with photos of her best friend and of the wedding of a man with whom she had had a passionate affair, "The true love of my life." She looks at the book, "when I'm thinking about Donald and his short life, anniversaries of his birthday, of his death, and I show the kids that this is Mommy when she was little. My ex-husband and I went through many crises, and we're still in touch with each other."

Her living brother, her dead brother, her twin children; next Amalia moved on to a possession from her mother. Her reminiscences became edged with a certain sharpness. At first the box was produced primarily for its contents, but gradually its full story emerged. "I believe it was something that either [Mother] had, or an aunt gave it to her, and it was her great aunt's." Painted on the lid are two women in ball gowns and elbow-length gloves, magenta flowers draped around the bottom of their long skirts, their hair swept up and black velvet ribbons around their throats.

I never wore dresses. I hated to wear dresses. I never thought of the dresses. It was more the colours; the skirts were like a landscape, a hill, or maybe clouds. I used to admire it. She had it on one side of her dresser, the old-fashioned mirror dresser. She used to keep letters in it, from my dad and from her ex-fiancé who was killed in the war. It was symbolic for closeness with a yesteryear, and I have carried it on in the same light, respecting the tradition of the box.

Her mother gave Amalia the box, she thinks, in a perfunctory gesture, shedding her own past, saying, "I don't really need these letters any more."

It was very symbolic for me. I was part of her little ceremony, getting rid of the contents. We sat on her bed and were very close. I was her confidante during my teen years, which ended up being a problem for me ultimately. She allowed me to enter her world of the letters, and told me how she really loved this man, the guy who was killed in the war, and how she was pressured into marrying my dad by friends. She was thirty-four, and was told this was her last chance. She liked Dad well enough, but he wasn't her sort. He was – well, he was just who he is. Her intuition was right because he was not somebody to nurture her and to treat her with dignity. She was the wife and the servant, and she was very hurt by him.

So, she gave it to me in her early fifties. She decided she had made her lot in life and was going to have to live with it. The box is so full now. When I close it up I love the feel of it, in that ceremonial closing up. My mom never had it that full, so I appreciate.... Gee, I have a full life. I'm allowing myself a fullness that my mother never allowed herself. I'm still connected with – allowing myself the connection with people from the past, like Sam. I appreciate when I hold it. I think of my mom and I have sadness for how she's lived her life, that she hasn't had or made herself the allowance to be as full as she would have liked, as full as she might have been.

So Amalia creates her own life through her long history with her mother; she creates the "fullness" she desires, treasuring old ties as much as current ones. She does not break with her mother, but learns from their relationship the dangers in abandoning connections.

The original letters have disappeared. Amalia has her own letters in the box now, and her eighth birthday cards, and her sixteenth, and a letter from Donald written the summer before he died, and her old modeling portfolio in which she looks, as she said, "vampish" – quite a contrast to her current unadorned and fragile beauty. "It was a life I hated. It was really good money, and afforded me a life, like traveling, which was important to me. It was prostitutional. I did it for the money." She never forgets who she was, while knowing who she has become. And, finally, one more connection: the twins again.

This is the positive pregnancy test. I was working at the Women's Health Clinic in my spare time, and one of my colleagues did the test. She said, "Look at that, it's got two dots. Isn't that the strangest thing?" It didn't mean anything at the time, but eight weeks later I found out I'm having twins. Two little blue dots. "You must be real pregnant," she said, you know, joking. It's not that it's got any special beauty, and I wouldn't take it on a cruise or on a trip to Europe. But it was the first sign that I was getting an incredible gift.

Amalia has re-created herself as a mother different from her own. She has accepted and grown beyond the limitations imposed on her mother's life, but she also acknowledges the limits her mother herself created. In common with so many women we interviewed, she seeks to understand her mother, as well as to know her, to gain the empathy that will allow her both to look for her mother in herself and to understand their differences. For many women, that quest begins with photographs of their mothers taken before the daughter's birth. She is a mystery. The mother-daughter nexus begins with the daughter's birth, but the mother was born and had a life before that, and remains to some extent unknowable.

Carole has a picture of her mother at the age of four on her mantle, right next to her own wedding picture. "I love this picture, and when my mom died last summer I asked my father if I could just bring it home. I thought he would want it back. But when he was here last month he decided

I could have it." Every day she glances at the photo and sees her mother as a child, as a separate person whose nature was formed and developed before her own birth.

Frieda, a German immigrant, never knew her mother at all. She died at Frieda's birth during World War II, and all Frieda has of her is one photograph taken shortly before her death at nineteen, a little glass bear that belonged to her, and one more possession, about which she is clearly ambivalent. It is her mother's membership pin in the Hitler Jugend, the youth branch of the Nazis. Living now in Canada, and thriving, Frieda clearly does not know what to make of it. Her own daughters have told her to throw it away, but she cannot. She keeps it at the very back of her jewellery box, and showed it to us almost surreptitiously, wondering no doubt what we would think, perhaps wondering herself why she keeps it. Frieda was raised by her grandmother, about whom she knows more, and received gifts from her mother-in-law, including a superb set of china with a gold rim. "The whole set comes out when we have a special occasion and you have to wash it all by hand." She mourns these women too "now that they are gone;" but her mother will remain forever a mystery. She cannot even speculate about her.

Suzy has a happy reminder of her mother as a young woman, sixteen years old, in Yugoslavia. She treasures the photograph of three dark laughing women in bathing suits standing at the edge of the ocean. "This is the original; Mom would kill me if she knew I had this. She is the middle one. I think she looks so sensuous there, something real honest. It's not crudely sexy. They have tummies and they're allowed to." The three friends do not look at all self-conscious, and Suzy is thrilled at such a legacy of physical comfort and acceptance. Another photo shows her mother again, this time with her father, sitting in front of his car. "Maybe that was his first car, because the license plate says 1955. I just noticed that Mom must have been pregnant with me here which makes me kind of sad because it was before they were married. They were married three months before I was born." But she does not know the exact story.

Robin is also confronted by mystery. Her mother moved frequently. "With each move she gave things to my brother and myself and to grandchildren. But through it all she kept this little bundle with her. Didn't even risk it in the memorabilia that was stored in her brother's for a short time. So for some reason it had particular salience for her. I don't recall her ever talking about them to me." When her mother died, Robin found a small package labelled "Treasures" in her mother's dresser. Reviewing these treasures, Robin came to a completely new and different understanding of her mother and consequently of herself, having restrained her own ambitions in order to follow an itinerant husband and to bear several children. She now sees herself as very like her mother – sharing her intelligence and her enormous frustration at postponing her own academic and professional aspirations until very late in her life.

Peg also sought to know a mother figure, her mother-in-law whom she never met. She keeps a ring that belonged to her husband's mother.

I think the significance of it is largely that it was his mother's. I have probably three or four pieces of jewellery that belonged to her. This one has added significance in that it is also my engagement ring. I think I've created a fantasy person. From the little bits of her own writing and from her pictures, I think I would really, really have liked to know her. I think I have sort of created a relationship with her in absentia. Her jewellery is almost a spiritual connection with her, and so I have a relationship with a person I've never met. I owe her such a debt of gratitude that she managed to raise her son.

This mythic figure truly belongs to her in a way that the other women who seek to peer into their mothers' lives do not own their mothers. As an invention, she can be anybody Peg desires her to be, connected to her by a son and husband.

Connections with godmothers also suggest women's intricate relationships. Gabrielle is fifteen years old, and one of her prized possessions is a porcelain doll, an angel that stands on a shelf in her bedroom, given to her by her godmother. "She's supposed to give me guidance. I kind of look up and I'm okay." Gabrielle's language about her godmother is not sentimental, but she seems nonetheless to find her a source of security, expressed in the angel doll. She said only that the woman "is very special to me. I'm always welcome at her house." That acceptance may well suffice.

In fact, there is no reason to look for sentimentality in mother-daughter relationships, or in relationships with women who represent mothers. Many such relationships are not easy, and while our culture may choose to gloss over their complexities with the banal sentiments of Mother's Day cards, women themselves do not. Sometimes women simply have bad relationships with their mothers; sometimes they are just less warm than cultural verbiage would lead us to believe. Women may be aware of their distance from their mothers or may signal it by their use of language. Ann, for example, told us that she has very little from her mother, partly because

> my mother would not have had a lot of things to give me and I am from a large family. I'm one of six. If there was anything that my parents could hand down, there would've been six of us to distribute to. Before I was born, my parents apparently moved several times. You leave things behind. That means the things you do keep have some particular meaning, which we're not always sure what they are. I don't hardly have anything like antiques or what we would call heirlooms. The only thing I have from my grandmother is a candy dish. It says "Empire England" on the bottom, and these women on it look like they're having a lot of fun dressed in drapery. I didn't think I had any attachment to this particular item, but it is the one thing that I'd want to grab if there was a fire. It's special to me because my mom passed it on. I moved out of the province for

seven years and from what I understand my mother, who is not very emotional, or at least doesn't allow herself to be, it turns out she missed me. When I came back she gave me this.

Another thing I have from my mother is a pincushion and it's something that I've loved all my life. I know that my mom used it when I was a child and I'm not sure why she gave it to me other than she knew that I loved it so much.

Ann's mode of expression is hardly extravagantly emotional, yet the pincushion is important because it brings back memories of childhood.

I think as a child, I looked at it as being in the place where things happened, I suppose. The sewing corner. Things got made, aprons, pillowcases, and so on. I took my mother for granted for my whole life at home. I see now that I respected her industry as opposed to her, and her frugality. They were very poor. She's the oldest of fifteen children and then had nine of her own, losing three.

We would be mistaken to assume homogeneity in relations between mothers and daughters. In contrast to her mother's scarce attention to such things, Ann has "drawers full of things that my children have given me. I have all their class photos and I have all the Mother's Day cards they made and bought for me and I have writing and art work that they did." Did her mother's poverty influence the distance in their relationship, as it influenced her mother? Ann herself certainly has more latitude to be expressive with her own children. What story will they tell?

Ambivalence is not reserved for mothers; mothers-in-law also evoke that response. In Carmen's case, we wonder if even "ambivalence" expresses too much warmth. She has many, many English antiques from the mother of her now-dead husband.

> I have so much. I have lots of antiques and furniture and lots of really old china. It's just amazing, all that stuff. She was English and she sent over a lot of things from England, old china, antique christening dresses. I still have all that stuff. I am moving next year, building a house, so I'll be going through everything and taking out what I really want to keep and giving things away and donating them to museums. Because I want other people to appreciate them too.

She will keep what she wants; others can appreciate what she does not want. We asked her whether she feels burdened by these possessions; she had conveyed her mood, perhaps her impatience with "all that stuff," quite clearly.

> No, I don't feel burdened. I just feel like it's too much and it makes it a little bit cloudy because it's so much. I feel like these things have been passed on to me

and I want to pass them on to somebody else. I don't want my son to wait till I die and then go through it and wonder what to do with all this stuff.

Is she angry about her husband's death? Her ambivalence escalated to impatience.

I have my husband's grandparent's diaries. I love reading through those. My husband kept all that stuff. Those things are priceless to me and I will keep some, but there are a lot of things that smell musty. They're just lovely, but I'm going to get rid of them.

And finally, Carmen tried to make amends for her anger. "I still have this old picture of my husband's mom right by my bed. This is when she was quite a bit younger. She was this beautiful woman. Even after my husband died, she'd come to me in my dreams." Clearly, we were hearing a chaotic story full of unreconciled emotions.

Many women treasure gifts that suggest merely that their mother was thinking of them. They are often satisfied with very little. Susan saves a thimble. "My mom had come up to visit; she went up to the health food store, and bought me this. It was so unexpected that she got me that, and I just love it." Peg has kept a cushion "for a very long time, and the reason why is because my mother made it for me. It is the only hand-made thing I have from her, so it's important." And though she has designed whole rooms to go around the cushion, "I don't think anybody else would recognize it. The kids wouldn't know where it came from.

I don't know if my husband knows where it came from. It's just my own connection." We wonder, does her mother, unlike her other family members, know the importance of the cushion?

Another woman showed us her christening dress, "awful yellow-looking now but my mother made it and I had it for all four of my children and Mum made it and that's what made it so special. This has gone with me everywhere." Aimee, a student in her late twenties, wore silver earrings that made her feel singled out in a special way by her mother.

> I had always thought that these were hers. But on my twenty-fifth birthday she gave them to me, which in itself I was touched. But then she told me that they weren't hers at all. Her best friend had given them to her on the day of my birth to give to me when I was twenty-five. I assume when I was born my mother didn't have much, and neither did her friends, in England. Word that was going around when she said she was going to keep me was that I would never have anything of value or amount to anything of worth."

And here she is, reminded of her mother's love and her mother's fidelity to her own friend. Connections indeed!

Betty expressed, both in how she spoke and in the content of her narrative, the stiffness and emotional distance between herself and her mother. First, she told us of her grandmother, her language betraying ambivalence. On the one hand, she showed us her grandmother's bench on which the telephone sat. "My grandmother had this habit of rubbing her finger on something while she was talking. You can see the corner of the furniture, worn down, where she was rubbing it with doughy fingers." This evidence of her grandmother's mannerisms gives her a living presence in Betty's house. On the other hand, when showing us the crystal bowl from her, she said, "Before she died, she sent my mom home with a bunch of stuff and I got this. Every year at Christmas I throw the cranberry sauce in it." Her

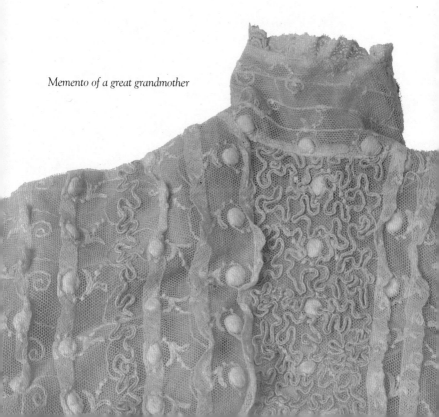

Memento of a great grandmother

language – "a bunch of stuff," "throwing cranberry sauce" – suggests the distance among the women in her family. She then became more explicit.

> Because my kids live all spread out, my mother figures our family is breaking up. But she did the same thing. Times have changed and people are moving on. My mother was one of these women who get a day's work done and nothing frivolous and of course we had nothing extra in our house, just the essentials. We thought they were fine. My mom didn't share stories with us about her past, just the odd cryptic remark about some aunt or another. So we weren't given a lot of connection to what her life might have been like. My mother is not one to hug or kiss any of us, never did, any of us kids. She's a real Margaret Laurence character. My father, however, is very gentle and we heard lots of stories from when he was a boy. Then, nine years ago, my mother had a heart attack and found out that she had a very inefficient valve. She had an operation where they inserted an artificial valve and all of a sudden she felt like a new person. She could breathe deeply, she could do things she had never been able to do before. All of a sudden she started to tell us stories.

Betty's mother – poor, frugal, emotionally distant, silent, and obviously unwell – began to talk. "I never would've asked her before, and now she's quite willing to tell me these things. It turns out now that she really didn't think her life was significant. She thought there would be nothing interesting about a young woman who lived in the prairies." From the story's beginning in coldness, her mother took on a new life. Voice was restored to her.

Betty did not lapse into nostalgia or sentimentality. She concluded by telling us that her mother lives close by, but that she does not see her often.

> There are issues here. She puts too many expectations on me. It would be nice to have a mother you could get along with, play with, and do things with, but for my mother her house is her thing. She won't drop her ironing and go help somebody or have coffee with anybody. She is not a social being.

And yet, though the relationship may have been difficult, virtually every woman possesses something that belonged to her mother. Women become the keepers of their mothers' stories. In the possession of one small artefact, a woman tells another woman's story, so that her voice, however silent, however distant, is still heard. These are mostly women whose lives are recorded in no book, whose material presence exists in no museum, and yet whose daughters keep them alive. Women are the archivists of each other's histories. Even if they are hidden from public history, their collections are faithfully kept, their stories retold again and again.

Possessions also bespeak warmth, love, respect, a thousand happy emotions. Mary Grace brought her collection of storybook dolls. "They are precious, quite simply, because my mother put so much care into them. It's not the dolls, it's what she did with them. She put them in a place where they seemed almost sacred." She still follows her mother's rules about them. "I just look at them. They're in jars, because I don't have a cabinet like she did. I will probably ask my daughter, she was close to my mother, if she is interested in having them. It'll be in my will: Do Not Touch!" She continues to honour her mother's requests and perpetuates her mother's daily presence by keeping the bright hat her mother crocheted for her. "Immediately when I look in the closet, that's who I think of."

Betty showed us a photograph of her mother, young at the time, her older sister Jenny, and her cousin Bunny, on the reserve.

My mother died three days after my sister. Jenny is the baby in the stroller. My mother always took care of Jenny, so when she passed away I thought to myself, " she is going to take care of Jenny," because Jenny was always the weak one in the family and my mother was always there for her. Jenny died of a drug overdose and my mother, well she was an alcoholic. My auntie raised me after that, Bunny's mom. She was the one that taught me all my values and morals. She was a really nice lady. When I got older she would send me post cards from wherever she was up north, cooking in the camps up north. She gave me this picture just before she died.

Betty also treasures a picture of herself as a child, saying, "That little girl has come a long way. I look at this every now and then and realize how far I have come. My mother must have done something right." Indeed.

Paddy treasures her mother's presence by her attachment to a linen bag that her mother embroidered, the only needlework she ever did. "I love it because she's so pleased that I use it and treasure it." The bag gives them the opportunity to laugh together, to reminisce together. "Every time she comes she turns it over and says, 'Whatever possessed me to put that colour on it? What an ugly colour it is. I probably had only that colour.' And she says the same thing every time. I find that very dear." Her connections to her family emerged at the same time. "These things are personal, things that I love to feel. You take your family for granted when you're younger and then you get older and you realize how important it is to come from something and pass something on." As Paddy lovingly recalls her connection to her mother, she wants to pass on her own presence in turn.

Women keep objects from their mothers in order to affirm their continuing presence, but they keep the stories of the objects too. Micheline began the story of the hope chest her Quebecois mother gave her in her adolescence with a narrative about her mother. Micheline keeps the small cedar chest at the foot of her bed. Beautiful white linens cover the bed, and the chest fits perfectly into the antique country look of the room.

My mother was very close to her father, because he had more time to spend with her than he did with his subsequent children. I don't think she felt that she had a lot of attention. She used to talk about how she had a very bad temper when she was little, would get upset when the kids didn't wait for her. She would scream and cry and yell. She was a pepper hothead. Demanded attention and probably didn't get enough. Her mother died when she was two. Her mother was twenty-seven, and there were already four children in the family. Her father married her mother's sister, who proceeded to have a very large family. My mother didn't talk much about her growing up years except to say that they were poor and there were many of them.

There was not a lot of time for them, or affection. My mother was not an affectionate woman. But would have killed anyone who touched us. My father loved us and thought I could do no wrong, but I resented the fact that he had made my mother's life very hard. He was a very good provider, we never lacked for material things, but he was a man who drank and couldn't deal with the day-to-day situation of a family. He could only get involved in family discussions if he was drinking.

My cedar chest was in my bedroom and my mother used to make jokes about it being such a small hope chest because I probably didn't have much hope. She had a biting wit like mine. I was still living at home, about nineteen or twenty. I began to think about leaving home and striking out on my own. I knew my mother would be devastated because I was her girl, and she would be left alone with five men. When I was twenty I got the courage to talk about it, and I was really asking for permission. When my own daughter decided she wanted to leave, she simply announced that she would be leaving, as though it was a fait accompli. I finally got the courage to tell my mother that I wanted to go work in Montreal, only an hour away from where we lived. But it meant leaving home. She was, as I expected, devastated, and said, "Please wait until you are twenty-one." I reluctantly agreed because I felt I didn't have any choice. She reminded me years later that I pouted for weeks.

The interesting thing that happened, the link with that little chest, was that she began to buy little things like tea towels and face cloths for when I left home. It was her way of saying that she was reconciled to the fact that I was leaving home. She was letting me go. It taught me something about letting go. I always thought to myself that I would have to remember that when I have my children. And I did.

When I was growing up I felt very special in my family because of being the only daughter. But I also felt I couldn't give my mother anything to worry about because she had enough to do with the boys. There were difficult periods in my life. I didn't share them with her because I wanted to protect her. Maybe she would have loved to share with me.

I didn't even go home from Vancouver to get married. I deprived her of something. She never told me what to do. My mother was great that way. She had immense faith in me. Everything I did was fine with her. I always felt that I lived up to whatever expectations she had, which I think is a very good way to grow up.

Micheline concluded her story. It is her mother's story and her own, and includes her own daughters: three generations of women's narratives contained in her small cedar chest. Her mother's story guides her in her own child rearing. Her mother's love and respect strengthen her. She remembers her every time she sees the chest at the foot of her bed.

Mothers are the people who, more than anyone, are kept alive in their daughters' lives. Diane has a framed set of two pictures, one drawing of a boy, another of a girl. She wanted these badly at her mother's death. "As a child I really identified with these, just that it was a boy and a girl. I liked that she had children on the wall." In a not particularly affectionate relationship, Diane found a place for herself in her mother's heart through those pictures, which now hang on her own wall. Her mother lives on, too, in a glass butterfly given her by a man who made her very happy after a long unhappy marriage with a husband who finally deserted her and disappeared. "She always said she would come back as a butterfly. When she died, each of the kids took one butterfly. Whenever I see a butterfly, I feel like I am seeing my mother."

We knew that the chapters of this book concerning women's connections to other people would be long and complex. Amalia's narrative prepared us for the varieties of emotional experience that would be expressed in the stories about relationships. We must admit, however, to some surprise at the capacity of women to resist the stereotypes, the greeting card sentiments, that describe our culture's view of ideal relationships. So much of their language is unsentimental and original. Even though the demands of a culture script the acceptable emotional responses of its people, many of the women told unexpected stories of connections to those close to them. North American popular culture has tended, through television, songs, and greeting cards, to reduce intimate relations to childish simplicity and unadulterated love or worship. Words like "mother," "father," and "grandmother" evoke automatic pictures of love and loyalty, as if those were simple emotions. The realities are complicated. They also include betrayal, rage, neglect, and disappointment. Knowingly, and sometimes unintentionally, women exposed the complexity and the difficulty of their bonds with other people.

We heard recollections of fathers and grandfathers, though not as many as we had expected, knowing that so many families are ostensibly organized around the presence of a man. By telling us about the important people in their lives, women were in a sense creating a culture and a mythology of the family. Their stories represent the ways they form the idea of family; these are not ideals necessarily sanctioned by the culture. They tell stories to make real or imagined families for themselves: stories of love or of loss, of caring or of cruelty. They may conform to or resist our culture's ideas about families. Despite being immersed in cultural meanings, each woman told her own story, her own way. The narratives are framed by each woman's social and historical realities and are lived as particular choices and actions. We can listen to their stories and find there both collective and individual realities expressing the grip of culture and the capacity to break out of it into personal thought and action.

Nancy's possessions evoke both the everyday nature of connections and the almost mythological ties within families. The first article she showed us was her grandfather's cigar box, which she described as "symbolic of something you want to remember.... It was always out on his mantle, and he smoked, and he kept his cigars in there, so I remember him." Her next item is similar:

> I kept my mom's glasses! My grandmother's glasses: something that is definitely her, there's no mistake. They are of an era and dated; mind you, they are also pretty cool because I think this style is coming back. But she wore these glasses, every time I saw her, or ones very similar to them. They remind me of her; I see her face.

The objects that were used daily by her grandparents connect her to them. The continuity became mythic when she showed us the family seal, which looks like a silver knife handle. "You would put wax on the letter and stamp it with the seal. My mother gave this to me when I took her maiden name. This was her father's, so she was really excited, and said that the family was dying out." Now Nancy has reclaimed the name and the heritage; she said modestly, "So that's nice for me."

Libby's story of her father is equally mythological. An eighty-three-year-old Mormon woman, now comfortable with herself and with her life, she invented a cast of characters to populate her early life. She began her narrative by showing us a small jewellery casket from her mother. More important than the small box, though, are the engagement and wedding rings inside. They were all her mother's.

My parents were divorced when I was four years old. I never saw him again. Mom just took up and moved to California and that was that. I tried to contact him and I never got an answer, so I didn't push it. It's a mystery, and when I was twenty years younger I would've liked to know the answer. Now, I figure I'm getting older and pretty soon I'm going to be on the other side where he's at and I'm going to go looking for him. In the meantime, I'm not going to worry myself or anybody else about it.

I was told that he had died and I accepted that. It wasn't until I got to be thirteen or fourteen that I learned he was very much alive and that I had a half-brother. Oh well, that's in the past. One can't change things. If you think you can re-do the past, you are badly mistaken; it's gone.

The rings have caused Libby to consider the nature of regret and her capacity, at eighty-three, for the present. She continued with her story.

As long as she lived, she kept that always on her dresser. She never married again, but she always kept it there. I knew, from being around my mother all those years, that she was still in love with him and nothing would change that. To me there had to be something very special in that relationship, even though it was broken. Even though I haven't had a father, I've had a father in my head. Somehow I knew that Mama couldn't mentally part with my dad.

I didn't know much about him, just how he loved the outdoors and how he was gifted in taking care of any kind of animal that got sick. When I asked Grandpa what my dad was like, he said to me, "He was the smartest I ever met in my life." "Then why did they get divorced?" He said, "I told you all you need to know." He never said another word.

Libby learned early about life's elusive mysteries, about reticence, and about privacy. Out of that knowledge she fashioned a mythical father, a fantasy figure, creating thereby a perfect family saga based on her belief that her mother's love for her father endured forever. "Mama loved him very, very much, and nobody she ever met could touch him."

We were amazed to discover that grandmothers are more important in women's lives than any of the literature we have read has suggested. Mothers, yes, that we knew, but not grandmothers. And yet, there they are, playing a large role in so many women's stories. Much like mothers, they are real or mythic figures, actually there in their childhood and adult lives – but also invented for the warmth they can offer. Just as women feel an obligation, a desire, to become repositories for their mothers' histories, so too do they save their grandmothers' objects. These grandmothers, whose histories may never have been recorded anywhere, find a place in the hearts of their granddaughters. In this way women create a women's history. It may not be a very public story, but this unrecorded history provides women with markers and signposts to direct them. The stories of grandmothers become a narrative that embraces the lives of women who come after them. The presence of grandmothers, whether they are described as real people or almost as inventions, connects women to a past, a continuity in which they know they have a place, even if the public realm of history does not contain their stories. Grandmothers give women a signpost toward making a future.

Reminiscences of grandmothers, evoked by their possessions, were not uniformly blissful by any means. As with stories of mothers, anger and resentment emerged occasionally, and sometimes feelings were mixed. Suzy, forty-two years old, showed us the teddy bear with hinged and movable arms and legs, its paws split from the years. Her maternal grandmother sent it from Austria when Suzy was a year old, and it sat on her dresser all through her adult years. One might expect, then, to hear of great attachment to the grandmother who sent it. But no: it represents something of an invention on her part, a way of filling a void. "It's my connection to my grandparents because I didn't have a relationship with them. I didn't have any grandparent stuff. If there was a fire this is what I would grab. Everything else is replaceable." A sense of loss permeated Suzy's narrative. She met her grandmother only once, on a trip to Europe at fourteen.

> She was cooking all day. She was quite big, had chipmunk cheeks. She would've been a great grand- mother to curl up in her lap. She was very cuddly. I really missed having that. With my mother coping with three kids, it would've been nice to have a grandma who had time for you.

Suzy wanted a grandmother to make up for the mother who apparently had no time for her. "I felt the loss of my mom. She works till she drops. Martha Stewart drop dead." The softness she wished for in a mother she received in imagination from a grandmother.

Patty was more overtly angry. "My grandmother was a controlling and miserable woman." Patty is a thirty-three- year-old university student, a single mother whose son is five. Her own life is not easy. "At best, her most endear- ing quality was her constant bitching." But she has some sympathy.

> That is not entirely who she was; I would have to say that the circumstances of her life led her to act

that way. In some way, these few pieces of jewellery remind me that she was not altogether a nasty woman. They also remind me that my past is part of who I am.

She obviously takes some pleasure in identifying with her mother through a diamond ring her mother bought for herself in the fifties while working in a jewellery store in Toronto. She started there as a clerk and ended as the manager. Patty likes thinking of her determination, her capacity to think of a career when middle-class women were not in the paid work force. "When I wear this ring, I like to think of how difficult it must have been to work full time when her children were so young and her husband away so much." Patty's own story is not entirely different from her mother's, and it was her mother who gave her the ring; she understood how much Patty would cherish it. "My grandmother would have made some snide comment about how I would lose it or trash it." Patty received a pair of earrings directly from the grandmother, in compensation, she thinks, for the sewing machine she had promised her but gave instead to an uncle, "I like the earrings but have only worn them once. Their real value is in reminding me of what I didn't get from her, which was kindness. But to be honest, I don't give a shit. She means little to me and mostly I detest her for treating my mother the way she did."

More women, though, recall grandmothers with warmth. Donna recalls hers with a certain amusement. She has what she calls a "bag of junk" filled with possessions from her teenage years. Her Jewish grandmother – this is how she labels her, clearly adjusting her memory to fit with a cultural image – gave her the bag when she was fourteen.

> I was going on the plane to visit Grandma in New York. She wanted me to bring some kosher meats and bagels home for my dad. She packed them in this little blue bag. I tried accidentally to leave the bag behind in the airport because I thought I would be arrested for trying to smuggle food into Canada! I had just settled into my seat on the plane when the stewardess came running on with this bag in her hand, saying, "I think you forgot this." And there was Grandma waving to me from the tarmac!

Donna's other prized possession is her grandmother's gold Star of David. She wore it to her college graduation to remember her, sad that Grandmother did not live to see her granddaughter realize her aspirations.

Adulation enters memoirs of grandmothers too: Jeanine, a social worker close to fifty, has her grandmother's pendant.

> She was an incredible seamstress, made beautiful quilts. She would wear this every day. She dressed quite elegantly, had her hair long to her waist, and she would wind it around her head in coils. This cameo reflects the feeling of her grand elegance. My mother doesn't have her elegance. My grandmother's life too was much more dignified. She really made a

statement about not working outside, for pay. That was a line she drew.

Jeanine has created a grandmother who was strong, principled, and effective. While her own life as the single parent of two adolescents cannot replicate her grandmother's, she cherishes the image of such a dignified woman in her life. She, like other women, creates the kind of grandmother who can inspire her, a mythologized, idealized person.

Linda had a close connection with her grandmother and praises her for being "very elegant, even as an older lady, but she had never been a kind loving woman." Despite this, "I have a real connection with her. I can' t explain it. It's almost a spiritual connection." Her grandmother, long dead, having committed suicide, is clearly a presence in her life, kept alive by a locket she wore.

Joyce, now sixty-five, also venerates her grandmother and makes every effort to keep her memory alive in her children. The first object she discussed was a replica of her grandmother's wedding dress. And yet, she told us, "Although she stayed with us on and off until I was sixteen, when she died, I wouldn't say that she was an influential figure in my life. She was there, just Grandma, and I didn't know I was lucky to have one." Joyce also has her grandmother's sewing machine, which she offered to her younger daughter, the fourth child of five. Her daughter, thirty years old, politely declined it – for the moment, she said. Joyce wants to impress on her the importance of family.

Grandmother's wedding dress

I certainly hope that is the way my children continue to feel, that they know family is important. It is of prime importance to me. And I think everybody knows it, because my aunt had the sewing machine and said that "this article is an heirloom and used to belong to your grandmother, and we are giving it to you." They know I like old family things.

Her grandmother serves, perhaps, as the quintessential embodiment of family – distant enough to be no danger, intimate enough to serve as a connection through the generations. Joyce has created a family story. It gives her a history, makes her part of a history, and prompts her to create a history in turn for her own children.

"She was descended from royal blood and was making sure that I would carry on the family tradition." In fact, it is not clear in her narrative what that tradition is: rather, her grandmother serves in memory to prompt Laine's sense of her own uniqueness, how special she felt in her grandmother's presence.

and her sewing machine

When I was a little girl, my mother went to work when I was three. She left me with my grandmother, and every afternoon we would have a nap. When she put me down to nap, she would cover me and bend over to kiss me. I'm the only one of her offspring that remembers being kissed. When she bent over to kiss me, I knew that I was loved beyond anything. She always wore this brooch, at the neck of her dress; it sat just below the pulse point in her throat. I always saw it when she bent down, and I knew that I was totally loved.

She is a strong and vibrant woman, whose memories of her grandmother are sensual and intense. In fact, Laine's grandmother takes on magical powers.

Laine also has a nightgown from her grandmother,

... all hand stitched with tiny embroidery stitches, and tiny buttonholes. She made nightgowns out of linen and kept them in her drawer in case anybody was ever sick. When I was fourteen, I was bitten by a black widow spider, became very sick, and got encephalitis from it. When they decided at the hospital that I wasn't going to live, my grandmother arrived at the hospital with this linen nightgown. And I got better. I miraculously got better. I always keep it in the bottom drawer of my dresser, which is the same drawer my grandmother kept it in. And whenever my children got sick, when they were small, I would wrap them in this nightgown and they always got better. Now, listen. My older son is a very large child. When he was eight, he was probably the size of a normal fifteen year old. That year, he was hit on the head with a baseball bat, which left him with epilepsy. He had grand mal seizures. Well, when he was older, he had a grand mal seizure when we were traveling in the van. We had to lay his 6'4" form down in the little tiny space in the van and to travel for almost an hour to get to the hospital. As he was coming out of the seizure, becoming conscious, he asked to be wrapped in the linen nightgown. And of course I didn't have it with me, and he's never gotten better. He still has seizures. Even though I know it's a coincidence, it seems as if something could've been done, as if I could've done something.

> Yes, my grandmother did that all by hand, I feel very
> close to her, because that is something she left me.

Frieda was raised in Germany by her grandmother, who thus was virtually her mother. She showed us the silver she inherited from her, with an "F" on every piece. "Was that her initial?" we asked. "No," she answered. "She thought I would have it someday, so she put my initial on it." It was marked, then, specifically for her, making her feel keenly the connection her grandmother had with her.

Jane also felt singled out by her grandmother, connected to her by a book of poetry they used to read to each other. Her grandmother was the only person who supported her, unmarried and seventeen, in having a baby. She had herself been a single mother and became a model for her granddaughter. Vanessa also had a model in her grandmother, who went to university at forty. She gave Vanessa a copy of Mary Wollstonecraft's *A Vindication of the Rights of Women*, which she said gave her "something to fight back with" against her very religious husband. She wanted Vanessa also to find power in this book. It is on the bookshelf with Vanessa's own women's studies books.

Susan is connected to her grandmother and reminded of her daily by the small embroidery scissors, the initials almost worn off with use, that her adored grandmother used for crocheting tablecloths.

> She used to keep them on a string and I wish the
> string was still there. My grandmother loved me just

as much as I loved her. She would sit me on her bed and tell me that I was her favourite. She adored me. When she was put in a home at ninety-four – she remained there for two years and then she died – I used to hitchhike every day to where she was until she died. I even skipped school to go to see her.

Her grandmother's dedication and commitment to Susan were returned and turned into Susan's connection to a women's history. She fondles the little scissors, her own hands holding her grandmother's in the powerful bond among generations of women who tell each other's stories.

Marsha, who lived with her grandmother for a year, thinks of her as a model to this day.

This is my grandmother's Passover plate. When my grandfather passed away, in his will he said he would take me and my sister to Israel. We bought her this Passover plate when we went because we wanted to get her something from Israel. They worked tirelessly for Israel, and were never able to go because of their health. When she died, I said I needed this plate. Granny was always my ally. [Because of her] I thought that women could do anything. She worked all day, did books all night. She had a style. And she just didn't quit.

And so she brings her style into Marsha's memory and her energy into Marsha's life.

Women's stories about their mothers, fathers, and grandmothers speak of the child coming to know herself through close relationships and of the woman who affirms the centrality of relationships. Moving between her own life and the lives of women important to her, she understands how her connections provide an essential foundation for her own independence. Their stories support her freedom to build what is uniquely her own by understanding the characteristics she inherited and recognizing their place in her life.

*C*atherine is a visual artist, a painter who has created her narrative, her world, and her choices from
textures, colours, and feelings. She has made careful,
conscious decisions about the kind of life she must have.
Many of them are unconventional choices. They have led
her to unexpected places and people, sometimes causing the
people close to her to shake their heads. Still, she is calm
and tranquil, in control of her life and her art, motivated
by her own needs, impelled by her own aesthetic, finding
her direction from within herself, and truly happy. She was
not always as balanced as she is today, but she has learned
through her fifty years to heed the knowledge of her senses,
of her body, and of her own desire. Her relationships with
men now begin and end when their beginnings and endings
work for her. Her friendships with both women and men are
long lasting.

Catherine's fidelity to her mother is part of her life's
fabric. Her activities, from ocean kayaking to hiking, painting, cooking, and reading, warm her. Her clothing is functional, suited to her island life, and yet the colours are her
own, the occasional pieces of jewellery enhancing her
appealing, slender, dark-haired presence, quiet and potent.

She reaches out, touches the world, hears her desire, and makes her own choices. She lives a conscious life, true to herself.

Catherine carefully unpacked her collection of objects, fondling each tissue-wrapped piece as she put it on the dining table. She could hardly wait to begin. Like many other women, she began by explaining that she had selected things that were "one of a kind and couldn't be replaced. So, although my computer is extremely important to me, and in some ways right now is at the top of my list because it keeps me in touch with people I care about, I didn't include it because I could go out and buy another one if I had to." Instead, she carefully drew a quilt from its white tissue paper.

> This is something I've carried with me wherever I have lived for thirty years. It is a quilt that my grandmother and a couple of great aunts made. It is a modified log cabin design, smallish pieces in velvets and silks, very rich burgundies, greens, and blues, the range of colours that I really like. This is at the top of my list because I think that both genetically and from our family tradition, I really identify with my paternal grandmother. Apparently I have the same body build and I know that my aesthetic sense is very similar to hers because everything I have ever seen that belonged to her, I have loved.
>
> I remember being very happy with my grandmother. When we were out at the lake in the summer, she and I shared a bed. She had long white

hair, and she braided it at night. I can remember her long flannel nightgown and her hair braided down her back. She must have had a sense of humour, because I remember being happy with her. When I was very small I can remember sitting on the kitchen counter and watching her make cookies. And I remember riding on the front of the carpet sweeper, seeing the little light on the front; things like that.

When I first got the quilt I was living in Regina. I had that on my bed, sort of an iron bedstead. I noticed that some of the threads in the silk were beginning to fray, and someone said that if you have people smoking in your apartment it's not going to be good for the fabric. So by the time I moved to Pennsylvania, my boss, who was very good at working with wood, said, "If you will pay for the materials I will frame this for you." He constructed a simple, strong, wonderful frame for the quilt. When I left New York, I took it out of the frame, folded up the quilt, and took it home, back to the same basement I took it out of twenty-five years ago!

Catherine's family remains a vital part of her life today. She foresees the time when she will own a set of Limoges china, once her grandmother's and now her mother's, "a creamy colour, hand painted with flowers in the same range of colours I seem to gravitate toward. It is tied to my immediate family and all our meals together, setting the table, serving the food." In fact, in surely one of the most unusual answers to our inevitable questions about who might become the recipient of the favourite piece, Catherine answered, "I would probably give it to my mother, who will be eighty-four the day after tomorrow!"

Her next prized possession – and she was very clear about the order in which she would talk about the artefacts – was a ring, an opal, still in its natural rock setting, set in gold. The story she told about it further intensified our awareness of the consciousness, the deliberateness with which Catherine chooses to live.

It is a replacement for a ring that my brother had given me for my sixteenth birthday, which I lost climbing in Pennsylvania. So, after several years of being separated from my husband, I discovered that I still had his wedding ring in my jewellery box. When he first got it he complained that it gave him pains up his arms and they then traveled down into his chest! So at some point I said, "Oh well, give it to me," and I put it in my jewellery box. So, since I had his ring and my ring, I wanted to do something constructive with it. It took me years, because it seemed like violating a taboo, you know, to melt down your ex's wedding ring and do something else with it.

So, I was going on vacation in the Virgin Islands. I had found a jewellery maker down there, so I brought the rings with me and asked him if he would design something for me. "Yes, and I think I have just the stone for it," and he produced this for me. And just look, it falls right into the same colour

range. It really represents me. I feel I created it, and it
also represents that act of freeing myself from a very
constricting relationship.

For Catherine, creativity, art, and making beautiful
things all combine to become an act of freedom. "I have
other pieces of jewellery, some of them given me by men
about whom I cared at the time, and worth far more than
this, but none is as precious to me."

Her next possession is a wooden lamp, carved into the
shape of a stylized cat, each of its four legs decorated differently from the others, and with some movable parts.

> It falls into the same category as the ring, in that
> it was the first thing I invested in, or splurged on,
> depending on how you look at those things, after
> I left my marriage. It was under $200, but I would
> never have spent that in my marriage. I have gotten
> more pleasure out of this lamp over the years. I've
> had it in the bedroom, I've had it in the kitchen, and
> I've had it in the hall. Depending on where I have
> it, I change the bulb. When I made my many moves,
> even when I brought very little, I carried this with
> me. When the bulb in it is pink, the metal shade on
> top reflects backlight very warmly.

Light and sight unite with the knowledge of independence and the capacity to make one's own choices.

This shawl – heavy and fringed and the two sides are different, almost iridescent – was also my grandmother's. I have not worn it in years. There was a period when I wore it a bit, when I used to dress up, and especially if I was wearing black. My feeling now is that I will grow into it. There will be a time in my life when I will wear this quite a bit. In the meantime I'm just very happy to have it. I keep it wrapped in tissue paper in a box. My mother gave it to me after I was married. She said, "We came across this when we were going through things of your grandmother's and thought you would like it." And obviously I did. Why I brought it here to the island I do not know. But it was a conscious decision.

Now I want to tell you about something that isn't here that is a very important thing to me. It is a painting that I did just a few months after my separation. I had my first vacation by myself; I went to Stone Valley for the first week in June. I was the only person there and I had access to a rowboat and a canoe. There were hills, and trails, and the lake, and I painted every day. I was ecstatic, absolutely ecstatic. One of the paintings that came out of that week turned out to be one of those little jewels that you look at and think, "My God, I thought that was a conventional painting and it isn't at all." It was quite striking. When I left there for New York, I gave it to friends of mine, good friends; I did it with some ambivalence but I wanted them to have it. About a year later I got a letter from her saying, "You may think this strange but I'm writing to tell you that I want to return your painting. It isn't that we don't like it. We love it and so do our friends, but we feel it deserves a bigger audience and I want you to have it back." I didn't even respond to the letter. My nose was a little out of joint, actually, and I didn't know quite – and it was signed, "Sincerely," so I didn't know what it meant.

A few months later I got another letter saying, "Catherine, I don't know whether you got my letter, but I really meant it." I think she had learned that I was leaving New York and coming back to Canada and that I was going to be painting. She said, "This is very important now that you are beginning a new phase in your life. You gave this to us just at a critical moment when you had made a major change. Now you're making another major change, and we want you to have this. Tell me where I can ship it to you safely." I was overcome. I got it within a couple of days, and I was so happy to have it. It's hanging in my mother's house right now. It particularly represented the importance that this friendship has in my life, and how much my friends have understood.

For Catherine, the painting is about meaning and sensory pleasure, about friendship and connections, about the beauty of the lake and the trails, about freedom and choice.

The next object was a little wooden book with a hinged spine that opens to reveal a red suede heart. Sensuality informs its story.

That was given to me by the same man who made the frame for my quilt, who is someone I love very much. We were never lovers, although at one point that became an issue. I think both of us are glad that it never happened. I worked for him for eight years, my first working years. He influenced me very much. He is a woodworker, and a photographer, and a sort of natural Buddhist, not a religious person in any sense, but eastern in the way he views the world. We are soul mates. We give support to one another; he sends me photographs and I make little paintings for him. He is one of a handful of people I carry around in my head, and I think, "How would he react in this situation?" Once I got a little vase, and he gave me books, but this is the one thing I really treasure. It even has a little feather on the cover. I have another piece he did that has a teeny fluffy white feather attached to a little square of wood, and a teeny magnifying glass so you can look at it. Of all the thousands and thousands of books in our house, back then, my ex-husband being a bibliophile, this book is really a book of love.

He wrote poetry too, and I have some of it. It was he who encouraged me, gave me opportunities. He was a mentor in an informal sort of way, during very difficult years in my marriage when I was also pursuing a career, so he is inextricably linked with my working life. He would take me to a conference and then disappear, and I would have to sink or swim. That was before we really got to know each other. So he was a friend, and father, and romantic interest, and a very creative person. This is a book of love.

Catherine turned from love to death, because her next object was a wooden mask of the dead from Mexico. "It called to me off the wall in the shop, and I felt I had to have it. It is used for the feast of the dead." She described it first by its appeal to her senses, the green protuberances from its forehead, the red mouth, the splatterings of colour. She hasn't incorporated it, she said, into any of her paintings; it has only been there, wherever she has lived, at eye level facing her.

In the living room in my New York apartment, when I walked in we were eye to eye. It's warm to me, but it's also a memento mori. But it doesn't scare me. It occurs to me that I may work with this when my mother dies. I've asked myself what there is of my mother's in my possessions. And I think it's too soon for me to know.

Her mother is still living, but is elderly and unwell, and already Catherine feels the mask of the dead calling loudly to her, becoming more real. Death and the senses combine in an affirmation of the power that comes from never denying mortality, and yet never being less than alive and aware. Catherine and her mother do not share an aesthetic sensibility, but they are "very much on the same psychic wavelength, because we just are. These temporal things remind you of previous generations, keeping that person alive." Her focus on objects that appeal to her senses, her sensuality, her self-awareness, came together in her final possession, a Japanese calligraphy scroll.

I bought this just before I left New York from my sensei with whom I had been studying for the last year and a half. A very talented woman, a Japanese-American woman who was in the camps during World War II. What started as a very formal relationship between teacher and student became a friendship. I miss her very much, for her instruction and for her presence. She was tough. She carved out her own little space down in the Village.

Right after my back surgery, the first day I went out for a walk, my friend and I passed her place. "Oh, look, I've been wanting to check this out the last couple of years. I'm really interested in this woman's work. I'll do it next time." My friend said, "Catherine, the door is open." So, I walked in and I ended up going home for lunch and going right back. I studied with her three times a week during those six weeks I was recuperating, six hours a week and I was also working at home on calligraphy. Then twice a week, then once; but she was a very strong influence on me. Every time I put the brush down, I feel that I'm much more conscious of each stroke, where it begins and where it ends, and the intensity with which I use the brush. She is another person I carry in my head. She was one of the very strongest influences of this last phase of New York and of my leaving to become a full-time artist.

I came to value myself as an artist, and I owe that to her to a large extent. Before I left I wanted to buy one of her paintings. She said, "Oh, artists don't sell to other artists." That was the ultimate compliment. I said, "But that is not the relationship here." I know she charges a lot for her paintings, in the thousands, and I said, "I have $400, and if you would select a few things that you would be prepared to sell for $400." She put out a stack of pieces and I sorted it into things I liked. At some point she pulled this scroll out and added it to the pile. I thought, "This is the one she wants me to have, and it is the one I want too."

Her senses, her art, and her life have come together as conscious choices made, departures experienced, relationships entered and ended: love and death and the will and the body.

As we see through Catherine's story, objects are not only meaningful for the stories they contain or the thoughts they evoke. Many have a strong sensual and emotional presence. They support a woman's knowledge of herself as an emotional, physical, and sensual being, one to whom colours, shapes, textures, sounds, music, and light are deeply pleasurable. Certain treasures are saved because they convey meaning through the body and its senses. They symbolize a woman's connections to the natural world and her vision of herself as continuous with nature.

Almost all the women talked about a few special items that serve strongly sensual functions, calling the past forward by smell or by sound, recreating a moment, a place, or a person. Some women, especially those who artists or whose careers emphasize the physical care of others, impressed us as having particularly strong predilections for possessions of this kind. Virtually every item in these women's collections contain multiple, layered sensory meanings.

When a woman holds such a possession – a shell, a book, a shawl – in her hands, she engages with it physically and emotionally. She may close her eyes as she holds it, her fingers moving in long strokes over its curves and textures, her senses attuned to its sensual qualities, her body and mind relaxing into unguarded recollections of special moments. She may gaze at it, transfixed, losing herself in its beauty and experiencing it as if it were an extension of her own body. Certain objects have the power to move women out of the mundane into another reality where the body is powerful and knowledgeable. They may escape for a time into some essential aspect of the self, the bodily self that is often submerged or obscured by daily obligations. The meditative aspects of such objects allow a woman to focus on and confirm an authentic, immediate sense of what is important, of what sustains and nourishes her.

Susan picked up a small box and turned it slowly in her hands. It is an oval, cherry-red cylinder closed at both ends, with four little legs, and a rounded lid, enamelled in vivid colours, clicks quietly into its latch.

This was our matchbox, but now I keep a lot of other little things in it. It was my mom's and she had it above her kitchen sink. Mom used to smoke; she'd take out a wooden match and strike it on the box without holding it. I used to play with this match-box. I would sit on the counter in the kitchen and listen to the CBC "Kindergarten Every Year," which came on every day at ten. Mom would be busy doing things around the kitchen and I had the matchbox to play with, along with some clay figurines of lady-bugs. I wasn't actually allowed to play on the coun-ter. I can't believe my mother actually let me play on the counter, but she did. She always let me. It's a sunny memory. My sisters had gone off to school and I was home alone with Mom for the first time, and it was wonderful. She'd give me a piece of whatever she was baking, which she would never have done if my sisters were home, because she would have had to give everyone a piece.

Holding the box helps Susan fully recover a memory that sustains her. The feel of the box, the sounds and smells of the kitchen, the baking, the colour of the box, return her to a place of safety, security, beauty, warmth, and love. The box encapsulates her happiness and the sense of specialness she had before things changed when her mother went to work.

> She went to work when I was ten and it broke my heart, a very sad time for me. It was so hard on me, so devastating; and it still is. Before that the house was warm. At the end of the radio program, I would step across from the counter to the other counter and go to the sink to put the matchbox away.
>
> I told my mother about the memory one day and I think that she was quite touched by it. I can't believe my mother gave it to me. She just reached out and handed it to me. She has a lot of things that I covet. My mom is funny, because anything that I like, she doesn't really want me to have. But she gives me strange things that nobody else would want to have, probably because she knows that I'll keep it forever and cherish it.

The kitchen memory obviously elicits mixed feelings. Susan's memory of her mother avoids mere nostalgia or sentimentality because it is complicated by loss. She peers at her childhood uncritically and unblinkingly, and emerges with her mother's love and trust and the physical memory of their presence in her life.

Marsha's embodied memories also allow her to enter her childhood again and to physically experience nostalgia and longing for the grandmother who knew her best and who granted her wish for beauty and magic.

Memories from a mother's kitchen

You can see every detail in this little Dutch painting from 1700. It was in the hallway and I used to stand and watch it. I would get lost in it; I used to think I was on that bridge going to that castle when I was a little girl. And one day, a carton came from Windsor, and this was in it. I cried and I cried and I cried. She knew that was the one thing that I had said, "Granny, when you go I'd love to have that painting." So she made sure I got it ahead of time.

Gerry recalled another kitchen memory as she fondled a small brown English jug from her grandmother's Nova Scotia farmhouse table.

It's about seventy years old. It always sat there when we were kids, on the big table in the kitchen, and always an oilcloth on it. They didn't clear off the table – the salt and pepper and molasses – because they didn't have fridges. We didn't have running water, just a dipper for a drink of water. This molasses jug was always on the table. When Grammy gave up housekeeping I asked her if I could have it. "I've always loved that, Grammy." "It'll be yours." But an aunt took it. She had it awhile and then when she died it came back to me. This sits on a small table in my dining room; I've had it for about twenty years. My kids know how happy I was when I got it. It'll be going to my daughter because she loves it as much. Most of the people that would know the history of it are dead now. It makes me think of Grammy and the

farmhouse. That's all you have left are your memories.

The molasses jug maintains Gerry's link to a vanishing
past, returns her to a place of simplicity and warmth. She
hopes that her children can keep her memories of the
farmhouse, her tenuous but real connections to a distant
past; she knows, though, that these connections can
never be as real to her children as they are to her.

Holding a mortar and pestle, Jindra evokes a happy
childhood in Hungary with a kitchen memory. "I used to
love sitting in front of the stove, the place where people
interacted a lot. To this day I like to sit in the kitchen.
Smells go back to my childhood. I was so happy."

Sometimes such objects are connected to a not-so-
distant past. For a much younger woman, Karen, the touch
and sight of a small sparkling grey rock reminds her most
directly of friends but also evokes many sensory memories.
She picked up the rock on a camping trip, taken during
final exam period with three friends. They spent their
days on the beach, sleeping, talking, drinking, feasting
on mussels they picked and prepared. She had only one
exam left to write, in political theory, which she hated.
Her professor had clearly let her know that she didn't have
what it took to pass. She should go into feminism, he said,
because it was easier. The trip was an escape from school
and its limitations, and the rock keeps the moment. The
freedom, the relaxation, the scent and sound of the sea, the
company of her friends are all made real and available to
her when she holds it.

Jane treasures a loudly ticking Canadian Pacific Railroad clock taken from her father's collection. "The sound drove my mother crazy," she tells us. "They used to negotiate: 'Don't wind this one, and you can wind that one.' He gave me and my sister a choice of whatever we would like to have. This one is very comforting." She and her father were close, partly because he seemed to understand how important the natural world, the life of the senses, always was to her: "I'd go to him and say, 'I cannot go to school today. I have to go down to the river.' And he'd say, 'OK, but only for today. I'll give you a note, and don't tell your mother.' I could tell him stuff like that, 'Dad, I'm going to play hooky today; would you write my note?'" We listen to the clock tick as Jane tells us how her father still comes weekly on the ferry to visit her at her farm now that her mother is in a nursing home.

Sounds, smells, and textures are essential ways of knowing for Danielle, a young blind woman who has never seen. Her possessions are treasured not for what they look like, but for their sensual qualities and meanings and for their connections to people in her life. She began by telling us that she doesn't put much "stuff" on display, in order not to clutter her house. Her possessions are few in number and kept always in the same place. Several times during her interview she repeated, "Mom will divide her stuff up, but it means more to her than to us anyway." Clearly, Danielle does not want more possessions. Her grandmother's china "means more to Mom" than to herself, although she probably will inherit it. Her need to keep her physical environment easy to navigate takes precedence over her desire for possessions.

She does have special possessions, though: a potholder shaped like a sheep dog, a china fridge magnet shaped like a dog. She outlines them with her fingers. These are both from her mother and her sister, who know that she loves dogs and who understand that touch is one of Danielle's best ways of apprehending the world around her. Her sister gave her a brass candlestick with a textured candle she made herself. A friend gave her a domestic scene in paper tole, its layered paper creating a picture that can be easily revealed through touch. Her friend carefully inserted extra layers of paper so that the picture would feel particularly pleasing. Danielle and this friend used to volunteer together in a social service agency. Danielle now works there, for pay, and the two women remain friends. Danielle has another gift from her, a small gold box, its lid covered with raised leaves. She keeps special earrings from a high school friend inside it. A piggy bank, also from the same friend, is kept inside the plastic bag in which it arrived. A teapot shaped like a house from an old European village completes her tactile collection.

Carole treasures a gift from her husband, given to her a year before they were married, perhaps before they knew they would marry. They were both in their early thirties and had been friends for years before becoming lovers. The gift is a silk scarf, made by an artist in New York of one thousand pieces of silk woven together.

This was Kenny's nicest gift. I am very attached to it. As a matter of fact, I – yeah, I love it. What it signifies is that one of the things that brought me and Kenny together and perhaps keeps us together is that we both love textured things. Together, these textures are our environment. We have created it together. When we moved into our first house there was a flood, and that's why this scarf is stained in places. Our roof leaked, but there was nothing I could do about it. I just thought, well, I guess this is part of our history. Now we are creating our own family, and these things will find a home after I'm gone. This scarf is something that will outlive me.

Clearly some women keep whole collections that connect them to their embodied knowledge of the world, of relationships, and of themselves. These women seem to us to live their lives, the good moments and the bad times, in the most vivid colours. They avoid neither deep pain nor dazzling happiness.

We were interested that few of the possessions that evoked sensuality were reminders of sexuality, or more specifically of sex itself. We do not take that to mean that women are uninterested in sex, but rather that when women are free to express their innermost desires, these seem not to be about lesbian or heterosexual sex, but rather about sensual encounters, a sexuality more diverse and more broadly understood as intense experiences that reside in the body. The objects women keep allow sensory experiences to emerge as vivid memories. They capture a moment in time in all its detail, recollected through the memory of the senses. Smells, sounds, touch flood through the years and emerge as stories. The memories become the catalyst for these women's knowledge of themselves in the present. They are a source of intense feelings that emerge from the body's knowledge.

Murie also lives through her senses. Sight and visual memory orient her. Her quest is to turn what she experiences, what she sees, into art.

> I have always been very visually oriented and I've always loved rocks, so rock and leaf collecting are a very distinct part of my life. One of the ways I could give myself pleasure was through nature. Nature has always been very significant. I would collect things to nourish me. When my six children were little I would point things out to them but they were never much interested. It was a tremendous frustration to me.

Her past and present join in the first possession she described, a lamp she calls Aladdin's lamp.

> It represents something very magical from my child-hood, the wishfulness of a child who is unhappy. I love it, the feel of it, the design on it. I've drawn it. I've painted it. It represents playfulness. It represents the freedom I never acquired. I'm divorced now for ten years, and I bought this around the same time. Even if it was expensive I still would have bought it.

It sits there and I delight in it. I keep it in my studio, and it goes with something else I have to show you, a little gold ball, which I collected when I was a weaver. I'm such a magpie. I wondered why I love this so much; part of it is the texture, and both the lamp and the gold ball are shiny, and both have magical qualities. I think about the fairy tales and here I have my own gold ball. I laugh at myself for my little objects. But we need the lamp, so Rapunzel can escape. All those story figures are prisoners, spinning for mothers or fathers.

Let me play you these meditation bells. I wouldn't have thought of them as very precious but they really are and I want to play them for you. They're very powerful, they cleanse me in some way. They are not really sacred, but they have that quality. And look at this Indian mirrored fabric, embroidery and sequins. Sometimes I have it lying out on my table and sometimes I put it away. All these are in my studio, on the top of my house, my private little domain. They're symbols to me of constructing my life.

Although they are kept in plain sight, Murie sees these possessions as her own secrets. Their hidden meanings are very important because, as she said, "I don't really have any privacy." Her ownership of these things rests in herself alone. Others may see them, but she alone constructs and knows their meaning. Next she discussed four oil paintings, placemats created out of one of her large paintings.

Isn't that a sign? That I would cut up a painting to make place mats. I mean it's horrendous; I never thought about it 'til just this minute. I would consider that trivializing. But the paintings weren't successful. So within paintings I find little compositions, so that's what I did with these. They're useful. Cutting up the paintings is very rebellious. It feels like some other script about women and domesticity. These are very rich; I love the colours.

Her rebellion against limitations is expressed in deep, deep colours – no pastels here. Strong secrets, kept in a secret language, expressed in colour. Colour – this time bright orange – is evoked again by a black and white photograph.

My mom and me. I guess I'm about seven. I only got this picture this year. My relationship with my mother has always been very awkward, but she's quite ill now, and it's bringing some reconciliation between us. I like this picture so much because I'm smiling and my mother is smiling; most of the pictures of either me or my mother, none of us is smiling. And then my mother says to me, "Oh, your Aunt Joyce made you that little coat. It's bright orange." It's still one of my favorite colours, so I was just thrilled.

A series of objects – candle holders, a ribbon, some broken pieces of art, all set up in her studio as "a kind of shrine or a ruin" – tell the story of a sexual reawakening,

an affair and the pain it brought her.

> I've drawn them and I've photographed them. I had
> a tremendous infatuation with a man younger than
> me – it started a couple of years ago. I was finally
> working through this infatuation. It was so incred-
> ibly painful; he was the kind of guy that actually
> encouraged it. They are sitting there like a shrine,
> a shrine to remind me that I don't need to do that
> anymore, and to remind me of the pain of it. No
> one will know what this is about. But somehow it's
> a circle. It's come to the end if I put this along with
> the picture of my family. I had to go through this
> before I could claim my inner consciousness. I don't
> think I'll ever go through that again, not to say that
> I won't meet someone that I will dearly love, but I
> don't think I'll go through the process of self-anni-
> hilation.
>
> It is a monument – if I photographed it and blew
> it up no one would know, it could be Stonehenge.
> My little piles of monuments – they are all over my
> house. People come in and say it looks like a museum
> and I'm smiling to myself, because I know what it
> represents to me. It's my life. These are not trivial
> things. This is my life on the floor. I value this pain.
> I am conscious, thank God.

Murie wants to experience her emotions fully, to escape
a life that required her to suppress her artist's sensibili-

ties, to see that her life now is consciously chosen. She lives now in full awareness, whether of pain or pleasure, in contrast to her years of grey depression and isolation. The only regret she has about her collections of artefacts is that she didn't save more visual, tangible markers of her life. "I'm sorry I haven't saved more clothes, because they are tremendous markers. I can look back to one pearl grey suit I bought in my early marriage, the only article of what I would call good clothing I had. Last night I was thinking of coming here for this interview and bringing a suede coat with a fox collar." The early marriage years are a reminder of pain, but they also contain the memory of the pearl grey suit. The secret may go public, turned into art.

These are women who know their world best through their senses, through their bodies. Their worlds are complex and many-layered. One sense leads to another. One memory leads to another. One thought creates another action. They live their lives, the good moments and the bad times, in the most vivid colours.

Judy's home west of the city is a perfect setting for a woman whose experience we came to understand as being organized around the body and its senses. The high ceilings and many windows, the beautiful views, and the mother-of-pearl quality of the light that fills and surrounds it, all reflect its owner's love and appreciation of touch and beauty. She hugged her younger daughter, three-month-old Avalon, who was nestled nursing in her lap, reflecting her comfort with and pleasure in the physical. Judy had already arranged the things she wanted to talk about on the table in front of her. Picking up a photograph of herself and her older daughter, Savannah, Judy began to describe its importance and meaning for her.

> A lot of the things that will come out here have to do with mothering and being a mother. Of everything I have accomplished, what has brought me the greatest joy and where I have contributed the most has been as a mother. This picture was taken in 1990 by the fiancé of the young woman who worked as my office manager in California; we were showing them around the area up here. This picture of me and Savannah seems so joyous and carefree, symbolizing the closeness and connection we have, have always had. I was a single mother with Savannah since she was a few months old. I have this picture enlarged and framed on the wall going up the stairs. I almost always pause as I go up or down the stairs – she and I, happy together.

She shifted the baby to nurse on the other side and, once Avalon was settled again, drew our attention to a beautiful heavy gold and silver pendant around her neck, a slightly abstracted, oval-shaped mother, her back rounded, neck bent, arms enfolding her baby.

> This is my favourite possession. A very dear friend made it for me. It has as much to do with my profession as with being a mother. My true love is with mothers and babies. You can see her breast here,

and that's very symbolic of the breast-feeding, the closeness of the relationship. I grasp it a lot. It was very important for me that I was wearing it when Avalon was born; I found when I was pregnant with her I did not want to take it off. When I'm working, the children really connect with it. I've had very young babes that can barely grasp reach for it when I lean over them, mesmerized by it.

She told us that Savannah, who is eight, assumed that the baby in the pendant, disappointingly bald, represented her, and she agreed that, yes, this piece would most certainly go to Savannah were she to give it away. Judy gave voice powerfully to her connection to her daughters and to other mothers and children in her personal relationships and in her practice as a chiropractor. She understands bodies and the life of the body. She surrounds herself with physical comfort and, in her professional life, seeks to make other people comfortable, sturdy and strong. Her knowledge of the world comes to her not only through her intelligence but also through the medium of the body and all its senses, all its ways of being.

My absolute prize possession, a little too big to put on the table, is my piano. I couldn't do without it. That is the essence of who I am. It's always been there in my life. My mother played a lot when she was pregnant with me; the thing I remember with the greatest clarity is the music in our home. The parties centered around music; my father was a saxophone player.

When I turned fifteen, I went to Switzerland on a piano scholarship and stayed there for a year, ended up doing concert tours, but because I specialized in Bach and Mozart I was kind of burned out because I was too young. I went into jazz instead, which became the springboard for a lot of the work I did in nightclubs, which was my money to go to university. I traveled a lot, had a contract with Club Med, played at the Four Seasons Hotel, the jazz Sunday brunches. I love my piano on a lot of different levels, the physical structure of it, the sound of it; it's taken me to a lot of places, not just geographically. And now I play more than I practice. When I was pregnant with Avalon, I played Chopin every morning. We have a new tradition now, since she was born. After dinner, Savannah and I play the piano, she plays cello, she sings. We have at least half an hour of making music.

Another of Judy's treasured objects is a CD – a gift from a patient, a musician – which has what Judy calls an exquisite rendition of "When You Wish upon a Star." Savannah has gone to sleep to it for many years. "My whole body and soul just melt when I hear it." Her next memory is also connected with music, but shows the extent to which sensory memory is natural for her. It is a book, *The Prophet*, given to her by her voice teacher's husband before she left for Switzerland.

On the outside, he was a cranky fellow, a grizzled old man, who didn't show emotion. He would sit in the same chair and listen when his wife played for students' lessons. She had incredibly long, gorgeous, copper

Memories of an incredible relationship

red hair. The story was that she made her debut in "Lucia di Lammermoor," and he, a young Italian count, fell in love with her, married her. They ultimately came to this country, where he became very interested in the Indian ways in the Kananaskis region. We evolved an incredible relationship. He became such a mentor for me. He was a moving force in my growing up, in my love for books, in the way I look at education. He treated me as an intellectual as a young child.

Judy was taken seriously as a young child; she received respect, learned early how to be respected. Here, in this context, the sensual appeal of music and the life of the mind came together in perfectly complementary ways. "My life has been touched by some really incredible people," she said. Recently, a museum contacted her to borrow some of her photographs of her mentor. "I had no idea he was this famous; he was just my friend."

Judy moved on to another book, *Touching*, by anthropologist Ashley Montague. She read it first in 1976 and has since read it through perhaps thirty times.

> It has to do with the way I believe we should be treated from the time we are born, how we should live our lives, parent our children, and be health professionals. I'm glad that that was natural to me as a parent to Savannah. It was very soul shattering for me when I first read it, and has become an old friend now. I would describe these books as my soul mates. They nourish me.

Even books become a bodily presence, as they nourish the mind. Judy is so confident, at home with herself as an intellectual force and as a physical force, not beset by self-criticism. No accident, perhaps, that Judy's demanding professional life is dedicated to the physical and emotional well being of others. No accident, either, that she moves on now to an object through which all of her various aspects are connected.

> Me, as a mother, me as a personal individual, me as a professional. This is the manuscript from my textbook on paediatric chiropractics. It is 1,400 pages long in manuscript. That's achievement oriented. That's me professionally. My own chapter is dedicated to Savannah; that was really important to me.

She does not back away from her pleasure in her own achievement.

> Another little thing is representative of what I did in school and in my education as a chiropractor. It's a funny, cheap little plaque, my chiropractor's "Graduate of the Year" award, from when I graduated. That was very meaningful to me, because it was very haughtily stated when I went there, "Don't ever expect to win this or that, because they've never been given to a woman and they never will be." I was one of four women in a class of one hundred fifty. I felt nothing but support and camaraderie going through it, but that was mentioned a couple of times, and guess what! It was shared; a man in my class also got one. They couldn't decide between us.

Judy's mementos entwine the many aspects of her life, showing powerfully the clear desire to live an intentional life, a conscious life, which we found so often in women who emphasized sensory knowledge. She treasures videos of her two girls. "Savannah watches her video every year on her birthday." She communicates the centrality of mindfulness to her daughter, helping her keep a journal of her emotions and her physical progress. Judy's own mother did the same: she tucked pieces of paper recording her daughter's words, phrases, and questions into a white Bible that Judy remembers seeing as a child.

She devotes attention to her surroundings, going to a great deal of trouble so they will be "just right." Everything on her walls is meaningful and was carefully sought out to express her own visual aesthetic. She points to a clock in the kitchen whose arms are a fork and knife, and whose numbers are vegetables. "I always wanted to have it. I became obsessed with wanting this clock, couldn't find it anywhere. I was in Carmel, on my way to the airport, walking by a store, and there was the clock. The store was closed. I quickly scribbled down the name, and when I got home, I quickly called. I love that clock."

Judy and Savannah had begun decorating their house for Christmas when we arrived. The tree would be covered with ornaments collected to commemorate events over the years. One is a pair of hands in the position to do a chiropractic adjustment, made for Judy by a couple whose babies she delivered. She owns her own past, makes her own present, lives in a deep knowledge of her self and the meanings held in her body, in those of her children and her patients. For Judy, that knowledge creates emotional certainty and social stability. She knows who she is and how she will live, purposefully and mindfully and with respect and love for bodies.

EASTER SUNDAY, 1955

Why should anything go wrong with our bodies?
Why should we not all be beautiful? Why should
there be decay? – why death? – and, oh, why damnation?
                          Anthony Trollope, in a letter.

What were we? What have we become?
Light fills the picture, the rising sun,
The three of us advancing, dreamlike,
up the steps of my grandparent's house on Oak Street.
My mother and father, still young, swing me
lightly up the steps, as if I weigh nothing.
From the shadows, my brother and sister watch,
wanting their turn, years away from being born.
Now my aunts and uncles and cousins
gather on the shaded porch of generations,
big enough for everyone. No one has died yet.
No vows have been broken. No words spoken
that can never be taken back, never forgotten.
I have a basket of eggs my mother and I dyed yesterday.
I ask my grandmother to choose one, just one,
and she takes me up – O hold me close! –
her cancer not yet diagnosed. I bury my face
in the soft flesh, the soft folds of her Easter dress,

breathing her in, wanting to stay forever where I am.
Her death will be long and slow, she will beg
to be let go, and I will find myself, too quickly,
in the here-and-now moment of my fortieth year.
It's spring again. Easter. Now my daughter steps
into the light, her basket of eggs bright, so bright.
One, choose one, I hear her say, her face upturned
to mine, innocent of outcome. Beautiful child,
how thoughtlessly we enter the world!
How free we are, how bound, put here in love's name
– death's, too – to be happy if we can.

Elizabeth Spires, *The New Yorker*, April 3, 1995

In an earlier chapter we told stories of women who developed a particularly strong sense of identity and personal values by observing and retelling how their mothers, grandmothers, and aunts survived childhood hardships. In this chapter, women who have endured great hardships without an example before them tell their stories of survival and recovery. Those who were able to find ways to manage their childhood pain alone, or were supported by one or more key adults outside their families, became strong and accomplished. But unlike women who learned early from strong mothers or grandmothers, their self-descriptions still speak of uncertainty and self-doubt. They have built a structure for their lives, but it is often a fragile and vulnerable one that takes energy and courage to sustain. Some decided against having children of their own, fearing that they would fail as mothers; others, confronting the ghosts of the past, took the chance and struggled to give their children what had been so painfully missing in their own lives. Women who had unexceptional childhoods, neither well-supported nor particularly lacking in support, neither rich nor poor, but who encountered tragedies in their adult lives also tell their stories in this chapter. Events tested them to their limits and either forced them to develop new strengths or turned them in upon themselves and away from the world of relationships.

When we first began talking to women about the artefacts of their lives, we expected to hear mostly about objects associated with happy events. We ought to have known better, since our own personal collections certainly did not conform to this prediction. As our research progressed, we realized that women's objects often house memories of very painful moments and difficult passages in their lives.

In most instances, the suffering they contain is not apparent simply from viewing the object, as might be true of a funeral announcement or a divorce decree. The meanings of these possessions can only be understood if the woman chooses to share its story. Most of the objects women keep have secret or hidden meanings that no observer, however astute, can hope to decipher without their help and cooperation. Anne's dolls, Elaine's etchings, Kate's letters from her grandfather – all could be seen, superficially, as interesting curios or objects of sentimental or historic interest. In fact, they represent narratives of these women's most profound and meaningful experiences, written in a secret code. Some meanings may be more transparent than others, but most defy the attempts of the merely curious to understand them.

Many coded stories, especially those containing grief and despair, are never shared with anyone. Others are shared only with a few. Most are never fully understood by anyone other than the woman herself. Women's suffering is not a topic that our culture chooses to valorize except in reporting victimization. We are usually expected to be silent about the great losses we experience and about the effort of will asked of us to continue meeting the day-to-day needs of the people we care for. Individuality is not much encouraged in women as a general rule, and our individual suffering tends to be written off as part of our lot in life. The quieter we are about it the better.

This silence, or silencing, is part of the secrecy women maintain about their cherished objects, a secrecy that becomes a matter of considerable pleasure to some of them. Such special things are kept tucked away and contemplated only in solitude. Others may be displayed in public areas of a home where anyone can see them, and yet where their profound stories are completely and routinely overlooked. It is as if women are smiling and saying: You think you know me, but you don't. I have a life apart from what you know of me. The mementos kept by women whose lives have had more than their share of sorrows are particularly likely to be kept hidden from others' sight or understanding, whether they are packed away in a closet or attic or hidden in plain sight.

Carol is a young woman in her twenties who was a graduate student at the time of our interview. The objects she chose to share with us were remarkable for the fact that they included nothing from any female relative or friend, a pattern notably rare among our participants. Her keepsakes, of which she has a great many, are kept stored away, with the exception of a few particularly important things that she always carries with her to remind her of who she is and what she values. She gets out her boxes and goes through them about every six to twelve months, following no particular pattern or ritual.

> I don't use these things to relive old times, because actually I don't like to do that. It's more I go through them when I am in a down mood. When I'm in a transition in my life because I'm moving boxes or I'm repacking boxes, and so I've come across this stuff. Often when I go through a transition it's leaving relationships. And so it is a sad time and a time when I'm feeling like I've failed or something like that.

She reviews the contents of the boxes at such times partly to seek out the memories of good things, "when things went right." Cards or notes from friends, keepsakes from travels, photos taken on vacations, form the positive side of Carol's collections.

The things she shared at our interview, though, were the ones she considers to be most central to her sense of who she is. These objects – a plaque, a set of dog tags, a Bible, a scapular, and her wedding ring – all help her to access childhood memories. She remembers the lessons for living that she has taught herself over the years. Holding them helps her to calm herself when life feels overwhelming, and particularly when she is flooded with self-critical thoughts. Each object shows signs of much handling, and each is kept near her at all times in case of need.

The first of these objects, a small plaque, she keeps on her bedside table where she can see it when she goes to bed and read it each morning when she wakes. It is a poem called "Desiderata," and it reminds Carol of her philosophy of life, a set of guiding principles that she uses to make sense of her sometimes chaotic world. She purchased the plaque for herself seven or eight years ago when she was a teenager. It is a symbol of her early efforts at independence, her attempts to break away, at least psychologically, from a turbulent family life, and a guide for how to live.

> I think it has such a valuable thing to say about life, and it's a good way to look at the world, I think. So if I care about someone, I will always give them a copy of it. It is about acceptance of others and acceptance of yourself. And it has a spiritual tone to it, which is a very big part of my life: spirituality. And yet it doesn't throw it at you, it doesn't force you, you know, it doesn't talk about God and things that turn people off often. It's just, I think, a reflection of whatever God is, a reflection maybe of how God would like us to see the world – that we are part of the world, but only part of it, and we need to accept other people and be good to each other and to ourselves. I spent a lot of years working so hard to be perfect, and I beat myself up all the time emotion-

ally, so this really grounds me when I read it. It is a source of strength in the morning when I have to go out and face the world. Even at night when I go to bed, and I feel like, "Oh, I messed up today," I can read it, and it has a calming effect.

The poem acts a form of meditation for Carol, a ritual that she can use as an antidote to constant self-criticism. It is a kinder "recipe for living" than the one that taught her to be so hard on herself.

I was raised Catholic and actually I am still a practicing Catholic, although I can't say I am a good one, whatever that is. I was raised in a strictly religious home, but so much of religious dogma, including Catholicism or any other institutionalized religion, it's so silly in some ways. They get so contradictory, it doesn't make sense, it confuses people and the consequences are a lot of guilt feelings and anger, and following rules that you don't really understand. The "Desiderata" is a simple philosophy that, if there is a God, it's probably all that he or she would expect, for us to live by such a philosophy. Not all this garbage about do this and don't do that. I think it just makes people feel very confused and feel bad about themselves.

Not much that Carol to say about the other people and relationships in her life was positive. She has had only a few human connections of any depth, and few that have lasted for long. Instead, she has turned to animals to find stability and comfort. She showed us a set of dog tags she keeps attached to her key chain, telling us about her first dog and about how she views animals in general.

I am a complete and total unchained animal lover. I grew up on a farm and we always had several dogs and countless cats, and they were my best friends and my comfort. Even my pets today, they all have voices and I talk to them. It's crazy I know, but they are very close to my heart. The first pet I ever owned when I left home was a little dog. He was a little poodle. I named him Alexander, because I thought I'm never going to have kids and I always thought if I had kids my first child would be named Alexander. I got him when I got married, and then when I separated from my husband, I couldn't take Alex with me, so I found a home for him and I just keep this dog tag. It's very painful. I loved him so much.

When I left my husband I was living in a small town. I had to move to the city to take my night classes at the university. I got a job as a nanny and I couldn't take him with me. So I found a really good home for him. In fact, I still keep tabs on him, like I know how he's doing because I gave him to the mother of a man I used to work with at the hospital. She is a wonderful lady who lives by a big golf course and so he just has a wonderful time out there. But I sure miss him. There was a lot of guilt associated with giving him up, and keeping his tags is part of my way of being loyal. And it's a reflection, too, of just my real commitment to animals. Some people, even my very close friends, think I'm strange about animals. But I just think they have a great value, they're quite spiritual to me. I always thought – maybe this is stupid, but I might as well say it – I always thought that animals were kind of, maybe represent what God had hoped people would be more like, not vindictive and cruel and conniving. I mean I guess animals can be that way too, but they just seem more pure. Human intellect, I think, has messed itself up in so many ways and gotten into so much trouble. I mean, it has done wonderful things too, but it has made life so complicated in some ways. So in animals I see a more natural way to live.

I don't go to visit Alex, but I send him cards. It's been about – how long since we've been separated? It's about five years ago now. I remember the day I left. My husband and I took him out there. I thought my heart was coming right out. I hadn't sobbed like that, well, for ages. So I don't think I want to see him because I don't want him to remember me and then think, "Well, are you leaving me again?" I know that he is happy, and I would just as soon leave it that way. I think I knew at that time that I wouldn't have children. I'm still pretty sure about that, I feel like I don't want to mess up having children. I guess I pretty much messed up with Alex. Oh God! I guess I kind of abandoned him in a way.

Carol's thoughts about the "Desiderata" and her thoughts about her relationship with the lost Alex came together in her next comments:

> I just think that children, you have to be so careful and so sure that you want to have them, otherwise you can hurt them so much, you know. You know, with animals you can find a home for them and if it is a good home they can go and be happy. But a child, if you abandon them obviously it is a whole different ball game. There is this simplicity of relating to this animal, as opposed to the complexity of a child. There's the sense that I know I can do this well, this little undemanding creature.

After the discussion about the plaque and about her lost Alex, Carol was worried about whether she would find the remaining objects too upsetting to talk about. She felt that "we're moving along into things that are more sensitive – I hope I don't cry. It's like this dog tag, I hadn't thought about it for ages, and yet when I start to think about it so many things come up – my marriage, my family, spirituality. There's lots of things attached to this little dog tag."

Carol chose to continue, handing us an old Bible. We saw many Bibles in our interviews. Sometimes they were passed down through generations. Their pages contained childhood drawings, dedications from relatives, bookmarks made by children or by a dear friend. Carol's Bible came from her parents as a gift for her confirmation, when she was nine or ten years old. It became a comfort to her in the turmoil that was her home.

As I told you, I was raised in a strict Catholic home. Often, I guess this happens in religious families, there was such a lot of hypocrisy that was going on at home. But from a very young age I felt I had a relationship with God. I just refer to it as God because it makes it easier. I used to love going to church and I still go because it is such a good time to reflect and be in touch with your spirit. I don't often take time during the week. I'll pray or whatever, but you just get so caught up in life that it is very rarely you take an hour to just be inside yourself.

I've kept this Bible by my bed since I got it, so for about twenty years. I grew up in a violent home, and I was so, so afraid of my Dad. I would go to bed at night and I would be so worried about things and afraid of the yelling or whatever going on outside my bedroom. I used to read my Bible every night before I went to bed, and maybe I'm not remembering the times when it didn't work, but all I remember is that every time I had a fear I would open my Bible randomly and would come to a verse that seemed to specifically relate to what my fear was that day. I took such comfort in it. I didn't feel as alone or as afraid, because I thought, "There is a life outside of this house and it's going to protect me. And nothing that happens here can hurt me permanently." So it was such a source of strength, such a source of strength, and it increased my faith because whenever I opened

it this thing would always happen. I felt someone was taking care of me. In my mind I always say that this Bible saved me. There were so many times when I thought I would just kill myself, and it kept me safe. Because nighttime is so awful sometimes.

Carol's Bible was like a parent, one she could count on to keep her safe, to understand her fear and to comfort and love her. In the absence of parental guidance, or at least of guidance that was inspirational as opposed to punitive, it taught her how to live. As a child and a young adult, she filled it with underlining, folding over the corners of pages to mark especially important lessons. Between its pages are a bookmark she bought when she was a child, a little pamphlet about nuns that she picked up on a trip to Montreal, and scraps of paper with the locations of special messages that spoke to her situation. One message means to Carol that "if you go against your own conscience, that's when something becomes wrong. And if you go against your own spirit, that is what causes problems for you." Using her childhood interpretations of Bible passages, Carol was able to assemble a moral code for herself that allowed her to withstand the abuse she experienced. She could acknowledge that her father's way of being in the world was wrong, and understand that she need not become like him. At the same time, the Bible and the "Desiderata" plaque helped her to accept him. "You know, everybody has their own story, as the 'Desiderata' says, and their own conscience, and you can't interpret it for someone else, only for yourself."

What her Bible couldn't give her, of course, was the experience she needed of human relationships that worked, of people who knew and valued her, of loving and being loved. Carol's childhood experience of her parents was mostly about obedience, punishment, and demands that she live in a particular way. Outwardly, she tried to comply, but inwardly she developed a rich private life that let her separate herself from them and use her understanding of God as her parent.

> And it's like, a new Bible wouldn't be like my old one that I had when I was a little kid and so scared. I can hold it and imagine lying in my bed in my room, and exactly what my room was like. I can hear the angry voices, imagine the darkness, how worried I was and how this Bible comforted me. It brings everything back so clearly. Especially the feelings. I can see the bedroom, and where the Bible was lying. The feeling I would have of just being so afraid, so hopeless, so scared. And just to open the Bible, and it would be like – how is this happening? I was so grateful, that's the best word I can use. It's ironic that Mom and Dad gave it to me for my confirmation. They gave me this lifeline.

The third object Carol showed us was a scapular, given to her in a rare moment of insight and affection by her father.

I went on an exchange trip when I was in grade twelve to Trinidad, and, as I was leaving, my dad went out and bought this for my birthday. He always used to give my mom money for Christmas or birthday presents, and she would go shopping. I can still remember sitting in the house, and he just made me so nervous, and I remember sitting there and opening it and he said, "I got that myself." And it still chokes me up because he – it just made me feel good to think that he was thinking of me and because he recognized that the spiritual part of my life was important to me. It was like his way of saying, "Stay safe." It's so sad. And it's important to me because it keeps me close to my dad. Plus I guess it is a statement of me, my identity statement, because spirituality is so important to me.

For Carol, this single gesture of affection in a lifetime of anger, violence, and fear meant so much. Through it, her father seemed to say that he loved her, "without actually having to say it."

Because he was such a hard and angry person. But he had such a soft part of him that he hardly ever showed. And yet, this was a time when he showed it and it was directed at me. And that was really wonderful. So I always value that memory. Later, when I got separated and divorced, he and my mom disowned me, so this kind of keeps me close to him too.

There is an unmistakable longing in Carol's words and expression as she talks about the crucifix. She wears it around her neck on a chain and handles it frequently throughout the day. It has become a sort of talisman that tells her that she was once found worthy of her father's love. Even in the darkest moments of her isolation from her parents and her memories of their harshness and cruelty, Carol can find some solace here. It reminds her that everything was not black, that there were moments of love and acceptance that strengthen her in difficult times.

> I wear it all the time, hold it and rub it. Which is probably why the chain always breaks. I've had this chain fixed countless times. The chain is still the original one he gave me, though. I just get it fixed. I don't know if he ever knew how much it meant to me. That he spent time looking for it, that he paid attention to me. Even though I can't talk to my dad, I should write him a letter. I know that he knows he was, well, quite frankly, not a very good dad and I think he should know what he did that was good. Maybe he forgets that this meant so much and that it was a good thing and I haven't forgotten regardless of everything else. It might be good for him, for his spirit you know, to know that.

Carol's final piece was her wedding band. It, too, has many meanings and contains memories of bad times and good, happiness and sadness; insights into her own nature; and perceptions of the people with whom she has had important relationships.

My wedding band does have so many things attached to it. I married my junior high school sweetheart. I met him when I was eleven. We dated all through junior high and all through high school. He was the only guy I ever went out with except for one other man who I went out with for a year when I was nineteen. He turned out to be quite abusive, and it was actually Alex, my ex-husband, who saved me from that situation. This fellow that I was dating was black, and so when my parents found out I was dating a black guy they had nothing to do with me. He was also a good friend of my elder sister who I was living with at the time. So Sid, this guy, when he beat me up – it only happened a few times – and the last time it happened my sister came home and I was bleeding and she said, "Well, you probably deserved it." I had nowhere to go. I was living in the city and didn't know it very well at the time, and I was only eighteen or nineteen anyway. Alex was the only one I knew. I didn't really expect him to help me because Sid had already kind of gone after Alex and harassed him for no reason. And I had let it happen. But yet Alex helped me. Sid had kind of stalked me around the city trying to find me and Alex gave me a place to stay. He let me stay there and Sid never found me. I was so grateful to Alex.

When my parents found out that Alex and I were communicating again, they immediately acknowledged me again because they loved Alex. And Alex really is a wonderful, wonderful person, very steady and focused and kind – just a really decent individual. So, after he saved me from this situation, I started dating him again and the next fall we were engaged. When we got married, my parents were so thrilled, it was what everybody had thought would happen with Alex and I. We got married. It was the worst marriage I ever saw. We were just no good as husband and wife. And besides, I was quite sick. I had been bulimic since I was twelve and it seemed to be getting worse and worse. I was twenty when we got married. I was an emotional wreck. I developed this obsessive-compulsive disorder, became very withdrawn and was basically a hermit. I would go to my work and I would come home. My pets were my life. I kind of forgot about Alex. I think, in retrospect, that I believed that marrying Alex would make my dad love me and make my parents approve of me. It never happened. I was angry and I felt jilted and hurt.

It wasn't Alex's fault. He tried so hard to be good and patient with me, especially with the bulimia – that was hard enough for him to take. But the obsessive-compulsive thing – I used to check locks and so on until it drove both of us around the bend. And he was starting to do it too, poor man! I just see him as, he was just so good. He tried so hard. But we were not meant to be married. Once we were married, I discovered that I wasn't attracted; we didn't have any sexual interaction at all the last two or three years of our marriage. I just couldn't be touched, didn't want to be with anyone. Alex was so incredibly patient, but clearly things were not getting better. We had actually a quite amicable separation. He helped me move and we just decided that it was not going to work and we were destroying the friendship we had. And he wanted to have a family and I wanted to get on with my life while we were still so young.

We separated and it was a really good thing. I don't regret it at all. I learned so much in that marriage and it set me free. I moved back to the city and started again. But what really set me free was when my parents disowned me. My three brothers didn't talk to me for three years after that either. So I had my two sisters, but it was great. Because even while I was married, when I was being a hermit, the one relationship that I did pursue was still this relationship with my parents, which was not working. It was just beating me down. I couldn't please them. So they set me free in a way. My life has done nothing but get better ever since. They had done their worst to me. There was nothing more they could do to hurt me. There was no reason to live any other way than how I wanted to.

I miss them. Well, I always say I miss them. Because my dad had some great qualities and I was very close to my mom. So that part hurt. More than my dad, because I kind of expected it from him. He disowned my other two sisters as well, for different reasons, so I was ready for it from him. But not from my mom. She didn't disown my other two sisters. That really threw me off, but it made me be strong and it really made me think that I'd just been grovelling for the past twenty years. I was really angry.

And this was the other thing that was so important about this ring. When I was growing up, I never got angry at anybody or anything. I cried a lot, and a very intuitive psychiatrist said to me once, "You cry in every session. I wonder how much of that is anger and not sadness." He was probably very right. I think he was. But when I was married I was very abusive toward Alex, verbally abusive. I had the worst temper and I'd never seen that side of myself. Who I reminded myself of was my dad. I could finally have some understanding of why my dad behaved the way he did. Your anger gets out of control and you lose all sense of rationality and logic and you do and say horrible things. I thought, "This was what he went through and this is why he was this way. And I can be this way too. He's not some evil demon. He's someone who didn't get help and didn't learn to control his temper, that's all." I think he felt trapped. When you have kids who you see are cowering and crying and terrified, I can only imagine that would make him angry because he must have felt so bad about himself. So it really gave me some compassion for my dad and some understanding.

So I wear this ring, and when people ask me why I still wear it, I say, "Because it keeps me humble." Now I'm not sure if I need something to keep me humble, because I tend to be fairly self abusive, although I think I'm getting over that. But I think what it really does is remind me that my dad is human, and I know that, because I behaved very similar to how he behaved. But the important thing is that I got over it. That's where I still have trouble with him. He could have gotten help and he didn't. But he grew up in a different generation than I did too. It's not easy for him to tell all. So anyway, it's like his bad behaviour let me forgive myself for mine, and I could say, "Okay, you have a choice now; you can go on the way he lives, or take charge of your life." And it was about taking charge of my life, because I had to get control over my temper.

And the ring does remind me too of Alex. He actually married one of my best friends, and it was wonderful. He has a family and she is good for him. So it reminds me of a good choice I made in my life. It's not something that I want to put behind me. My marriage was about friendship, and about learning and growing and understanding. So many things actually.

The stories attached to Carol's objects tell of personal resilience in very difficult circumstances. Her actions as a child and adult show characteristics of this resilient individual. By finding something to believe in, she found a way to believe in herself. Faith in a personally defined

God helped her to get through her childhood fear and confusion, gave her a safe retreat, and taught her about forgiveness, acceptance, and hope for the future. She found she could be different from the adults around her. She came to take herself seriously enough to form personal goals and to recognize her strengths and use them toward making a better life.

But Carol is still very vulnerable. Her confidence is shaken and she does not trust herself to succeed in relationships. At the same time, she has great depths of compassion for people and struggles toward realizing peace and self-acceptance. By keeping these objects around her, she reminds herself of who she was, what she has learned, and who, through her many strengths, she intends to become.

Emily is also a young woman whose mementos function to contain grief. Like Carol, Emily is in her mid-twenties, and not yet at peace with herself. Her history of being silenced in her family and ostracized and criticized by her friends at school has left her profoundly mistrustful of human relationships. It was difficult for her to engage in the interview. She spoke very little at first and, even later in our discussion, tended to be much less forthcoming than most participants. She avoids engagement with people because based on her experience, she believes they will eventually turn away from her.

Emily is part of an extended family of women, but she feels alienated from them. She does not rely on them for support or comfort. She keeps many things stored in an attic to which she retreats in difficult times. One of these is a puppet her mother made "way back when I was a kid." It looks like Emily at three, and she remembers playing with it, when others were not around to laugh at her, associating it with "having fun. [Which was] not a reality." Her sense of being constantly criticized and found wanting has been with her, it seems, since infancy. The puppet story is one of abandonment and fear. "My brother had to go to the hospital when he was four, so Mom and my brother left and dropped me off at Aunt Mary's house for a month, and that's when she gave it to me. I was six years old. She told me to be careful of it. My mom always said she would light us on fire if we weren't careful."

A shiny reflector from Finland, given Emily by a high school friend, was next. "She said that if you put it on a piece of string and pin it to your shirt or pants and let it hang down, you will always be seen…. High school was a pretty tough time." Emily was a very athletic young woman and very different from everyone around her.

I was the first female Little Leaguer in town, and the first Babe Ruth player. It singles you out a whole lot. Some people thought it was pretty pathetic to bring women into baseball. And I was an ugly kid, I mean really ugly. I was taller than all the boys, I had a monstering head and buck teeth out to here. I played all the sports – baseball, basketball, track and field, javelin, shot put. People used to try to beat me up for it, because you can only be named most valuable player in basketball for so long.

Emily's memories from this time are still very bitter and angry. She showed us the baseball glove she wore – she keeps it to remind her of her achievements in sport – but she no longer associates with the people she knew at school and no longer plays baseball.

Just basically, you're out to play the game and people don't like that if you do a good job. Being in a small town, too, people know you, they know what you used to look like at school. They know what you used to be. Even if you're twenty years old. I'll keep the glove, and a ball in it too, to make sure it keeps its shape. I remember playing with my dad and my brother, we used to play catch across the street. A bunch of us would get together to do that. It was a fun game, a good game. But you could never play first base if you were a woman. I played first base in Little League for a while and I guess everybody got so darn upset that I got kicked out in the field again. "She's a girl, she can't do it. She's not tough enough." I got beaned by a ball. This pitcher wanted to get me. I was up to bat and he pegged me right in the side, right in the boobs. And then some of the guys on the other team started to tease me, so I just stood there and could not move. It hurt, holy God did that hurt. Anyway, I just stood there, and once I could breath again, I walked off the base. Basically stuck it to them, because I made it to first base. The coach was going to pull me off, and my mom was screaming, she was watching. And I made it around the bases.

Basketball, too, I was one of the tallest ones at
that time and I've got scars on my shins, my back.
High school was brutal. And then when I was in
Babe Ruth, I didn't see anybody. It was just me and
a bunch of farting guys. They used to fart and spit. I
could talk to a couple of them, but as soon as another
guy saw us talking, it was over.

The fact that Emily is now a tall, beautiful woman doesn't
help her come to terms with her memories of being singled out because of her ugliness, her athletic abilities and
her difference. Still hurt by these rejections, and by her
knowledge that men and boys would go to any lengths
to have her removed from the teams, she still feels "alone
in a world that doesn't want me." She lives in the same
small town of her childhood, though she believes that
the people there categorized her when she was a child,
and will never change their views of her. Most of Emily's
support these days comes from her relationship with her
partner, Jean, with whom she has lived for the last six
years. Other than that relationship, though, Emily said
that she would "rather just be a hermit" than try again to
connect to the people around her.

Although Emily loves music and used to play the violin,
she avoids getting her violin repaired so that she can play
it again, because playing it has "too many other things
associated with it." She brought a tape to the interview
because some music "takes me wherever I want to go." But
other tapes bring her back to her despair about ever being
loved and her fear of taking that chance. Some kinds of

music "just drive me crazy. It takes me way in a dark spot. Just depressed, sit in a corner and bawl." She has been in treatment for depression, but so far it has not helped her to break through her sense of isolation and difference.

Emily next showed us one of the rocks that she has picked up because something special about them – a colour, a pattern or shape – has caught her eye. A favourite came from England, where she and Jean went on a holiday to trace her partner's family genealogy. This relationship is the one bright spot in Emily's life. While she continues to be in touch with her family, she gains no emotional sustenance from them. Her father lives just down the street from her, but her interactions with him are superficial and none of her keepsakes are from him.

Emily told us about other things she keeps tucked away in her many attic boxes – a faded T-shirt she wore as a child, the windshield washer from her first car, a set of old license plates.

The stuff I have in cardboard boxes is more consoling to me than anything. I would rather just sit and look at that stuff. Because my life is basically, you know, the old "to be seen and not heard." My brother was in the spotlight. He was there because he was allowed to be. I brought it up to my family and they say, "No, no, no, that's not true. I'm not doing that!" but yet they'll be the first ones to interrupt when I'm trying to say something. I see a lot of people's backs. I don't understand. I don't give people hugs, I don't give people kisses on the cheeks. I don't touch

Childhoods left behind

people, because it is too dangerous.

The keepsakes she showed us, and the twelve attic boxes, provide Emily with her only stable source of self-knowledge. So much of their emotional content is negative, though, that it seems hard for Emily to move through that period of her life and develop a sense of self that is based on more recent experience or on her apparently successful relationship with a partner. Rather, these keepsakes seem to act to prevent change; they are constant reminders of the price of being different, of the need to surround herself with an almost impenetrable wall of anger and despair, and to isolate herself to stay safe.

Phoebe struck us as being very like the person Carol may be twenty years from now. She too has memories of a very difficult childhood, but many of the objects that embody her memories of that time are packed away and rarely visited. When we met at her house, she began by saying that she did not consider herself to be feminine like her mother, who had collections. Phoebe takes pleasure in keeping her life stripped down to essentials. She refuses to keep anything that isn't "really important and necessary." She showed us a little shelf where she keeps "the accumulation of forty years of life." Each of the things on the shelf has "a whole lot of significance. They're things I

collected on my travels, or things given to me by someone
who is important to me."

Later, Phoebe went to a bedroom closet and took down
two boxes of mementos from her childhood. She hadn't
looked at the things in the box for about five years, and
probably wouldn't look at them now, she said, except for
this interview. And yet they are clearly important to her.
She has kept them for many years, taken them with her on
extensive travels, brought them from one house she lived in
to the next, and restored them painstakingly after a flood.
"I was really upset; there were a lot of things that I lost. I
was most upset about the possibility of losing these things.
Everything had to be taken out of the boxes and dried
out." She apologized for their appearance, saying:

> They are sort of silly looking. They aren't really
> something you would want to have out on display.
> And my attachment to them is very subjective. I
> think they give me a feeling of roots or connected-
> ness.
>
> They represent to me – I came from a kind of dys-
> functional background, a lot of alcoholism. But I'm
> at the point at this time of my life where I've been
> through a lot of personal development. So I'm quite
> able to discuss it and understand that in my imme-
> diate family there's alcoholism, and with my grand-
> parents as well. For me, it was my dad who had the
> problem. He became really bad when I was a teen-
> ager. I don't have much from those years of my life,
> but what I have is in these boxes. I was very unhappy

then and very sad. I really idolized my dad when I was a child. He was quite special to me, so his going off the tracks was ... I think the reason that I don't go into these boxes is that I'm happy and adjusted at this point. There isn't any longing, you know, or wanting. I know myself well. I used to need them to help me cope with unhappiness.

Carol's strength and resilience was built on her childhood relationship with God. Phoebe's came in large part from her special relationship with her father's mother. Her grandmother lived common-law with a man whose mother Phoebe described as

... a fabulous knitter, sewer, crocheter, embroiderer. She could do it all. When I was a kid, I loved to skate. I never took lessons, but I could skate very well; Grandma noticed this and had her husband's mother make this little skating outfit for me. I had white figure skates, red leotards, and a white sweater, and I looked pretty cool!

The skating outfit she pulled out also included a blue velvet skirt, short pants lined with red silk, and a hat with a red pompom attached. It was easy to see how a little girl might feel "pretty cool" in it.

So I kept this because I was so close to this grandmother, who is dead now. She took such an interest in me and what I was doing. And part of what I liked about her was that she wasn't a traditional kind of woman. She had her own thoughts, and she didn't really care what other people thought. She would say to me things like, "It is important to be athletic and it's important to achieve things academically, but what you look like or what men think about you is not important."

Another thing about her was that she lived with this man that I thought was my grandfather. She lived with him for years, until she died, at least twenty years. But she had been abandoned by my real grandfather – I never met him. She was still married to him, but she lived with this common-law husband.

After the flood, the skating outfit was dry-cleaned by a special process to prevent it from falling apart due to its age. Phoebe has kept the outfit for over thirty years, and the thought of ever losing it is insupportable.

The second item Phoebe showed us was a lamp, a childhood gift from her father. It no longer has a shade, but it is still treasured as a memento of him and of her childhood. It was on her bedside table for many years, until she left home at eighteen. "I couldn't stand what was going on there any longer, so I moved the hell out of there." She also keeps a doll bed and a tiny wedding gown her mother gave her as compensation for not being able to afford a real Barbie doll. Phoebe remembers how touched she was that her mother had gone to so much trouble.

Another keepsake shows very clearly how Phoebe managed to keep herself safe from the chaos her father's alcoholism wrought in her adolescence. It is a school binder, originally her mother's in the 1950s. It reminded her mother of "the man she should have married instead of my father," but she agreed at some point to let Phoebe have her treasured notebook. At about the same time, Phoebe says, "[I] discovered I [was] really a girl and not a boy like my brothers." She spent a great deal of time in her bedroom creating a journal in her mother's binder about how to become a "good" woman. When things were difficult in her family, Phoebe could retreat to her room and work on her journal, incorporating sections on posture, grooming, manners, cooking, nutrition, exercise, makeup, and other attributes of being a woman. The journal includes clippings from magazines; photographs; tracings from magazine pictures, carefully coloured to look as much like the originals as possible; and her own extensive handwritten notes and lists of rules and advice. There are lists of "the seven points about what makes a true beauty"; descriptions and pictures of elegant hair styles and pearl jewellery; pointers about how to maintain health, how to be physically fit through yoga, how to be well nourished, how to choose clothes and apply makeup, all meticulously recorded.

> My grandma was gone at that point, so this was an attempt to organize chaos. I remember that I had a very strong thought as I started this that, no matter what was going on at home, I was going to

be detached from it. I still had to live there and my parents still had control of me, but I had decided that this was not going to drag me down. This was not how I was going to live. This journal was about how I was going to live my life. This was the start of that. I was very goal focused, very determined that no matter what they were doing that as a child and teenager I couldn't cope with, that was not going to be my life.

It ended up being the start of a healthy lifestyle. And I have continued to live this way, very active physically, watching my diet, being careful about my appearance, and this is where it all started. They say that there are people who, no matter what the situation they find themselves in, they can rise above it, and I've often wondered if that was the case with me. I have never had a problem with stress because of what I learned to cope with when I was growing up.

Phoebe's journal also contained personal schedules for her hygiene and fitness routines. She set herself certain goals, researched them, and compiled a schedule of activities to reach them. "It was like, I was not living that way and so I will research and I will know what I can aspire to."

Phoebe started cross-country running at age twelve, coincidental with the worsening of her situation at home and the loss of her grandmother, her role model and confidante. One of the treasures in her cardboard box is a trophy she won in a race that was particularly important to her.

I kept this trophy because that was a really significant race. That was just after my father had come back from a peacekeeping mission. It was a really bad scene at home involving having to call the military police. My parents were having a terrible fight and it looked like my dad was going to kill my mother, so I said, "I have to do something even though I am just a kid." So I went to the neighbour and we called the police. I really feel to this day that if I hadn't intervened there would have been something terrible as a result. But that was the beginning of the end of the close relationship I had had with my father. Because even though he was ill and it was primarily his fault that this had occurred, he never really forgave me for – as he saw it – squealing on him. You don't do that in those kinds of families. You're supposed to keep quiet, keep the secret. But I had refused to do that.

Anyway, I ran this race without any training. I had this rage in me at my father, and what he had done, and how he had turned it around on me. I remember having so much power that I could have run twenty miles. I was passing all these people, and I'm a small person as you can see. I was passing girls twice my size. It was like I was possessed. People – my coach, my gym teacher – were shocked that I could have won this race. I remember having to go to the awards assembly and get this trophy. People were amazed that this little person could have done that. But I was so angry and it propelled me. So it is more than just a trophy for a race – it's almost an assertion of power, a child's power. I realized what I could do for myself. I don't have to be powerless, be a pawn to someone else's feelings. It is a symbol to me that no matter what's going on, I ultimately have control of what happens to me. It's up to me.

When she lost her grandmother and her closeness to her father, Phoebe had no one to turn to, so she took her life in her own hands, recognized her anger and her right to determine a different path for herself, and never looked back.

I always used to look at my mother, and I know now as an adult that often, and especially in those days, it was very difficult for women married to alcoholics or whatever. But even so, I know that I am a different kind of person from my mom. I know that if it had been me, it wouldn't matter what, I would have taken my children and gone. And she didn't. She was very passive and she chose to stay. I guess I think of traditional femininity and passivity and it adds up to victimization for me. I equate those things – femininity, powerlessness, and victimization. And I refuse.

Like Carol's, Phoebe's is a story of resilience, this time fuelled by special relationships with a grandmother and with her father, at least for the first ten years of her life. Because she sees herself as a lovable person, at peace with memories of her childhood, she is less vulnerable, more anchored in her life than one might expect, given her experiences. The childhood objects she keeps are important supports for her self-definition and her refusal of victimization. They are about the meaning of her experiences and her hope for the future. Virtually all of them are kept stored away in boxes, and Phoebe feels no urge to revisit them with any regularity. She is not currently engaged in reworking that part of her life. But they are there as a testament to her strength, as a reminder of her roots and of how she came to be the person she is now.

Jeanine's story, with its central themes of loss and confusion, is unlike those of Carol, Phoebe, and Emily. Her childhood and its artefacts contain warm memories. Only her adult possessions evince the grief and despair that became central to her sense of self. The first object Jeanine showed us was a pocket watch her father had given her. Once his grandfather's, Jeanine's great-grandfather, to whom she had been especially close as a very young child, it is inscribed with his name. Her father and mother told her stories about how she used to run out of the house to greet him. "He was a community leader, a superintendent of the Sunday school. Everybody seemed to have connections to him. My mother always talked about him so fondly, about how she would laugh with him so much." He died when Jeanine was only four, but she recalls him quite clearly. The watch has passed down through generations

of men in Jeanine's family, coming to her after her only
brother died at nineteen.

Jeanine also keeps a memento from her mother's side of
the family, her grandmother's cameo pendant.

> My memory of her is very sketchy because she had
> already started losing her mind when she came to live
> with us, so I can't remember carrying on a conversa-
> tion with her. She would point at things because she
> couldn't remember the words. Eventually she moved
> to a hospital. She had been a very intelligent woman,
> a schoolteacher, and I think she married late, at
> about thirty. She married an older man and had
> three children, my mother being the eldest. She had
> this incredible ambition. She wanted her family to
> be really well educated. My mother thinks she mar-
> ried her husband because she thought he had lots of
> money, and he did. The man she married, my moth-
> er's father, was a market gardener. She never worked
> outside though; that was not considered proper. She
> was an incredible seamstress and did beautiful quilts.
> All of the things she made were so special. I remem-
> ber her wearing this pendant. She wore it every day.
> Most of her clothes were handmade. She dressed
> quite elegantly and she had her hair long to her waist.
> She would wind it around her head in coils in a very
> elegant way.

Jeanine's mother gave her the pendant, along with some
other jewellery of her grandmother's, because she knew

that Jeanine was very attached to this grandmother. The combination of femininity, elegance of person and dress, and ambition seemed to Jeanine to provide an ideal model. "There's a sense of her life as dignified. She really made a statement about this business of not working outside. That was a line she drew. She was going to stay at home and teach her children. Even though they went to school, she still taught them at home. My aunt, the youngest child, didn't go to school until she was in grade ten or eleven." Her grandmother taught her daughters her skills at crafts and sent them to tailoring school so that they could make all their own clothes. "So these two, my dad's grandfather and mother's grandmother, were really interesting characters. The other two grandparents were not particularly strong." Jeanine relies on her knowledge of being connected to these two strong and interesting people to help maintain stability in her very difficult adult life.

Jeanine's passport is also an important keepsake. At twenty-one, she traveled for a year in Europe until her luggage was stolen. "I was backpacking, so I had things that I really wanted that I carried with me. It was terrible. I have very little to remember from that trip." The stamps in the passport show that Jeanine traveled widely in Europe, the Middle East, and Africa. It was an expectation in her family that after finishing school and working long enough to save up the money, each child would go traveling. Only one other keepsake from the trip remains – a ring purchased in Norway, which Jeanine was wearing when her luggage was taken. "I wanted to buy something for myself

to really remember the trip by, something I could have
with me all the time. Normally, I would hardly ever buy
something very special for myself."

When Jeanine came back to Canada, she met and
married her first husband. She showed us his wedding ring
as the next of her keepsakes.

When we separated, we had this little ceremony.
We went to the Empress Hotel in Victoria, to the
Bengal House restaurant, which is very lovely. We
had drinks, very civilized. He gave me his wedding
ring, I gave him mine, and I walked away. There was
never a negative word spoken. When I really think
about it, the whole marriage was done in such a civilized way. No arguing. If I was upset about something, I would go for a walk. I think that he had an
affair, that's what I think happened. From then on he
just couldn't cope and he started acting very bizarre.
You couldn't make head or tails out of what he did at
all. And then one day he came in and said, "Well, I
guess that's it, I guess we just have to go our separate
ways." And I said, "Yeah, okay."

By that time there was so much bizarre stuff going
on that I couldn't make any sense of it at all. He
seemed so weird, even when we moved to Victoria.
That whole last year he would come over and he
would be almost incoherent. He would come to
the door, his hair long and matted. He would wear
this long coat down to his ankles and he would
trail around the streets. I kept thinking that maybe

he'd be picked up and put in the hospital. When he arrived at the door, he'd just stand there and I'd say, "What do you think?" And then we'd go to bed. We would spend some days together and sleep together and after that he'd just go out again. But there was never a word spoken. I've seen him a couple of times since, and one time I asked him if he ever wanted to talk about what happened, and he said, "No, not particularly." I was twenty-five when we married and twenty-nine when we broke up. I went back to school after that. But I was very upset. It was totally shocking to me. I probably went through a year of mental breakdown.

Jeanine explained that she keeps the ring to remind herself "that there was a wedding and a marriage." She also keeps a ring from another man. In her confusion and despair over her marriage, Jeanine felt directionless. She had left her family behind in Ontario to move to the west coast, where she had no family connections. Searching for some stability and sense of normality, she began to see another man, a potter and silversmith. Instead of providing the support she was looking for, the relationship became very destructive, further weakening her sense of herself.

He was a very mysterious guy. He would go down to his studio and put a lot of things in to fire. He would set the timer, come over, we would sleep together and he would get up about five and leave to go unload his kiln. And then I wouldn't see him for a while. He gave me this ring, but then I was at a party and this woman said, "That ring you're wearing belongs to X" and she named this woman. She said that the ring was very distinctive; it had a green stone in it and she said, "That ring is so distinctive, I'd know it anywhere because it's one of a kind." The next time I saw him, I asked him if it belonged to someone else. I got the story that it belonged to the woman he lived with and he had taken it and she thought she had lost it. She was also a silversmith, and I never knew if she had made it or he had.

The stone dropped out at some point and that just adds to its ugliness. This ring to me is so ugly. It just looks like death warmed over. I keep it because it reminds me how deception is so complicated. It's filled with meaning about how deception has operated in my life. I could never really tell anybody about this guy. I'm not very proud of even knowing him. I wouldn't want to run into him in the street. But it is part of my life and I keep it fairly visible, it's downstairs in front of me when I'm washing the dishes. Since then, whenever there is another deception in my life, I go back to this ring and it adds on new levels of meaning. It's like a container for all those negative things. Every so often I think I will clean it up, put a new stone in it and wear it or something, but no, I don't want to do that. It's meant to be ugly. All tarnished and convoluted, and only an empty hollow where the stone should be.

The ring takes Jeanine back to a very dark time in her life but also reminds her that she has moved past it.

> I didn't know what I was doing. Not treating myself well. I didn't have any regular sleep hours, I wasn't working, I was living on unemployment insurance. That was the first year after my marriage broke up, and then I decided I could go back to school and that seemed to save the day for me. At thirty I went to school. But I went down to Mexico and decided to get myself something nice. The ring I got in Norway that I loved so much, I thought, "I will get something similar to that and it will remind me to do something nice for myself." I got this ring, which turned out not to be nice. It looked nice to begin with but it was very poorly made. It broke in here and I didn't wear it because it broke very early. It didn't have the strength and it didn't have the beauty of this one from Norway. It was just another sad story. I ran away to Mexico and it didn't solve anything. Nothing was working for me.

Jeanine moved back to be nearer her family in Ontario, where she found work. She began to regain confidence in herself and in the possibility of having other people in her life, but not long after she went home her nineteen-year-old brother died.

> He was the youngest. One of his friends gave me this Emily Carr print to remember him, because she

said that the picture reminded her of him. He had been around at the time I was going through all the problems in Victoria. He was really striving, but he was alone essentially too. Part of it was that we had grown up in a very tightly knit community, tightly woven family. And there we were, off in the wild blue yonder totally separated from our family, unable to have any real grounding. This painting signifies to me that absence of grounding. The tree is struggling to grow, trying its hardest. And I think we came from a rich background, like the one in the picture, but there we were, high and dry and separated from everything that had meaning. So I really identified with my brother, that he was in the same boat I was in, a bit lost, having no sense of who you were or what you wanted to do. And then he died.

After her brother's death, Jeanine began to see a man who had been her brother's friend. She eventually married him and had two children. Over the next few years, she felt that she was finally beginning to get reconnected to people. She settled into a life with possibilities and returned to school, studying massage therapy. Her next keepsakes were a cardholder from a close school friend who encouraged her to set up her massage practice and a small sculpture by another woman friend. The sculpture represents Jeanine's new sense of connectedness to a community of women.

The roundness of the sculpture. It's very evocative, an abstract female form. Having her there is about continuity too, a continuous connection between different parts of my life. I stayed in close touch with this friend. Her work has really grown into something special. She's become a very fine artist. But when I come to this, when I look back on it all and I think, "What a long road."

A small jewellery chest came from a woman friend in Ontario; white with gold trim, roses and violets painted on the lid, and letters spelling out "absent friends not forgotten." After a few years in her more settled life in Ontario, however, she and her second husband moved west again and her newly stable life unravelled.

I was in such a disconnected state again, and I still am. He got sick three months after we moved. He had a heart operation and never really recovered. I was very dislocated that first year, and he was too. He was in a lot of pain. Then he withdrew half our savings, which we were going to buy a house with, and proceeded to travel all over the place – back to Ontario, out to the coast – and spent it fast. I found out later that he thought he was dying and he was convinced that he had only been given a short time to live. By the time he wanted to come home again, I had bought this house and I was living here with our two children. He stayed for two more years. He was hardly working at all, and I was putting together these small contracts. I went back to Ontario to do a six-week teaching contract that summer, and while I was there he decided that he was going to sell the house. And he called me and told me that he was leaving. He couldn't sell the house, but off he went and moved in with another woman.

Since then, for the last two and a half years, he has sent me a hundred dollars a month. So there was a lot of deception there too, and what I've realized is that I've just been pouring all these layers of lies and weirdness into that ring. It's why I keep it in front of me. This deception in my life seems to just go on and on. I wanted to get divorced, but he said he wouldn't sign anything. Finally, after a year, I said that I would like to file for a no fault divorce. I said I would do all the paperwork, we wouldn't have to see a lawyer, we'd just make it a joint divorce. I sent him the first set of papers and he didn't sign them. Two months later, after a couple of phone calls, he did sign them and sent them back. The final set of papers, which also just needed to be signed, he altered before he signed them. Where it said "Husband agrees to pay main-tenance of children when he obtains," he changed it to say, "Husband will attempt to pay maintenance when he obtains." The judge didn't like it and she said it was ridiculous. She issued an order for divorce but deferred anything to do with maintenance and said it would have to be reopened. So I think, "How did this all happen?" I left the bosom of my family, and when I go there now I see all my relatives who

are still interconnected, and I realize that that's not
where I belong now either.

The last memento Jeanine showed us was a small candy dish given to her by her first husband's grandmother, who died while Jeanine was still married to her first husband. She left Jeanine

> three beautiful old antique things of hers. When it came time to separate all our belongings, I decided that I was going to keep this. It was my little rebellion I think, that I would keep one of his things. It was his mother who stayed in touch with me after the divorce, and when my daughter was born she knitted a wonderful outfit for her.

Jeanine continues to live with her children and supporting them entirely on her own through her massage teaching and practice. All of the positive memories she has, with the exception those connected with her great-grandfather's watch, are associated with other women, and she looks to them exclusively now for friendship and connection. One of her neighbours, Elaine, who tells her story in another chapter of this book, has "adopted" Jeanine and her two children. Jeanine provides a substitute family for Elaine as she adjusts to life without her husband, who was recently admitted to an Alzheimer's treatment facility. Elaine is a surrogate mother and grandmother to Jeanine and her children. They form their own small community, one that is slowly helping Jeanine to regain her sense of wholeness and confidence.

Many other women also told us stories of deception, tragedy, and loss. What made some of their stories different from those of Carol, Phoebe, Emily, and Jeanine was the fact that negative experiences were an occasional occurrence in their lives rather than a life theme. Although their tragedies were sometimes very profound, they did not consume their life stories.

Marie spoke of the locket her mother gave her that was meant to support her when she was sent away to live with her grandparents.

I think it must have meant more to her than to me, maybe because I was being sent away. I know her heart was in it. She put a picture in this little locket, of her and dad, and gave me this little ring with my initial. I know she was trying to do something for me. But it just reminds me of leaving home. I remember the night before when I was told I was leaving. My grandparents had come to visit and I guess the decision was made then. My dad was away at the war. It was hard to get to the school three miles away. We didn't have a car. But I remember the night before, realizing what was going to happen to me. It's one of the first major emotions I remember feeling, and I just felt sick. I called downstairs to my mom how I felt, but she didn't come up. She just told me to go to sleep, it would make me feel better. That would have been a time for her to comfort me, but I don't think she knew how to do that kind of thing.

I remember how, when we started driving, I cried and cried. When I would go home in the summers, she would be very sweet to me for about three days, but she was a very scolding type of person. She scolded a lot, especially me because I was the eldest. But I remember knowing that the niceness would end in two or three days.

Although this separation from her parents and her mother's difficulty in showing affection were very painful for Marie, her other keepsakes showed that there had been enough love in her life to make it possible for her to form a stable, positive sense of herself.

Kathleen showed us a handkerchief left behind by her mother, who died in her early fifties. It speaks to her about her mother's admirable qualities, about her suffering, and, in combination with other things, it provides a reference point for Kathleen's own development.

She had been a very lovely, gracious person. She always had hand-made, lace-trimmed handkerchiefs and used them rather than Kleenex. She used them mostly to cover the malformation of her hands from her arthritis. One hand was worse than the other and she would keep it covered with a handkerchief like this one. This handkerchief is partly about her daintiness, but it is also partly about her suffering. It's a good reminder of the kind of person she was

– very traditional, very self-conscious. I don't have a
lot of her things, but I sure have a lot of memories of
her. I would like to be like her in her personality, her
graciousness, her gracefulness. The handkerchief is
part of a sort of shrine to my mother. She was a very
important person in my life.

Bev's stories disclosed unresolved and continuing grief
over the loss of a brother to whom she was very close and,
even worse, over the death of her young son. She keeps
a cap, given by her brother to her baby son, with other
mementos of him in a cedar chest.

I have that full of objects from my son – boots, jack-
ets, things that I could not throw away, and I keep
all those memories in my cedar chest. And I never
go into it. I took that little hat out because it was
right on top, and it reminded me of both my brother
and my son. So I took it out and closed the chest
again, because I am not prepared to go through those
memories. When I go home I'll put that back in,
but I won't look at other things. After my son died,
I put everything in there so that I could heal more.
Sometime I will go through it.

Bev's losses have been so severe that she cannot yet risk
revisiting them. Most recently, the dog she loved as a surrogate child was intentionally shot and killed by a neighbour. She has two other dogs, one of which she acquired
in a confrontation with some young people who were

mistreating it. She has redirected her energies to protecting them, showing us photos and referring to them as her "family."

Bev told her litany of disasters quite matter-of-factly, but also spoke of her frequent panic attacks, which she confirms are probably about unresolved grief and her lack of stability. Her work in a mental health profession brings her in contact with many people who are grieving, and this contact only reinforces her avoidance of her own grief. "I saw a lot of people who drowned in their grief, and never ever came out. It terrified me to think that could happen to me. So that is not where I want to be. I do not sit around feeling miserable." Since her son's death, "I am married to work."

Jean, who emigrated from England at twenty-three, spoke of a childhood lived "in a very beautiful environment. There was lots of freedom, but emotionally it was constant pain." She learned to retreat from that pain into the pages of a particularly beautiful book, the story of Cinderella as told in a special Ladybird edition. Years later, she returned to England for a visit, accompanied by her partner, Emily, who took on the task of finding the book for her. They searched in every bookstore they passed until they found a copy, which Jean now treasures.

> This book means the world to me because I read it so many times when I was a little girl. This is the exact one. The pictures are so powerful, so beautiful. She goes to the ball three times, each time in a beautiful dress. The pictures are so bright. To me, it's about

transformation. Each time she is transformed, and
each time more beautiful than before.

For Jean, the book functions in much the same way
as Carol's Bible or Phoebe's adolescent journal do for
them. It calms her and reminds her of life's beauty
and of possibilities for a future unconstrained by her
unhappy childhood. Cinderella speaks to Jean of her own
transformation, after two failed marriages: the decision
to come to terms with her lesbianism and make her own
life.

> My first love was my girlfriend when I was eight
> years old, but I learned quickly that it was better to
> be a slut than to be a lesbian. I think it is things like
> this book – it's looking into beauty that allows you to
> survive these childhood traumas and pain. It's when
> you're in pain that you can open this book and look
> at this beauty and somehow put yourself into it.

We also saw many objects representing stories of betrayal,
almost always betrayal by a father, husband, or lover. One
young woman keeps her mother's family ring.

> [It reminds me of] one moment when my family was
> perceived as normal. It has a stone representing each
> of us kids in it. It reminds me of one time when a
> relative visited from out of town and was surprised
> by how much we all looked alike. He called us "the
> picture of a normal family." That has always stuck

with me. He was very wrong, but for one moment we were perceived as normal.

Other women, whose own lives have not been touched by grief and despair, treasure the mementos of a special woman whose endurance set an example against future possible hardships. One spoke of a tragedy in her grandmother's life that helps her to understand how strong her grandma is. She keeps a photo of a gravestone, with flowers set on one side, marking the grave of her grandmother's special child.

My grandfather was exempted from conscription due to a disability. He began an affair with a soldier's wife. When she became pregnant, she had nowhere to go. My grandmother took in her child after it was born and legally adopted it. I can only assume what this kind of betrayal must have felt like. But she said, "What could I do? Marriage was a forever agreement then. The option to leave was not there."

Having the baby to love became more important to her than staying angry with her husband. But at the age of two months the baby became ill and died. She told me it was the saddest thing that had ever happened to her. Her faith provided her with survival tactics. She gives praise to God for giving her the strength to go on, but I tend to believe that strength is what my grandma is all about.

Mary showed us a journal she had kept throughout the painful process of her divorce. She was married for almost

eighteen years to a man she thought of as her "best friend in the world." They had two children and an active, busy family life for many years until she became ill with multiple sclerosis. Her husband gradually withdrew from her and, after a final two years that she describes as "agony," ultimately left. Her divorce journal is a compilation of faxes sent to a sister to whom she is very close. It includes poems, sayings, and passages written to herself about getting through and about the meaning of her pain. One entry from the journal reads:

Dear Lou,

I got your FAX with no problem, so I guess everything here is functional – everything mechanical that is. The rest of the place is, as you point out, in a state of flux. I have decided that I am a victim of torture and that that is why I can never make a decision (she said as she made one) or feel one way about anything for more than five minutes at a time. I have just come through another ghastly weekend full of tears and misery and going-nowhere conversations with him. He apparently wants to act as my main support and comforter as well as chief torturer – I think that is how it's done in real life too.

The part of me that is unbearably lonely wants to accept this comfort and whatever shards of reassurance and hope may cling to it. The part of me that is supremely pissed off wants to scream at him and initiate divorce proceedings immediately (as well as arranging for various disasters to befall him in as humiliating a way as possible). The part of me that is trying to be a decent human being and a good mother wants to be patient, continue to give it time, try to keep things stable for my boys, smile and be pleasant while he turns the knife. I keep waiting for him to make his decision, while simultaneously trying not to care, feeling humiliated that I do still care, feeling that he is unworthy of my grief, feeling that I must make the only decision I can to end this impasse and escape from these vicious circles. So yes, I am, as you said, "oscillating markedly." Trying to bear it day by day, sometimes minute by minute. Trying to get on with my life the best way I can.

Sometimes I think that all of this agony is complicated by the fact that I am simultaneously dealing with my own issues about aging. I have never in my life (and I have had some pretty awful times) felt so "over the hill," useless, unattractive, discouraged, short on possibilities. I tend to think that I have used up my life on futile attempts at relationships and in pursuit of the wrong goals. I really do often feel that my life is over – that nothing of interest is likely to happen to me again, that I will stagger along in my grey dismals until I drop. How's that for a defeatist attitude? It must be almost time for the good fairy to arrive in some form or other to rescue our heroine (me in case you hadn't noticed) but I don't see any sign of her.

Oh well, one solution that has always been partly effective is to bury myself in work. Fortunately, work always cooperates with me in this, and the present is no exception. I have a million things to get done that I can focus on to make the time go by – but this approach does not fit well with the "take time off after Christmas" plan. Which reminds me that I am really dreading Christmas. And so around I go again! I am hopeless in every sense of the word. Well, enough of this moaning – eventually I do get sick of it and try to pull myself together and take some constructive action. Problem is, I have the attention span of a gnat. Still, I will try.

Mary said that the journal still serves some very important purposes, even though the divorce is now several years in the past. When she has bad days, and especially when she is experiencing a worsening of her illness, it serves to show her what she has endured and persuades her that she has the strength it takes to manage on her own. It reminds her, too, of the reality of her experience. A divorce is not "just a divorce," however common the experience may have become. It is unique to every woman and is often a watershed in a woman's life, precipitating her and her children into difficult economic times and a lengthy period of emotional turmoil and adjustment. For Mary, it required a complete change in self-definition, which, in concert with revising her self-image to include a chronic illness, made the struggle particularly difficult. As she put it in her journal,

I want to try to re-think all this, because the more I write in this journal the more I see the enormous gulf that exists between my inner thoughts and my outer experience. I realize that I am blaming myself for the loss of my marriage. I think it was my fault. I didn't try hard enough; didn't speak my anger in ways that might have moved us closer together. I lived to accommodate his wishes, and tried constantly to anticipate what those might be – he didn't like me to ask. I allowed him to terrorize me with his anger. I wasn't honest – I let myself down and made myself, over the course of years, into a person it wasn't difficult for him to leave.

Well, there is some truth in this, but not the whole truth. He had his choices too, and he always made the selfish ones. Never anything more than momentary compassion for me, even when (especially when) he knew how ill I was. I am on my own now – alone with myself and obliged to make a life for myself. I don't know how to even begin this process. There is no one for me to use as a referent – no one to accommodate to. I have to design my own life, not try to figure out what he wants and get it for him. This task isn't so difficult on the immediate, superficial level. I have many interests that I could decide to pursue – my gardening, cooking, reading and writing, piano lessons, etc. It's just that the heart has gone out of me. I feel so defeated. I feel like giving up and just drifting. Sometimes I think "I don't have all that many years left, why start anything new?" My life has

been lived, and lived badly. Why try again? There
is no energy for it. It looks like just a long, solitary
and exhausting climb above the tree line – no alpine
meadows to pass through, no turning around to look
at a lovely view behind me, no one's hand to hold.

The world often wants women to "just get over it," to
"stop exaggerating" their problems, but for Mary, and
for many others we met who were like her, this kind of
betrayal and loss was profoundly disorganizing. It stripped
away their primary support while simultaneously shak-
ing the foundation of their identity. The recovery process
was slow and painful and often involved the remaking of
a sense of self and of a life plan. Many women were left
alone with this task, as friends and family retreated or got
tired of hearing about it. For Mary, the journal became
a friend, a place where she could let go of her feelings
without worrying about what anyone else might think of
their validity or their appropriateness. Reading through
the journal now, she values the insights it still offers her
and its evidence of the gradual process of recovery. She
still reads over it occasionally, though she doesn't seek
it out anymore and no longer makes daily entries. "I
think of it as a sort of record, a year of days, of how I
got through that first year, and the one after that. I don't
really need it anymore. But I would be very sorry to lose
it. It is part of who I am now."

It was a very rare participant who didn't have some story
of sadness or grief, mediated by a special object, to tell us
about. There were differences in the extent or depth of

the grief they had experienced, but tragedy is common in women's lives. Those who had stable backgrounds and supportive relationships found these events hard to bear but were able eventually to incorporate them into a generally happy life, a personal narrative without gaps and without places that could not be entered. The few who were without these resources, whether of internal strength or of strength gained through association with other women, found that tragedy became a constant presence in their lives, interrupting their development and dominating their life stories.

*A*nne is eighty years old. She is a widow, a volunteer, a retired professor of psychology, and a stepmother to four children. She lives alone now, high in a condominium at the top of a high-rise apartment building. The rooms are large, the windows enormous, revealing long, beautiful views across the city and the mountains a hundred kilometres west. She is not one, she said, who likes clutter around her or who collects things. She prefers not to "have 'knick knacks' and do a lot of dusting," and does not consider herself to be a feminine sort of woman who might surround herself with "fussy" things. Rather, the objects she showed us came from boxes stored in a large closet, where she keeps them carefully wrapped in cloths and paper.

Anne is a woman of character. She lives a principled life; she is mindful of intentions and meanings and morals. "Character" is an old-fashioned word – a beautiful word, too – that we use here to describe a woman with clear personal values and strong commitments. Women of character live out a hard-won moral strength. Their achievements, their failures, and their tragedies combine to create a powerful sense of self. Women of character know themselves well. Not surprisingly, many of the women possessing this quality are elderly. The stories attached to their cherished possessions are complex, and often tell of the pivotal events and relationships from which they have derived their strength. Their achievements are often unusual for their place and time. Their lives rarely follow cultural expectations – or their own.

We met with many women of character. Our impression was that most women who move through troubles and tumult to a productive old age belong to this group. We certainly saw the beginnings of character in many of the younger women who shared their stories with us.

What do the stories of these women of character have in common? Certainly, it is not a simple matter of profession, of achievements in the world, or of having particular experiences, like marriage and child bearing, that are assumed to be central to women's lives. Rather, they share a strong, early connection to at least one remarkable woman, often, but not always, their mothers. That bond was an authoritative but mutually respectful relationship between a strong mother and her child, and was often supplemented by a similar relationship with a grandmother or another female relative or friend. The mothers, grandmothers, and aunts of women of character were very strong people by any definition. They were often heads of households; fathers were often absent, in wars or at work, had died early in accidents or from illness, or had left their marriages. In only a very few instances strong and expressive fathers or grandfathers also figured in these women's stories.

Women of character recalled many early losses – deaths of family members or loss of a family home and possessions. In response to these hardships, their female relatives showed resilience, persistence, and determination, and were never distracted from respectful and caring connections with their children. In such families, losses became challenges that tested and clarified their parents' commitments to certain values. Their mothers' responses to crises and the advice they gave their daughters left the daughters with a sense of life as an adventure, where setbacks are to be expected, grief and loss are unavoidable, but meaning emerges.

These mothers and fathers took their children very seriously, studied them carefully, and knew them as individuals, encouraging each child's personality and special abilities. Under difficult circumstances, often in the face of severe hardship, they invested time and family resources in the child's development. The mothers and, when they were present, the fathers had egalitarian views about both sons' and daughters' possibilities. Their child-rearing practices were not gender stereotypic; both sons and daughters might have dolls, for example, and education was considered equally essential for both.

The children in these families were expected to persist as their parents had: to do their best, to accept responsibilities, to make and honour commitments, and to accept difficulty and loss. These values were demonstrated every day in the life of the family. The developing child was encouraged to live by them, but also to make her own choices freely within this framework. The family "rules" spoke of and demonstrated the importance of examining and choosing values, honouring promises, taking advantage of opportunities for adventure, working hard, and living intensely. Beyond this, the child developed herself and chose where and when she would make her own commitments.

Like many of the women we spoke with, Anne began her description of her treasured possessions with remarks about their lack of material value:

> They're not, by and large, any material things. I mean of value. I know people who have a terrible time moving into condos because they want certain specific kinds of dishes or so on. I got rid of all that before I ever considered moving. They've been more of what you'd call almost silly things; well, I will say silly things. They are things that I can see now, looking back, have a lot of meaning.

Anne led us into her construction of meaning with her first story about a very old cloth doll with a china head and eyes that opened and closed.

> I have cherished this since I was this big, my baby doll. It was a time when our family, well, the financial situation was just desperate. My father had been a big successful farmer, and following World War I he lost everything in that crash. I didn't know anything about this. What did I know about it? I was happy enough. I know now that we were practically homeless. We were living in a house somebody let us live in, someone's summer cottage. We were really, really poor. Not genteel poor, just poor poor. But

they got me this baby doll. And I loved her. I must
have had her – notice she has a personality – when I
was three. My brother was born when I was almost
four, and Mother said she used to sit and nurse him
in the rocker and I would sit in my little rocker and
nurse my baby too. "Companions," she would say.
Well, when my brother got somewhat older, about
three or four, he was a curious type. He decided to
see why this baby's eyes opened and shut. He took
her head off one day and broke her eyes. Well, if it
were one of my real children I don't think I could
have been more devastated.

Now, you have to remember the circumstances
we were in. But my father said, and I think this is one
of the reasons I cherish this doll, "Now Anne, I have
to go into Regina and I know there's a place there
that I can get parts for dolls, and if I can find eyes I
will try and get you some and bring them back. Now
what colour would you like?" "Oh," I said, "brown
eyes, cause I'm going to marry a man with brown
eyes." I did, too! Sure enough, he came back with
the brown eyes, took the doll apart, fixed them up,
and to this day they work.

And of course I had other dolls. I always had
names for them, but this one was The Baby. This was
my baby and I think what it represents is, I suppose
besides a certain nostalgia for childhood when you
didn't have to worry about all these things, or at least
you didn't know what to worry about, it was sort of
the sense that some things were more important and

One of Anne's dolls

they weren't always the sensible things. We didn't
have much money and yet they thought this was
important.

Anne went on to explain that in her family there is a tradition of cherishing meaningful possessions. To emphasize the meaning she was talking about, and how she had
chosen the things she keeps, she told us another story
about the doll's clothes. Opening another box, she set
out the doll clothes that were made to fit her Baby. There
were nightgowns, petticoats, diapers – some store-
bought and some made by her mother. Speaking of one
special nightgown, she told how, on a particular family
Christmas when she was about seven, a snow storm had
prevented trains or any other form of transportation
from leaving the city to reach surrounding farms.

The packages that had been ordered from Eaton's
for Christmas didn't come, and the packages from
my aunt and from the people in Regina didn't come
out. So it got to be Christmas Eve and my mother
got frantic about what she was going to do, because
there were no real presents. She could make candy,
she could do things like that, but there were no
presents. She thought she had to have something
for the children. My brother had a doll too. So on
Christmas Eve she made these little nightgowns, just
like she was making for her own baby. She worked
away and sewed them up, put featherstitching
around the edge, finished the two of them. Well of

course, the piece-de-resistance of the whole thing is that at nine o'clock my uncle came down. He had gone to meet the train and got the stuff off the train, and had come down in his big sleigh with all this. So there were lots and lots of presents. But Christmas night my mother was tucking us into bed as she always did, and she said, "Now what was your very favourite present?" and without a hesitation I said "The nightgown for my Baby."

The doll embodies Anne's many warm memories of the innocence of childhood, of how little it takes to make a child happy, and of how important her happiness was to her mother and father. The fine handwork on the nightgown tells of her mother's love and the time and trouble she took to avoid disappointing Anne and her brother. Her father's special effort to repair the doll let her know that he understood her attachment to her Baby and her grief over its broken eyes, and that he knew her well. Her parents' attention to these seemingly small things taught her about the meaning of love and about what her parents found important in life. "The reason I have come through all the stuff that I have come through is that I've had this solid base of a father who would do this, a mother who would do this. When you'd think they might be preoccupied with just the necessities of life, they remembered their little child's sadness." The baby doll is a constant reminder to Anne, seventy-seven years after she first received it, of what was important then and what remains important today. It still has the power to move her to tears and continues to offer her assurances of having been known and loved. "Even as I am talking to you," she said, "I can feel my tears and I am aware of how much it means."

A second doll, thirty years older than the first and much smaller, came out of the box next. It was Anne's mother's doll, her own Baby. With head and shoulders of china, it wore a copy of a lady's dress from the late nineteenth century. Anne's mother was about eighty when she gave Anne the doll. Its painted face is still perfect, its costume complete with delicate buttons and hand-sewn details. Again, Anne's first comment was about the fact that the doll "is of no material value, but it represents – it's hard to find words – it represents love."

> My mother was a very unusual woman ... way ahead of her time in many ways. She had started out from a poverty stricken part of the Eastern Townships. She and her sister decided they were going to medical school. She started medical school and was over halfway through the course when she decided to marry my father. But back in 1913 you didn't combine a career with marriage. My father told her, "You can go back and finish your course but you can't practice, I wouldn't want my wife to practice." "Well," my mother said, "what's the use of finishing the course?" And she claimed she never regretted it, although I know she must have. She was a very bright woman, with great joie de vivre. I cherish a very special mother.

In fact, the women in Anne's family all supported and exemplified a tradition of women's education, scholarship, and community service. Named for an aunt who was one of the first women to graduate from Brandon College, Anne herself graduated from Columbia University, accepted there as a scholarship student. She later joined the faculty at Columbia and was one of the first women to hold an academic appointment. As Anne continued to talk about her mother's lessons, she brought out of the box a collection of her mother's speeches. Like the dolls, these much-folded papers show the marks of daily use. They are impeccably handwritten in a flowing script, with no sign of changes or corrections. The speeches are inspirational, passionately expressed evocations of the importance of a principled life, about tempering judgment with compassion and calling for understanding of the everyday difficulties women face in their lives.

It had been her mother's habit to involve Anne in preparing these speeches, which she delivered to various women's groups. She would try them out on Anne as they worked on household tasks together.

My mother was a very lively woman, a special person in many ways, and she did a great deal of public speaking, mostly in connection with the church. She was kind of ecumenical in her churches, went to whatever was handy, wherever we lived, whatever the church was. She wasn't dogmatic. There was no "you have to believe this and this and this." The content was not important, just the principle. She did a great deal of YWCA work; she was president of the board for a long time in Regina. She was a very community-minded, community-spirited woman. She had a really good stage presence. I used to tell her in later years, "You know you gave me all the vocational training I ever had."

These speeches represent that kind of thing, which began way back when I was three, the Christmas before I was four. We were in Regina and my aunt wanted to show off her little niece. She wanted me to say a piece, to recite at the Christmas concert. Mother said, "Oh, I'd better ask Anne." Which in itself tells you a little bit about how she raised her children. My mother told me, "Auntie would like you to say a piece at the concert." I said, "Well, what would I have to do?" and she said, "Well, go up on the platform, say your piece and bow. You know lots of little pieces to say." And I said I guessed I could do that. My aunt went down and bought me a new dress, I remember, and new shoes, which at that time we could use! Anyway, my mother said to me, and this is the point of the story, "Now, when you get up on the platform Anne, look at the people in the back row and say your piece to them." So this little bit of a thing brought the house down because they could hear me.

She went on to describe how, in later years, mother and daughter would be doing dishes together, when times were "really tough" after her father's death. Her mother had taken in boarders; work was unending.

We'd be doing dishes and she'd say, "Anne, we can't just chat tonight. I have to make a speech tomorrow night and I want to think it out with you." So I would keep quiet and she would talk out loud and plan her speech. These are her notes from speeches that she composed and gave and I've always treasured them. What they represent to me is – it's hard to explain what it is. Competent is not quite the word I want to use. This accomplished, strong, influential woman who, in the details of her daily life, was quite limited, but she had this outlet which was her way of speaking. And these represent to me what started me. This aspect of my mother that was my role model. And the speeches represent my enormous pride in her, and how she helped me to go on to do what I did.

Anne followed in her mother's footsteps from her earliest childhood. A very bright child, she was accelerated through school, entering high school at twelve. She was, she said, a social misfit, but the impact of that problem was lessened by the care her mother took to involve her in community activities with children her own age. She recalls having been chosen for speaking activities, like narrating the children's pageant, and consciously following her mother's example in carrying out these responsibilities. Anne credits her early training and the power of her mother's personality with developing the skills, the desire to excel, and the commitment to moral and ethical living that were the basis for her own later success. Anne admires her mother's speeches, too, for the way they reflect her mother's "lovely use of language," particularly their descriptions and their emotional intensity.

When her father died in the spring of her high school graduation, relatives advised her mother to let Anne get a job and help support the family. She refused. "Anne," she said, "is going on to college. How she is going is another story, but she is going to go to college. She may not go this year while she is so young, I may let her first take a business course or something, but she is going to college."

Later that summer, while her mother was away settling the affairs of a deceased brother, Anne, with the help of her formidable grandmother, was running their boarding house when she received a letter offering her a scholarship. Unable to contact her mother, she went ahead and enrolled in college and began to work on her first degree. When her mother returned home, she supported Anne's decision.

Reading her mother's speeches reminds Anne that her mother trusted her judgment and gave her the freedom to make her own decisions. They renew her connection to her mother, to the ideals and values that structured her life. They remind her, too, that strong emotion is an important part of living; emotions are to be experienced in their full intensity, clearly expressed, and managed by guiding principles. This latter lesson was of particular significance, since Anne's childhood and youth were marked by the experience of many deaths in her family. Her mother's example of passionate expression of ideas and of endurance in the face of tragedies taught Anne how to put losses into perspective, how to experience grief but not be defeated by it.

> I'm carrying, of course, a little bit of past grief. Everybody kept dying – all the grandparents, the uncles and aunts, my father. So, you know, we carried, even from early childhood, a burden of grief. But you go on with your life, it's not the worst thing that you could carry in your soul. And you feel it. You allow it to flow over you. But you move on.

Anne combined emotion with strength of intellect. Other women raised by their mothers shared this capacity – emotions were intensely felt and demonstrated, tempered with analytical thinking and self-conscious decision-making. They were not people who panicked or who fell apart under great stress. Instead, they thought through problems, turned to a community of women like themselves, and, when necessary, evoked the power of their will to endure.

Anne next showed us a small wooden bench made for her by her father. Looking at it closely, one can see the square nails and other details of construction that mark its seventy-five years in Anne's homes. The bench reminds her again of her father, a very quiet man who was widely respected for his wisdom and good judgment. He never, in Anne's recollection, raised his voice, and he "tempered mother's lovely qualities with calmness and good judgment." She saw her parents' relationship as "wonderful," especially considering the financial hardship of their years together and the fact that he was very ill for at least four years before he died when Anne was fifteen. She remembers asking her mother how she managed to maintain a happy marriage

Mother's speeches, father's bench

throughout these difficulties and in light of the fact that, when they first married, she and her husband lived with his mother. The response was typical of her ability to make decisions and her strong will. "Well, I made up my mind that I loved him and that I was going to get along with his mother and come to love her. It wasn't just exactly easy, but I decided that's the way it's going to be and you're going to do it that way." Anne's descriptions of her mother as strong-willed, decisive, persistent, joyful, and loving leave little doubt of her individualism and her determination to raise a strong daughter.

Rather than settling into life as a public school teacher after college, Anne went on to graduate school and became a professor at a time when few women held such positions. Her strong sense of adventure and need to seek out challenges for herself led her to travel widely and to enjoy a busy life as a single career woman until her late thirties.

A folded traveling chess set, perhaps four inches square, contains the story of her marriage and motherhood. It belonged to her husband for many years and represents to her the happiest parts of their life together. In her late thirties, Anne accepted a one-year posting to Nigeria to help develop the education system. There she received a letter from a man who had heard her give a speech at a school in New York. He wrote that he had been impressed by her speech and that his wife had also been there but had since died, leaving him alone with four young children.

I thought, "What does he want? I want nothing to do with this man. He's looking for someone to take care of his kids." So I wrote back a very curt, cool note, which he never got. So he wrote again. Persistent man! And this time he described the chaos in the house on Christmas morning with these four kids. The furnace went out and the whole place was freezing. And I suddenly thought, "You know, he has been awfully burdened, but he treats it with humour and compassion." So I wrote back in a slightly warmer tone and we corresponded the rest of the year. When I came back, I met him. We met at the Harvard Club, and he told me more about his four children – they were between four and nine when their mother died. I thought, "I don't want anything to do with this situation. This is not for me. He's looking for a governess." So, when I got back to my own place I wrote him a letter and said, "Thank you for dinner, it was pleasant to meet you, but if you are interested in a governess for your children, please look elsewhere." He responded to this with a huge bouquet of flowers, delivered by courier to my office desk. And I thought, "Hmm, he's kind of an interesting man!"

I wasn't thinking about marriage, but I was intrigued. So, I went to his place in the country. I got there and they were making grape jelly on the terrace – if you imagine this with four little kids! We kept seeing each other, and later that fall he phoned me up one night and said, "Anne, for heaven's sake, let's just get married and court afterwards. This is too complicated." Which I think is one of the stranger proposals you could get! Bill asked me if I would want to stop working if we got married, and I said no because I knew I could never go back. He moved his office into the house so he could work from home, and we had live-in help. So I became a mother at forty, to four traumatized little children. I didn't care for the house, but I was into the kids and into Bill, our relationships.

Anne married Bill in 1958 and began thirty years of marriage and child rearing that tested her ability to persevere, to refuse to allow anything to divert her from her task or from the commitments she had chosen. She "made up her mind," as her mother had done so many years earlier, to love her husband and her stepchildren, and she did. The chess set recalls memories of courtship, of marriage to Bill, and of their years of happiness together.

He was a great chess player, champion of the Harvard Club. And every day he would sit, usually after supper, and he would work out chess puzzles. And of all the things he gave me, of jewellery or other mementos, this is the thing that represents Bill to me. It reminds me of his one-track mind – his complete absorption in what he was doing. And there was a kind of enthusiasm in him, a whole-hearted enthusiasm for whatever he was committed to. He was intensely focused, and this set evokes that presence for me. And look at the pieces. When some got lost, like this little white one, he took a piece of white plastic and made a new one. You can see how much he used it, how often he held it. He had this long before I married him.

Looking at it, I can see him sitting in his chair by the fireplace with his chess, and taking his glasses off, and hanging them out of a corner of his mouth. I'd be puttering about, or reading student exams across from him in my chair. We'd have this nice companionable, peaceful time, and it just brings back the whole picture, the many good evenings we had. I think it also represents, on a more realistic or different level, Bill's complete absorption. He was one of those men, you had to get his attention. My love for Bill was not a blind, adoring love. I recognized where he was difficult. In my memory, looking at this chess set, I can see all that. He's a real, whole person.

This image of Bill soothes her and lets her focus on the man she loved and enjoyed, before illness changed him. Ann knew before she married that one of their daughters had been born with a mild brain injury and that the other three children had been badly hurt by their mother's

Memories of their years together

death. Together, she and Bill raised the children very successfully, but their son's problems were not ones that could be overcome by loving parents.

> I thought for a while that if I were only a good enough mother I could straighten this whole mess out. Well, I couldn't. Our son Robin, a brilliant kid and so nice, became schizophrenic when he was sixteen and was in and out of hospitals for the next fifteen years. He died when he was thirty-one. It was not suicide, as we had at first assumed, but a heart attack. Then, six months after Robin's death, Bill became psychotic. Fortunately, all of the children were grown and gone by then, and they were wonderfully helpful to me. Bill had become dangerous and we had to get him committed. He was in hospital for a year and a half. The thing for which I am

most grateful is that we were able to get the very best help for Robin and for Bill and I came through the whole thing with no bitterness.

Bill suddenly became convinced that we had to get divorced. He would say, "I love you dearly, Anne, but we have to get divorced." He was trying to protect me, really. There had been an incident where he had taken a vagrant into the house while I was away with our daughter while she gave birth to our grandchild. He wanted to leave all his money to this man. So everyone said, "Anne, for the children's sake, you have to do this." We were technically divorced, to protect the kids and for Bill's peace of mind. It was only a paper divorce. I don't think most people walk out of a divorce hearing holding hands! Then, a year later, he developed cancer, which had metastasized, and he died that May.

Throughout her recollection of these memories, Anne held the chess set. She treasures it particularly, she said, because when he became ill, Bill gave up chess. He didn't want the chess set with him in hospital. It remains an uncontaminated reminder of who he was before the illness changed him, in the years when they sat together through so many contented evenings.

The last of the mementos Anne shared – there were many others, each with its own story to tell – was a small sewing kit, made for her by her brain-injured daughter. Joannie's coordination, Anne said, was "perfectly wretched" so that most of the things she made fell far short of her hopes. But with Anne's help, she persisted and was able to make this memento as a gift for her mother.

Most of the time when she made things, she would look at them and say, "Mommy, that's just terrible. I can't make good things like this." But this thing was just what it was supposed to be. And I carry it when I travel. You can see it is very well worn. I've used it a lot because it represents for me my little girl's desperate effort and her pride. She is such a perceptive child. I can remember coming home after college one night, beat, bedraggled and tired. I sat down and Leslie came and said, "Mommy, can you help me? I have to do a paper," and Robin said, "Don't forget you said you'd make brownies for something or other tomorrow." And the littlest, Pamela, came in sucking her thumb and holding her blanket, upset about something and I was trying to comfort her. And Joannie comes in and looks the situation over and says, "Mommy, you look tired. I think I'll make you a cup of tea." And I always thought that was so typical. She was the one who would always pick up on my fatigue. The others were always so preoccupied with what they needed from me, so Joannie has a special place in my heart. And she tried so hard.

The signs in her daughter of willingness to take on challenges, to make the most of her abilities, and to be sensitive to the needs of others were particularly moving to Anne. Coming from this child, the sewing kit represents hard work, thoughtfulness, and persistence in the face of difficulties, as well as her child's love for her, her wish to make Anne's life easier, and the pride she was encouraged to take in so difficult an achievement. After Bill's death, Ann moved back to Canada, where she continues to lead an active life, involving herself in church and community activities for senior citizens, and in the lives of her daughters, her grandchildren, and her nieces. Her life remains an enactment of principled living, great determination, a sense of adventure, the fullest use of ability, respect for the life of the mind, and the capacity to love and nurture others unselfishly.

She has very clear plans for what will become of her treasures. Before she dies she will give them into the keeping of those of her daughters and nieces who show an interest in them and can be trusted to keep them safe, preserving the family stories they represent.

> My niece is the kind of person who cherishes this kind of thing, so when they get into their new house and get settled, she'll have a cabinet with treasures, kind of family treasures. And I told her I would give her my Baby doll. You know, there's no use waiting until I die. No one will know what to do with this thing. What I don't want is somebody to come in here after I either go into a nursing home or die or whatever happens to me, which I really have no control over and don't care about at this point, who doesn't know what to do with it. What in the world do we do with this old doll of Mother's or

Grandmother's, or whatever? She needs a home and my niece will give her one. She'll make her nice clothes too.

The values contained and expressed in these possessions will continue to enrich Anne's life and the lives of her descendants. They are the foundation of Anne's character; they have the power to inspire character in those who know their history.

Another participant, Elaine, spoke of a mother whose independence, love of life, resilience in the face of hard times, and commitment to education shaped her daughters' lives. Elaine began the story of her childhood by showing us a beautiful etching in shades of black, grey, and white. Hanging in a place of honour in her living room, it depicts a small group of people, including two men on horseback, who are apparently setting out on a trip. One mounted man speaks to a woman standing beside him while the other shakes hands with a third man, who is staying behind. Two dogs complete the group picture, and the whole is set against the background of southern Alberta's Porcupine Hills ranching country. The etching, given to Elaine by her youngest son and created by a young artist she knows, is, Elaine says, "a picture of my childhood." Its place of honour in her home reminds her, just as Anne's dolls and letters do, of a childhood spent with a very special mother.

I was a rancher's daughter. When you lead that kind of life, you are much more mature at the age of twelve than most children are today. We had great responsibilities and it was such a beautiful upbringing. We had animals and we had such a loving home. My mother and father separated early on. He wasn't able to carry on the way my mother thought he should, was pretty spoiled in his family, and a bad money manager. So he left but we still kept the ranch. At the age of twelve I had my own bank account, because if the money was in my bank account nobody could take it from my mother for debts. They were difficult times. My sister was three and a half years older than I was, and very conscientious. We were very close; we did everything together.

Sleeping in never occurred to us. I suppose we were just too busy. We were up early. In the beginning we had water and sewer in the house, but as the depression worsened, we weren't able to have them, because it took machinery to run them. We lived in a very deep ravine where a creek ran through, and every morning we would climb out and walk about a mile further to school, a tiny school with only a few kids. I went there until grade eight, but my mother was at odds with the school board. She couldn't accept the teachers they sent out. So she hired a university graduate for twenty-five dollars a month and set up a private school for us. She was a very strong woman who valued education and we inherited that.

Just as Anne's mother had valued her daughter's education, so did Elaine's. The easy way, keeping her daughters home to help out in difficult times, saving their very limited funds for other pressing needs, was not her way. An educated woman herself, she was determined that her daughters would be as well. Taking the same authoritative but respectful approach to parenting that we saw in Anne's story, she expected the best from her daughters, encouraged them to live physically active lives, challenged them with hard work, and included them in making decisions.

> She gave us a lot of respect, included us in every-thing. There were always chores to do, chopping wood, cows to milk, horses to feed, and we wouldn't come back into the house for supper until about 6: 30. Then we would do our homework while we listened to the radio, then get off to bed. Mother also read to us a lot. The three of us depended on each other. When there were problems between us, mother sat down in the kitchen and discussed them with us. Whatever the problem, it was always settled within an hour. None of this sitting in the corner. Mother never treated us like that.
>
> We were taught extremely good manners. We ate with the hired hands – some of them were pretty grim with their manners, but we were told that they hadn't been taught, that we must not stare at them, but just accept the way they did things. It was a complicated household, but it was knit. Mother was the matriarch and that was it! She was in a bad position, but she accepted that.

There was no room for self-pity, no question of giving up or giving in to weakness, either in Elaine's mother's approach to her own life or in her expectations for her daughters. A loving, demonstrative woman, she was always aware of her daughters as individuals in their own right. Elaine described a daily ranch life of hard work and high expectations. Hardship was taken as a challenge; competence and self-respect were the expected outcomes.

> So the picture is about my childhood until I was about fifteen. It was such a lovely, free life. It was very hard work; Mother didn't ever hide the responsibility that she was carrying. It was a large ranch – six sections, plus some lease. But it was a wonderful life, and I am so grateful to my son for choosing this picture for me.

Once Elaine started high school, she had to go to school in town. She rode the fifteen miles at the beginning of the week, stayed the week, and then rode home "if my horse hadn't jumped the fence and gone already, which she did sometimes." Elaine's sister went to university to study agriculture. After high school graduation, Elaine first took a business course, went to college in Calgary for a year, and then went into the Air Force as a civil servant. The war had started, and she was "living in heaven, because all the staff in the hospital where I worked were very nice young men who were so good to me." It wasn't long, though, before Elaine also made the commitments that shaped her adult life.

The second possession she brought to talk about was one that contained all the memories of her married life and her life as a mother. It was a 4-H club badge, a symbol of an organization that became a way of life for Elaine and her family. Her first husband suffered a serious injury in a ranch accident, making it impossible for him to continue ranching. Instead, he became a grain buyer, and he and Elaine moved into a grain company residence. They started a family, two daughters and two sons, all under the age of twelve when he died of a heart problem, possibly exacerbated by exposure to grain dust. Widowed, Elaine was no longer eligible to live in the company residence. After a few weeks, she and her four young children moved into town.

If you can name a job, I probably did it. I was fortunate. I had great aunts and uncles who were very good. I worked for the undertaker and I worked for the lawyer and for the district agriculturalist and for the veterinarian. I never refused work. I did a lot of typing at home. I transcribed books. The children and I had our Sundays together, and Saturdays they had lots of projects going. The kids were very responsible. When things like that happen, well, it's the bottom of the barrel. You either sit there and sink or you start climbing out.

Among her friends was a local ranch family, including a bachelor farmer, who now decided that "maybe he needed a wife."

It took us a while to decide, but it is a lonely life and I knew he would be so good with the children. But it used to really, really annoy me when people would come up to me and say, "Oh dear me, you were so wise to marry John. Now your children will have a father," in that pious, holier-than-thou voice. I would say, "I'm sure they will, but I would never have married him if I hadn't loved him." They used to sort of sit back and say that I was pretty crusty for my age.

I married him three years after my husband died. We went to the farm to live, but we built a new house. We were hailed out the day before we were to be married, and it was so funny. He called and I could tell right away that something had happened, and he wondered if it would make a difference. He thought that I wouldn't want to marry him then. I told him that if that was going to break up our marriage, then we had better not start. It was very difficult. I owned my own home, and we rented it out and went and bought milk cows, and milked cows by hand, seven of them. I let go of the other jobs, but kept one that I thought I could handle and still be on the farm. Whenever I got enough money, I would buy another milk cow. That's the way we carried on until my husband's health gave in, but we educated all our children. Three of them got degrees. One is a doctor, one an engineer, one is in television, and the fourth is a rancher.

So this 4-H badge represents to me all that life we had together with the children. John had good pure-bred cattle, so many people would come and buy their 4-H calves from him, but of course now he had children of his own and they got first choice. Our children did very well in 4-H, but the thing was, this badge is a symbol of how our whole life with John evolved. He was over forty when we married and had never had children. But we worked together on the farm all the time. He became a 4-H assistant leader, everything sort of revolved around 4-H. It made for a lovely home life, because not only did we work, we played. It bound us all together. The kids all had chores, and they did them willingly.

John was so gentle with the cattle, so gentle with the kids. And it just made all the difference in weld-ing our family together. We had a big garden. We would dash out in the morning, get things out of the garden, put them in big tubs in the living room. Then we'd turn on the radio for the afternoon and snip peas and beans. That's how we survived.

We always talk about our 4-H days and even now the kids have some of the same friends they had then. None of them are in 4-H now though. They've all got professions. But you know, you don't know what your children are going to do, and I don't think we have a right to make our children be what we think they should be. I guess I was independent as a youngster and I wanted to make my own way through things. If you have a gift it is a terrible thing not to use it.

Elaine now lives alone in a retirement community in British Columbia. Her husband, John, suffers from Alzheimer's disease and lives in a nursing home in the same community. Elaine spends time with him every day. At seventy-three, she still goes on horseback expeditions into the mountains. As she puts it, "I was born on a horse. I rode from the time I was three. My great aunt used to ride with us all the time back home. They were all great riders." She follows their example, remaining physically active and engaged with others in her community. She has "adopted" a young woman and her family Jeanine, who has appeared earlier in this book – a single mother with very limited income and two children to raise – and is closely involved in their lives as a mentor and role model.

Elaine's home is filled with memorabilia from her active, colourful life. She has "all of Mother's lovely china," but says that she doesn't need these things to remember her by.

I was with my mother when she died. My sister died in my arms. Those memories are etched in my mind as if they were yesterday, and that's all I need. And of course John is in a home now. It is a tragedy, and one could become very bitter, if you allowed yourself to. You wonder, when he worked so hard and was such a

good father and did everything that he thought was
right, then to have this kind of reward for it.

But, she says, giving in to bitterness is a poor choice.
Better to make the most of what there is. She takes John
old Father's Day cards from her assortment of the ones
they received from their children over the years, hoping
that they will help him to remember. In her home,
decorated in western style, are displayed many photos
from her childhood as well as pictures of her children
and her three grandchildren. Like Anne, she also has
expensive jewellery and other valuable things, but she
does not particularly treasure these, valuing instead the
things that remind her of her life, her mother, and her
experiences. Keeping informed about decisions and
passing along instructions to her tenants.

> I haven't lost any of my identity anyway. When the
> time comes, we will just switch over and the kids
> will manage it. I couldn't go and sell out from under
> John. I just couldn't. He wouldn't know, but I still
> couldn't do it. People ask how I can cope with it,
> but I always tell them, "But for the grace of God it
> could be me. He could be here, and he would go
> every day and do what he could for me." I do what I
> think is right at the time, and I think that's the only
> fair way.

Another woman of character, Vivian, evinced similar
strengths and courage. She is a retired school librarian,

the mother of nine children and grandmother of twenty-two, "the last time I counted." She began her story with a postcard from her aunt Lydia, who would become an important figure in her life. The postcard, dated April 24, 1918 and carefully kept in its original envelope for her by her mother, is addressed to Vivian on her birth at Riley Farm, Calgary. It reads, "Greetings to my new niece Vivian. May she grow fair, fat and twice forty without any more troubles than are necessary to make her appreciate her blessings." The postcard was recently a centerpiece, read by the many friends and family who gathered to celebrate Vivian's eightieth birthday.

Vivian was the first child in a family of eight children. Her aunt Lydia was special to her for many reasons, the foremost being her qualities of character, the same mixture of fortitude, expressiveness, humour, intelligence, and principle that Anne and Elaine found in their mothers. Lydia and her husband, a railroad engineer, lived in Saskatchewan when World War I began. He was killed in the fighting, leaving Lydia a widow with four small children. Vivian's parents, who had been working on a farm in what is now Calgary, moved to McLean to help her.

> So for the first seven years of my life I lived in a very small town, next door to my cousins, who were a good bit older than I, and my aunt Lydia. It was one of the only times in my life when I had any sense of family at all. I have a lot of memories of Aunt Lydia. Things that she told me, things that she did, things

that she and my mother got up to. They were full of mischief, the two of them.

Lydia and Margaret, Vivian's mother, were strong-willed women who needed all their willpower and tenacity to survive their difficult lives. They lived with their children, often without supportive husbands, through times when large families were commonplace and poverty widespread. Economic disasters were changing the social structure and politics of the country, as natural disasters changed its very landscape. Vivian was caught up in these events, and her mother and her aunt Lydia were her guides for how to endure and rise above circumstances, keeping essential principles before her as lodestars.

Like Anne's and Elaine's mothers, Vivian's mother and her aunt were committed to their children's education and passed on to their daughters a love of learning and a competitive spirit. Vivian showed us a grade one report card that her mother kept for her from this period, pointing out with pride the fact that it is signed by her mother, forging her absent father's name. Bureaucracy might set up barriers, but Vivian's mother had no compunction about walking through, over, or around them when necessary. The report card shows that Vivian was an outstanding student, the first in her class. She disapproves of ranking children as poor practice, still trying to reconcile her competitive spirit with her beliefs about equality.

Her mother forged her father's name

The first I knew they did that, I wanted to be first. And I succeeded in doing just that. When I look back on it, I've got a picture somewhere of this little group of girls I went all through elementary school with, and this little group of us were first, second, third and fourth in every class all the time. It lessened the pleasure when you knew there was a last, but I enjoyed school enormously. I was the eldest in my family, so I brought my brothers and sisters along as their turns came.

When Vivian was eight, her family moved to Cardston, leaving her aunt Lydia and her experience of extended family connections behind. As we spoke, she showed us pictures of her family and friends and of places that had figured large in her life. Photos of young women and men, leaning against a tractor and surrounded by barren fields, photos of babies, and photos of political figures were intermixed in her narrative.

We became refugees from Saskatchewan. And I
remember, of course, the terrible dust storms. I can
remember helping my mother use a knife to stuff rags
in all the cracks around the windows and the doors
to keep the dust out. We left and went to Cardston,
which was probably one of the biggest mistakes my
parents ever made. We had an extremely rough time
there, extremely rough. Left there and came to
Calgary and we had some terrible, terrible times in
Calgary. I was just starting grade ten when we came
to Calgary. At the time I was still a churchgoer, but
I met some young people who were in the League
Against War and Fascism. So I started going to that
and taking an interest in politics.

Vivian's experience with the radical politics of the
Depression era began when she was fifteen and continued, ebbing and intensifying, throughout the rest of
her life. Part of the lasting legacy of these experiences is
her championing of the poor and her life-long efforts to
combat injustice, whether at a political level or in the life
of a friend or relative. She was particularly moved, in her
teenage years, by what she saw as the threat of fascism in
Alberta. It was personified for her by the premier of the
province.

This photo is a picture of William Aberhart. He
began the Social Credit movement in Alberta.
He terrified me when we were living through the
Depression. He really did. He had Fascist written

all over him. The night of the election, the theatre where his speech was held was crammed to the rafters. If he had told those people to go set fire to the whole city they would have done it. I used to go to some of their study groups, and they were strongly anti-Semitic too, though they try to deny it to this day.

People starved in this country in the Depression. You couldn't buy a job, you couldn't get an education, you couldn't do this and you couldn't do that. People understand that, but they don't realize the extent of the repression. We were getting damned awfully close to fascism in this country. It was those experiences, when I was fifteen and sixteen, when I really became politically aware and realized what was going on in the country, and came to be what was later called a "premature anti-fascist." If you wanted to have things like unemployment insurance, things like old age pensions, socialized medicine, you were called a communist. And I used to say, "How come you give the communists the credit for having all the good ideas?"

When the Ottawa Trek came through, I was very active raising money for that, and for Norman Bethune's mobile blood unit for Spain. When R. B. Bennett defeated Mackenzie King, both of them spoke in Calgary and I went to hear them both. It seemed to me, with the arrogance of youth, that I knew it all. I became a flaming radical – went out and joined the Young Communist League. I remember having a blazing row with my father about it; my mother was treading a little more softly.

By this time I was in grade eleven, and I was a member of a right-wing church and simultaneously a pacifist and a young communist! I was a screwed up kid! I had a marvellous teacher, bless his dear heart, who used to stew about me. He took note of the essays I was writing, and he said, "My wife and I would like you to come over after school. We would like to talk to you." So I went, and he said to me, "How can you be this and this and this? These things are dead opposites."

As I read more I decided I had better find out where this whole religious thing was coming from. So I did a lot of reading along that line and thought, I can shed the religion. It was hard at first – I was maybe ten years old when I started being indoctrinated, and they did a pretty good job of it too. But I really started doubting the church, which was supposed to be a seat of righteousness. It wasn't. I found out that it wasn't safe to go out with the bishop's son because he could get drunk and wreck the car or whatever. The kid down the street, his father was a Mountie, used to tell us all his father's stories about the church hierarchy. I just got so I couldn't bear the sight of them. Another teacher who was very special to me tried to help me, explaining that the church could still be true even if some of its members weren't. So I hung in until I was about seventeen and I started questioning the doctrine, not just the people. I had had it.

Although Vivian's mother doesn't seem to have shared her daughter's political views and continued to be a member of the church Vivian had rejected, she did not stand in her daughter's way. Vivian was allowed to make her own decisions and shape her own life.

The next item Vivian showed us was a photo of her mother and her husband's mother together.

The reason that I picked that picture out was because I find myself at this stage of my life comparing their lives with mine. Those women had very hard lives, and both raised large families and did a pretty good job of it under the most difficult circumstances. I felt, when my children were young, that we were having a really rough time – and we were by almost anyone's standards. But not compared to these two women and what they had to endure. My mother-in-law and her husband came to Alberta from Illinois and homesteaded in the Palliser Triangle. There is a book over there about that area, called *Empires of Dust*, which is just about what it was. They were living in a place called Tide Lake, which is now non-existent. I guess the lake filled in with dust, if there ever was a lake. But I remember my mother-in-law telling stories about how she and her sister-in-law lived. They acted as each other's midwives at the birth of their children, this sort of thing. I remember my aunt telling about the birth of my husband's brothers. Remember those old trunks with the sort of rounded tops? Well, apparently she delivered the baby and wrapped him in something and put him on top of this trunk and then turned back to take care of the mother. When she turned around again, the baby was nowhere to be seen. He had rolled off and down behind the trunk. It is a wonder he survived.

So, now I can sit here on some days, not too many thank goodness, if no one phones or no one visits or I haven't got a place to go, or I am tied up with this stupid back or whatever, and feeling sorry for myself, and I can say, "Oh my God, you've got running water in your house, you can turn on the electric stove, you've got a TV and a VCR and a radio and every comfort. These people couldn't get out of their own back yards." My mother had things a little easier, living in a city, but not much.

The photo reminds Vivian of the time she spent with her mother-in-law and of the lessons she learned from her.

My mother-in-law was important to me. I lived with her for about a year and a half fairly early in my marriage. I can't imagine for the life of me how she put up with me. I was so young and stupid. I learned a lot from her. I never made much of a rural woman, I can tell you. I valiantly tried to adapt to that life, and I guess I succeeded up to a point. Then my mother-in-law's oldest son, Roy, went overseas for the Second World War and died of peritonitis after an appendectomy in England. He left behind a wife, Helen, and five little children. His twins were two, and his wife was pregnant as well. My mother-in-law had told Roy that she would look after Helen until he came back. Well, he wasn't coming back, so they moved out to the west coast to help her. We kept in touch, of course, and she came to visit us fairly regularly, but she died younger than she should have, at about sixty-five. My mother's mother lived to be a hundred years old, and her mother lived to a hundred and four. My own mother died at eighty-six. These photos of them are very important to me, you see. They remind me that I come from a long line of tough women, survivors, real survivors.

Other photos continued to accompany Vivian's recollections. She told us about how she had married at twenty and temporarily moved away from politics to be "sunk in darkest domesticity." As her nine children grew, she continued to work in leftist election campaigns for friends, but, she said, "by then I had about used up my capacity for righteous indignation. But just when I think, what is the use, then something so outrageous happens I get all fired up again."

The relative lack of contact with relatives that Vivian experienced in her childhood made her particularly focused on holding her own family together and on making sure that her children and grandchildren would know one another well. Because of the Depression, she left school in grade eleven, but her strong focus on education and achievement is realized in the lives of her children and grandchildren. The box of photos shows them at various ages. Of the nine children, five girls and four boys, all completed high school and took post-secondary professional training. Two are nurses, one a medical librarian, one a university professor, another a lawyer, one a physician, one a psy-chologist and two are paramedics with specialized training in emergency response computer systems.

I compare their lives with mine

Vivian raised them all in a two-bedroom house in intense poverty. When her husband became disabled and unable to support the family, Vivian completed high school through home study, rising out of her own depression to graduate shortly after her last child was born. She went on to university and became a schoolteacher and later a librarian. She now has twenty-two grandchildren and six great-grandchildren. One of her greatest pleasures in life is the large family gatherings, where it is not unusual for twenty-five or thirty children, grandchildren, and great-grandchildren to get together for dinner and celebration. Recently her children began a scholarship in Vivian's name to honour her lifelong commitment to education and social welfare. She remains closely involved with politics, primarily at the local level, most recently championing the cause of refugee physicians who are often not permitted to practice their profession in Canada even after passing the same examinations as Canadian doctors take. Her "family" is made up of her own children and their descendants plus her "adopted" children in Cuba, Central America, and the United States.

Many women besides these three have the qualities we think of as constituting character. Young and old, they spoke of making decisions, of feeling empowered to affect their lives, and of treasuring strong connections to the women in their lives. Robeka, showing us a picture of herself as a child, remarked that "it is not one of those posed pictures. I am after something. I am very determined. I keep this on my dresser and I look at it a lot. My childhood was very special. What I got from it was a constant struggle towards an ideal." She also keeps a statue of the Chinese goddess of truth and beauty, Sun Yin, given to her by a friend more than twenty years ago. The statue stands in her bedroom as a reminder of "a female icon or ideal. I think of my mother and grandmother always striving, and it all fits together."

Maria, speaking of her childhood in Mexico, told us of her mother, who was quite an entrepreneur.

> She used to sell gold, clothes, eggs. We never had much money, but we all went to private school. My mom used to say, when we were young, "Don't care for clothes, for houses." She wanted to give us an education. She never had that, she only went

to grade two. She was very smart though! She told us "Go to school and get an education. If you get married to a good man, you can walk beside him. Never in front, never behind. But if he is no good, you can leave him." I never understood what she meant then, but now I do!

Some women, when they had no such female model to fall back on, chose a female ancestor who seemed to them to have character and modeled themselves after her, filling in knowledge with invention where necessary. Paddy, for example, spoke of her great aunt Molly. She showed us both Molly's wedding blouse and a picture in which she wore it.

This is the great aunt who left me her diaries and who I am writing a play about. I feel such a sense of connection with her. She must have had a waist like this! When I was much younger I did actually wear this blouse. It was decided when she died that I should have this, because of her fondness for me, and vice versa. The greatest event in her life was her marriage. She kept a diary in 1914 when he went off to war, and she followed him. It's full of her adventures as a very, very young woman all by herself. He was the love of her life and they lived happily together until he died.

She lived until she was ninety-four, but he was her life and she made no bones about it. She was a kind of a character; eventually she moved to a nursing home and I used to smuggle in her bottle of brandy. She never wanted flowers or anything, but she wanted brandy. She also gave me a set of Dickens, which she treasured. I like to think that I inherited a bit of her flair. She was also an admitted liar, of course. She told the most outrageous stories, so you never knew what was true and what was a lie. She claimed that she was the first woman in Winnipeg to wear trousers. She would make statements like that and dare you to contradict her. So I like to think there is a little bit of me in Great Aunt Molly.

Gerry, too, spoke of a favourite aunt to whom she had been very close.

I stayed with her for two summers, once when I was twelve and again when I was fifteen. She was someone I really wanted to become. She was so loving and non-judgmental. As much as I loved my parents, there was a lot of fear of them. They were very strict, almost afraid of letting us try things on our own, go out into the world. But she brought out the best. She believed that I was the best girl that ever was. And so I wanted to be this girl. She was also a very brave woman. She had three boys and two of them had haemophilia. She lived on the edge of death all the time, just waiting for one small thing. She was very open to the world, even though it had hurt her. She showed me what is possible.

We found only one instance of a woman whose memorabilia told of a similar relationship with a male relative. Kate's grandmother and grandfather, her mother's parents, were central figures in her life. Her grandmother was an artist, and Kate has many beautiful examples of her clay work and quilts. Her grandmother's ability to blend the practical and the beautiful has been passed on to her granddaughter as a shared aesthetic sense and a profound appreciation of the beauty that can be found in small, everyday things. But it was Kate's relationship with her grandfather that most developed character in her.

> My grandpa worked so hard and was so generous and he helped my mom so much. The house where I live is because of Grandpa's generosity, and I will pass it along to my children. Grandpa wasn't subtle in the least. He was very open. This is the kind of life you should lead, the good life, this is the way to be a decent person. Study, choose your friends carefully. You are so important to us, treat yourself well and be responsible. Heavy on "be responsible!"

Unlike the female models we were told about so often, this grandfather was a strict disciplinarian. As Kate put it,

> I never thought to question him. I would have got a cane across my rear. He did have a tough side. My mother was a very quiet person. She doesn't communicate, doesn't talk much. And my father was

almost like a stranger in the house. But Grandma and Grandpa had this energy, this way of living that came right down to my sister and me. I spent every summer with them. Grandpa built a cabin the year I was born, thinking that he would need something for the grandchildren and so we had these beautiful summers, riding and swimming and stuff.

Among Kate's collection of memorabilia is a series of letters written by her grandfather when she was away at school. Like the mothers in our other stories, he was a great advocate for education for women, and insisted that Kate should do her best and use every opportunity to learn. We offer one letter, sent to Kate when she was fifteen, as an example of the communications that Kate regularly had from him.

This is a letter just for you. Your Grandma and I were very pleased to get the pictures of you and Jane, which your mother left with us when she was here. You are a very good-looking young lady, my dear, and we are very proud to have you as our grand daughter.

Now the real reason for this letter is that when I asked your Grandma how you made out on your last trip to Vancouver, she said that you had not said very much about your trip, and that she did not know whether you enjoyed it, and did not know just how you got along and what you did in Vancouver. She also said something which disturbed me very much, that your teacher in school reported that you did not take much part in discussion in your class at school.

Now, if true, that is a pity, because it is a very great accomplishment to be a good conversationalist. And no one becomes a good conversationalist without practice. By taking part in the discussions in class, you can do at least two things.

First, you can get to be good at asking sensible questions, and that will all at once call you to the attention of your teacher and she will soon take a special interest in you. And it will also enable you to get more information and develop your understanding and possibly solve some of your doubts or problems. In the second place, it will give you the confidence to express your opinions. Confidence is most important and can only be developed by practice. Of course, no one has much use for someone who is always talking and really saying nothing, because there is no sense or anything of interest in what that person says. To express good opinions also requires some practice. You really have to plan what you are going to say and how to say it. Here again, a person who expresses good and sensible opinions attracts attention and acquires influence over others and automatically becomes a person of some importance.

I for one was much interested in your trip to Vancouver and I wish you would write and tell me all about it. Please do that right away. To help you do this, I will try to help you as to what you should tell me. I would like to know:

Who organized your trip?

How you came to be one of those chosen to go?

How you were taken to Vancouver?

How did you like the scenery, and did anything of interest happen on the trip?

Who else went along with you?

When did you arrive, and where were you quartered when you got there?

What you did and saw in Vancouver. Did you see the ocean this time, and what you thought of Stanley Park, the buildings?

Who you met in Vancouver and how you got along shopping in the stores?

Describe your trip back, and were you very tired?

Did you have enough money to pay your way?

Now this is quite a list, but you will notice that I have started with questions as to how the trip was organized and followed on from there. You should have no trouble in planning your reply and in putting in some incidents of your own.

Your Grandma's arm was examined by her own doctor here, and he found only a fairly severe sprain or pulled ligament. The pain is pretty well gone, but there is some swelling and it hurts if she puts some extra strain on it. I'm wondering how you and Jane liked the new car your mother picked out? I hope you all like it. I will be much interested in your reply and will be awaiting it with some eagerness.

Incidentally, your reply should be something of an essay and it will be good practice for you.

With love,

Your Grandfather

The tone of Kate's grandfather's letters is more admonishing and authoritarian than inspirational, in comparison, for example, to Anne's mother's speeches and the conversations other women reported having with their female mentors. Still, it is also clearly very loving and supportive and, perhaps even more importantly, it speaks to the child Kate without condescension and with the expectation that she is a person worthy of his efforts to help her. These letters, in her grandfather's writing, can be read and reread as a chronicle of her own development and of the time and patience he was willing to expend to see her become the best she could be.

Taken together, the stories these objects tell are lessons to their owners about how to raise a child successfully and about how to be a person of character. Their depth of feeling, their expressiveness, and the model they provide for living a life of integrity are priceless to these women. They reveal a pattern of strong women living as equals and in intense connection to one another, engaged in meeting and mastering difficulties and using their lives to express their strong beliefs through action. Women who develop in this context have no doubt of their value. Because they were fully known and loved as developing individuals, trusted early with responsibilities, and empowered to make their own decisions where possible, they know they have important contributions to make to the lives of others. They are powerful people.

The lives these elderly women describe have been hard, inevitably perhaps, given the tumultuous times of their own childhoods, but hardship has been surmounted and no longer counts for much. Their sense of adventure and eagerness to engage fully with life has seen them through trouble and sorrow; they treasure their memories of both suffering and success. The objects they cherish and pass on to female relatives contain a rich individual and social history which our culture may not know, but which creates the narrative foundation for other generations of women.

Exile and Community: Preserving Connections

This chapter was written at the end of December, a time when many people express their desire to preserve connections with their traditions, their heritage, and their communities. Chanukah, Christmas, Ramadan: their celebrations are learned and require enactment by women. Because of our culture's emphasis, especially at this season, on the notion of a certain kind of normal family, we tend to overlook the many ways that women learn, and in turn express, their connections to traditions: not necessarily in order to serve the interests of husbands and children, but in their own behalf and in the interest of communities, varied and diverse. Different as they might be – in social class, ethnicity, status – we heard women expressing an urge to create communities of their own making into which they can fit. Elly was especially drawn to the topic and the stories in this chapter. Preparing to write the first draft, she recorded the thoughts below.

At this season, I feel particularly connected to my own tradition, to my Jewishness, through the lighting of Chanukah candles. I write now in my house on an island off the west coast. It is evening – very, very dark because there are no lights or other houses nearby, just the forest surrounding my house. Night comes early, and soundlessly, even the bird sounds muffled by the deep snow on the cedars and on red pyracantha berries outside the dining room window near the table where I write. Candles for me, Christmas lights for other people, reach out into the darkness to unite us with the night and with our ancestors, whether real or imagined. We have learned how to be communal people from them. Women preserve their ancestors' lives, and even create them in order to have a tradition. They guide us. They give us meaning. They give us our place, to fit into and to resist. They give us a place to begin and a new place to create.

I want to begin this chapter with the words of Jewish women. Rather than being drawn from individual interviews, these accounts have a different origin. Two years ago, I was invited to address a Jewish women's organization, Hadassah, at the beginning of their membership drive. Since we were then very much immersed in the work on this book, I asked the organizers to send out, with the invitation to the event, a request that the guests each bring a treasured possession that they felt expressed their Jewishness. That evening, I first spoke about the book we were writing and about the private and public meanings of possessions. The group of one hundred and twenty women then divided into tables of ten; the women removed the prized objects from their bags or cases or purses, and they began to speak to each other.

Each woman spoke in one way or another of her connections to her tradition, to her ancestors, to the historical past, and to her own present. For many of the women, that connection carried with it the great weight of history. One woman's prized possession showed this, though it was only three months old.

A mezuzah carries the weight of history…

I recently received a pair of handmade slippers from a ten-year-old girl from a school where I was invited to tell my story about the war. I talked to them how we were cold and hungry in the camp, and how we were not much older than them. That child sent me a pair of slippers with a note. "I hope that you will never be cold again." I keep it in my china cabinet with my good stuff and every Friday when I light the candle I kiss both of the slippers. It brings tears to my eyes. I feel that I am alive again. Red slippers, and she put on it a "P" made from beads, and wrote a note that she will always remember my story.

Another woman has been deprived of a family history because most of her family was killed in the Holocaust. She has created a history, fitting herself into the past she knows she must possess.

... and so do a mortar and pestle

I grew up not knowing old people and not having anything old around the house because there was nothing. There were no family pictures, no family dishes, or anything from my grandparents to my parents and then to me. But now life has been good. We have accumulated a lot of nice things, but nothing to remember or to continue the legacy.

Last year my father-in-law visited Israel and brought back from Israel a *kiddush* cup, a very gorgeous antique one. I thought, "I don't have anything old, but this is very special." I cherish it because somebody Jewish has used it for the most significant prayer that we have always said as a Jewish people. In a way I'm carrying somebody else's legacy. I cherish it for me because it's something old and I can pretend that it belongs to my family, and that I can somehow continue the legacy.

Jewish women might seem to maintain that legacy to perpetuate their families and their community; that, at least, is the stereotype of Jewish women. Like so many stereotypes, it is only partly true. In fact, many of them need to continue the knowledge of connection for their own sakes. Their bond with their religion belongs to themselves alone. Anna said, "My Star of David is something that I wear every day. It wasn't handed down to me. I bought it for myself to remind me of who I am and who I would like to be and that my faith is always with me."

A woman's connection to Judaism may not always be publicly proclaimed. The following story bespeaks an emphatic Jewish presence, and the speaker's prized possession, a tapestry, conveys her Jewish identity.

A friend gave it to me, a friend who is not Jewish, my best friend I grew up with in a very small town where I was practically the only Jewish girl. After I finished my Ph.D. she gave it to me, a tapestry of the Hebrew alphabet she made for me. What I like is that it shows how much my Jewish identity is shown to the world and how much it is a part of me, especially where I was labelled all the time as, "That's the Jewish girl," in my small town. So, it's part of my heritage and comes to me from somebody who recognizes that. It's in my living room so I see it all the time, and whenever I look at it I feel drawn to it. It is something I share, but it also is something that is private.

Her possession is first of all her own, reinforced by her best friend's acknowledgement of who she is.

Some women who told their stories that evening were choosing a tradition for themselves in an entirely self-conscious way. These were the women who had converted to Judaism, who were, as they put it, Jews by choice. Naomi's symbol of her choice was the lighting of candles:

> This is my candlestick. See, it says "Made in Israel" on it. I bought it myself. It sits there in my dining room, and catches the sun on it every morning. It identifies for me my choice to be Jewish. I keep this out to remind me that candle lighting is the light of the future for my boys. We don't have the Sabbath in our house every Friday. We haven't made that a commitment yet in our house, but sometimes it's been a few weeks and all of a sudden I see the sun streaming in and it catches on here. I think, "Maybe this Friday would be a nice Friday to have *Shabbat* in our home."

Another story of conversion also speaks loudly to a woman's choice for herself. Her precious object was a large framed embroidered copy of her marriage contract, called a *ketuba* in Hebrew; brightly coloured, it is powerful evidence of painstaking and loving care. She spoke first of her process of conversion. When her future husband asked her after they met whether she might be interested in converting, she wouldn't say yes or no. She had no Jewish friends, she said, though she had some knowledge of Judaism. She began taking lessons with the rabbi.

"As I took the class, still not knowing whether I wanted to become Jewish, I started stitching this. This is the very first stitch, right there." She pointed to the embroidery.

It was right around here, after taking classes for a year, that I decided I wanted to become Jewish. I can remember the different stages of the stitching and learning about what it meant to be Jewish, thinking also about how I wanted to start Jewish traditions. And when I did my conversion in 1990, everything had been completed except for this portion right here. I had saved that so I could stitch that as a Jew, and so I could put my Hebrew name at the bottom. I finished it the day after my conversion; this was my wedding gift to my husband.

But what we are talking about here is women for women. This was surely the most important piece of needlework I have ever done and that I ever will do. It is my first memory of being Jewish. People think I became Jewish because I married a Jew. But that's so untrue, because quite frankly nobody else is worth doing that for. I did it for me. And this piece too. Although I made it as a gift for him, it was something I did for myself. Had I not married him, I would still have become Jewish. It was a feeling of coming home. I knew I had arrived.

Many of the women know that, in an increasingly secular world, they are responsible for perpetuating their culture. A young mother told the group,

My mother and father are both gone now. It's up to me to start putting their things aside for my children so they will know that their Judaism is coming from my parents. But a lot of it is up to me now. Although my daughter is only four, I take her to Jewish school. We will do our best as Jewish parents." Not only as parents, but also as members of the clubs and institutions that perpetuate a Jewish identity, Jewish women desire to maintain a community. They are aware of it, in small cities perhaps even more than big ones, where Jewishness surrounds us.

In Toronto you can't get away from it. But here: I was dead tired but I came tonight because I want to know that I am an active participant. So I brought with me a little piece of Lucite, a key chain, which represents when I joined B'nai Brith Girls. These [key chains] were a fund raising project, and every time I look at it I think of how I was as a young woman joining that organization, first as a girl, then a young adult, then grown up. And when I moved here, joining Hadassah. It was just part of what I do. But when my daughter got married, she joined Hadassah on her own, and moved into a top executive position very quickly. Seeing what I did with my life, I'm very pleased that she did that. So this little key chain tells a very long story.

The Jewish women who met together that evening were very aware that they are Jewish not only for themselves, but also for the perpetuation of the culture. They are not hesitant in knowing their roles as mediators between past and present. Without their active participation in Jewish culture, they feel that Judaism in North America, conveyed as it is not so much by the rabbis as by families and institutions – what is known as "kitchen Judaism" – might be swallowed up by a secular society. These women are not shy about acknowledging their importance in the traditions. They know, too, the lengths to which they have to go for that tradition. Sophia told us that her son now lives in Israel, and what she brought was a letter he wrote her on Mother's Day forty-three years ago. "He is going to be nice, and be good, and he is going to love me. And every time when I go through my old stuff, I find this letter wrapped in nylons so it will stay, and I used to say 'I will read it to you on your wedding day,' and I did!"

Many of the other women, moved by the poignancy of her story, agreed that they had treasures from Mother's Day too, and talked about how when their children were little they didn't expect them to buy anything; their little cards were the true treasures. Theresa kept all her son's letters from the Yom Kippur War. "He was forty days in the war and I got forty letters. I kept every one. When he came home I didn't recognize him. He had a red beard from the sun in the Sinai. He didn't talk for forty-eight hours. He was twenty-one at the time. Twenty-one in Israel, already you're grown up."

The words of the women during this evening combined mothers and daughters, memories of the one leading to memories of the other, all the generations contributing to

Exile and community

each other's awareness of their place in a heritage. "I have here an antique frame from my daughter with my mother's picture in it, and I keep it next to my bed, so I start and end the day with thoughts of my mother and my daughter." Awareness is most often prompted by the ordinariness of the object, by its everyday use. It does not become prosaic because of that; rather, the everyday is elevated. "My mother passed on this rolling pin to me. Every time I roll out a dough for cookies or for an apple strudel, I can see my mother's hands on this rolling pin. I hope my daughter will one day like to use it too, even though she has one of those fancy rolling pins." Some objects connect the generations by way of the weekly rituals: "I think about my mother praying over the *Shabbat* candles every Friday night since I was a little girl. Now they're transferred to my home. I think of her as I stand and pray over them."

The traditions learned from mothers are powerful. They are often maintained even when their original meaning has been lost.

I have the end from an apple crate, from British Columbia apples. I grew up with that apple box under the kitchen sink with my mother salting the meat. It became a koshering board. She didn't know why she salted the meat, because we didn't even have a kosher house, but she still salted the meat because her mother salted the meat. And her mother didn't have a kosher home, but she salted the meat because *her* mother salted the meat. So I have my mother's koshering board, but it wasn't really a koshering board, but that wasn't important.

Yet another woman brings in her mother's pin from Youth Aliyah, in which she was active in her very small town. It speaks to her of her mother's "commitment to the community and to Zionism." More candlesticks, more Stars of David, more menorahs. All these ritualistic objects become personalized, imbued with the meanings that each woman finds there. Whether she is an observant Jew or not, each woman finds connections because her mother and grandmother filled the traditions with meanings as they might fill a ceremonial cup with wine.

And now this generation of women wants to pass those meanings, those objects, on to their own daughters. The daughters understand the need to connect. "My goal in life is to be sure my children know who they are and where they come from." One of Eva's daughters brought her candlesticks the first time she went to Israel, at seventeen. Her mother was profoundly touched: "She knew to bring me an item with ritualistic meaning." And another woman at Eva's table remarked, "That's right: we study our connections with other generations and then pass them on. My father used it thus, and I hope my children will use it thus."

The stories from that Hadassah evening made clear how objects connect generations of women through a shared heritage of traditions and religious observance. They confirm both a collective and an individual identity. After centuries of wandering and dispossession, these Jewish women are safe for the moment.

Some of the women we interviewed told stories full of present disruptions, forced emigrations and religious discrimination. Farah, a Baha'i, is an exile from Iran. She is about thirty years old, was married in this country, and has three small children very close together in age. Hers is a contemporary refugee story, one of the countless millions of such stories of hatred and banishment and the search for a country that will accept refugees. Her narrative began simply: "I escaped from Iran, so I don't have much."

She spoke quietly in an elegantly accented voice, her calm demeanour unexpected in light of the drama of her story. Her first treasure is a photo album, one of the few possessions she could take with her on her long trip out of Iran.

The pictures in there are my friends from high school in Teheran. This is my brother when he was eighteen. This is the night when I said good-bye to my parents; this is my dad; this is my mom; and this is my oldest brother and I love him very much. All of them are in Iran. I have my sister and this brother. We came out together. We left because there was no life for us. Our lives were in danger. We were expelled from schools and work. We had no chance to go to university. My sister had gone before the revolution. She wasn't able to finish her university because of the situation. My parents knew that we were leaving, but they didn't know when or how. We didn't tell them because we didn't want them to worry. They were living elsewhere. We went there for one night just to see them the last time. My dad knew. He held me tight.

Look. Here's a picture of my nephew. I used to take care of him when his parents worked. He thought I was his mom. He wouldn't go to anybody else but me until he was ten months old. I used to call him my boy, my son. They sent me his picture.

Another photograph reminds her of other losses. "That was my closest friend in high school. I've lost touch with her." These memories form the background for her migration. She depicted a large family, her relatives' lives entwined with each other's and with their friends. All of that changed suddenly with her emigration, which she undertook with four others. Each paid a man five thousand dollars in 1984 to take them to Pakistan, where they remained for eleven months until the Canadian government agreed to accept them. On their trip to Canada,

… we stayed one night in England. I hadn't seen my sister for over thirteen years, because she had fled there. She came to the airport and we went to the hotel and stayed up all night. It was so hard to let go the next day. It was harder for her because she was all alone again.

The Canadian government relocated Farah to a small prairie town after a gruelling trip from Toronto. Plans were changed; the immigration officials shuffled her about. Nonetheless, she had arrived somewhere that felt permanent. "I loved it. It was clean. People were friendly. I rooted there. I started my life there."

Farah's photographs serve to release her personal history. There are not many of them; nor does she need many. Each one is heavy with stories and memories. Her photographs do not merely provide pleasant moments. They become the way she makes sense of the drama of her early life in Iran and provide a means of preserving Farah's history for her children when they are older. "I want my kids to know. It's like a puzzle; you forget some of the stuff, but we help each other to remember and we talk about it around our kids so they'll know, because it's easy to forget." Hers is so typically the refugee story, with its need to reconstruct the drama of the past in the face of the seeming banality of the children's present, in order to know who they are and what their mother lost.

Farah's most precious possession, she said, is the doll she had as a child. Her mother brought it to her a year ago on a visit.

This was the first beautiful doll in those days. She's still beautiful. She has blond hair. They showed a Peyton Place soap opera in Iran before the revolution; there was a girl named Alison, so I named my doll Alison. My mom brought really, really nice stuff, but this doll was the most precious thing. She had six kids. She always knew what each one of us wanted.

Farah's thoughts turned again to the life she had left behind, prompted this time by her first driver's license.

"I was eighteen, wearing a headdress. You had to cover your hair. I heard horror stories. If they catch you with nail polish they would put your hands in a plastic bag full of cockroaches." At first she was uncertain why she kept it, and indeed why she presented it as one of her valuable possessions. "It's expired. Maybe I kept it hoping to get back." She thinks again. "I think maybe I kept it for my kids. This was my life."

Unlike most women who discussed objects related to cars, Farah's driver's license is not a symbol of her mobility or her independence. It is a reminder of who she once was. Her identity is further affirmed by the Baha'i identification card from her months in Pakistan and, finally, by her United Nations identity card. "I look like a jail bird. If we didn't have this, they could have taken us to prison." The fact of her having so many identity cards is the essence of the refugee story: she is nothing without those cards. They prove she is a person, not an impostor. But they are also reminders of her foreignness, wherever she finds herself. Perhaps as much as governments need her to be identified, she too needs reminding of who she is and of what she has survived. Certainly, her children need this evidence. She will pass on these pieces of paper, these identity cards, as artefacts and as stories to her children. "They must understand that life has many ups and downs, but you can get through and you will. You have to tolerate different things. I hope my kids will be strong." The talks will become lessons in acceptance and endurance.

Farah returned again to the refugee experience. She has another scrap from the emigration, a bus ticket from when she first applied to leave. She has a picture taken after a week of traveling from Iran to Pakistan. "You see that we are tired, very sad." Here is a book given her at the Canadian Embassy in Pakistan called *Living in Canada*. The immigration was made possible only by a long and complicated encounter with an official, aided by the desperation of her persistence.

And finally, another tangible reminder of who she once was and who she is today: the blanket her mother sent her in Pakistan.

That's my grandma's blanket. When we got to Pakistan we didn't have anything. In winter it gets a little chilly, so our parents sent us blankets. My mom kept it after my grandma died. I only let my mom use it when she comes here, no one else. These white hairs are my mother's hair. Some day my kids will say, "My mom used it." I feel a connection every time I touch this. I feel as though I'm sitting beside my grandma. After she died, I was the first person who dreamed about her, a spiritual thing. The only thing I miss about Iran is that I can't go to her grave and pray for her. I do pray for her here, but I miss going to her grave.

Farah's grandmother was a formidable figure. Her story helps Farah to recall the strength of the women she comes from, the standards of endurance they set for her. "She was a single woman but she took care of her own child. Now there are a lot of single mothers, but then she was a strong woman. My mom is a strong woman but not as strong as my grandma. It's hard to live up to her." Her grandmother died at the beginning of the revolution and Farah feels weakened by being so far from the tangible evidence of her life – her house, the graveyard where she is buried. Her mother's sensitivity in bringing her the blanket tells her, too, that she is understood.

Farah once had an identity bound up with the Baha'i community in Iran, which included the members of her large family. With only a few precious possessions brought from her other life, she is today a young woman with memories, making a very different life for herself and her sons, aided by the artefacts that keep them all connected. Central to that previous life was the grandmother-mother-daughter nexus. When her mother recently fell and broke many ribs, a daughter-in-law uncomplainingly looked after her. Farah admires a life aided by other women. She clearly mourns the loss of that other life, and yet hopes to recreate parts of it in North America. "I'm hoping that one day I'll have a granddaughter."

A story of exile is also a story about community – about its loss and its reconstruction in a strange land. The immigrants we spoke with were driven out – sometimes by poverty, sometimes by the prospect of a better life, sometimes by chance. Their former and their present lives are connected by their loss. Even when the departure is a choice freely made, the memories of home are often poignant – bittersweet at the least and painful at worst. The women we interviewed who had made abrupt or dramatic departures from their homes in other countries all felt some tugging at their hearts when telling us about possessions from their childhoods or youths.

Li, who left Singapore as a young woman to go to university and never returned, did not long for her native country. The opportunities she so badly desired, and which she created for herself in the new country, would not have been available for her in Singapore. She knows that if she had stayed her life would have been very different. "Probably get married, have children. I wouldn't have gone on with my studies. Hard to do that there." She is not filled with regret. And yet her first two precious possessions were photographs from her childhood. One is a photograph of her nanny, elegant and serious, whom she adored even more than her mother. The other is a picture of the seven children in her family, lined up by size from the smallest to the tallest, all wearing short white dresses or knickers, large white hair ribbons at the side in the style of children of the twenties, and knee socks. They stand in front of an expensive open touring car. The photograph presents a stunning contrast between the almost barren context of Li's apartment in which we spoke and the obvious luxury of her early life. Other mementos of that life are an antique teacup and a rice bowl with a spoon.

But she is not sentimental about her decision to leave. In fact, she said, "I feel that I'm pretty selfish to leave Hong Kong. Now that my mother died and my nanny died, I regret a little bit. I think I am too courageous." She meant, perhaps, that she is too individualistic to fit into the life that would have been demanded of her. She fled it. The symbol of her self-imposed exile is a leather pencil case. "I bought

She still has every stuffed animal her boyfriend gave her

this myself, when I come here to study." The red case is an apt symbol of her decisions about her own life. She decided to go to university, bought a pencil case, left the country – all from a decisive, "courageous" woman intent on making her life what she wanted it to be.

Li has also kept every stuffed animal that her boyfriend of ten years gave her. "I don't think he was a bad man, because he cared. We were just not compatible." Her closet overflows with the toys. "Probably I'm the type that can't let go," she said in one breath, and in the next, "I just don't take life seriously." Hers are the words of a conflicted life, vacillating between two worlds and two ways of being. Li may be in exile not only from her country but also from herself.

Teresita is from the Philippines; having left for more economic opportunities, she manifested a similar inner conflict between her own needs as an individual and her responsibility to her family's culture. She hasn't kept many things; "Maybe if I'm in my country, I could keep things, but I'm in a different country." She is on her own. One of her prized possessions is a valuable coin from her grandfather, which she said he kept especially for his children. Another is a small wooden sculpture of a carabao, the national animal of her country. "I like it because when my grandparents were farmers, these animals helped them plow." This and the coin are reminders of her grandfather and her country. And yet she has left, perhaps not entirely voluntarily, since her economic future looked bleak and her prospects better elsewhere, but she knows that she has gone, breaking down the strength of family ties. "I am the eldest in the family. In my country, anything that the family has, it's the eldest who takes it, more than the younger ones."

Cora and Felly are also Philippine immigrants, both working as nannies. They live together and share their space with other Philippine women, nannies too, creating a community of friends, fellow countrywomen, and exiles. "This house is theirs too." They arrived in 1985, horrified by what they saw of a cold prairie winter. "I asked my employers, 'How come all the trees are dead?' They said, 'No, Cora, it's just the winter time'." She thought she had come to a desert, spiritually as well as geographically. Nonetheless, she and Felly began to re-create a community, mostly of women who shared celebratory meals together, went to the Catholic church together, created joy, laughter, and friendship. Three photographs tell the story: each of the women has a picture of herself at work, dressed sombrely in slacks and very plain blouses, with the children she tends. The third photograph was taken at a party: here the women's hair is beautifully arranged and they are wearing gorgeous, extravagant satin dresses in brilliant colours and very high-heeled shoes. They both laughed. "Our employers never see us like this. But we Philippine women all are like Imelda Marcos! We love our shoes!" We were given a glimpse of a culture being remade by women, containing, of course, the pain of leaving behind families, even their own children, but also filled with the companionship of a new community of women who understand each other's past lives and present circumstances well.

Awareness of loss often permeates immigrant stories. Jindra came from Czechoslovakia at ten. Her story of migration is almost synonymous with leaving her beloved grandmother.

It was a great loss for me, and it certainly was a great loss for my grandmother. And now both of her children are here, my mom and my uncle. But she didn't want to stay here with us. At first she was all set to do that, and then she just couldn't. Her roots are there for her, the family grave.

We left in '68, illegally, so we couldn't take a lot of money. We couldn't really sell any of our possessions; everything stayed behind. My parents brought a little bit of gold, which they sold in Vienna. Soon we had to go on charity. Dad sold his wedding ring. When we came to Canada maybe a year later, my grandparents sent them new rings. Because we left with two suitcases, everything stayed behind. My grandparents sent a lot of things afterward, because we didn't bring anything out with us. Somehow they wanted us to feel like we have a home again. I have worn my mother's wedding ring for many years. It holds special meaning, the trip over here, the resettlement, a lot of losses, my grandparents and a lot of my friends.

Growing up in Canada, Jindra learned the language of her parents and grandparents, surprising her relatives when she went to visit them with her knowledge of Czech songs. "How can you possibly know that?" "I said, 'Grandma. She has been my link to my childhood; my ethnic identity and my childhood.'" Jindra expressed well the simultaneous sense of connection and separation of so many immigrants:

I realized, when I went back, that I am different from the average Czech person. But then here I feel different from the average Canadian so it's almost like I belong to a different cultural group. You take a little bit from both. I guess the Czech part of me is very important because it defines in part who I am and I don't want to lose that. The whole idea of continuity, or of some consistency in your life, an anchor. That is very important to me, but I don't think I could live there. And in terms of holidays, and rituals: that is a pleasant feeling for me, like when Mom makes a traditional Czech meal.

Learning Czech songs

She is sensitive to other's losses as well as her own, perhaps because she experienced profound loss early in her life and knows how small things can soften it. She left her favourite teddy bear with her mother when she left

home. "I lived at home until I was twenty-eight years old. When I moved out, this was very very hard on Mom and it was hard on me. So I left a lot of things behind that I guess defined me. I thought it left something of me that made it easier for Mom." The experience of exile can either destroy a person's compassion or intensify it. It can strengthen a sense of self or diminish it. New identities must be sought and reaffirmed. They don't come automatically.

Exile is a life changing, wrenching experience, an experience of tearing up roots. One can also be a sort of exile without leaving home. To some degree, probably, most women feel a certain distance from their culture since it devalues girls and women. Women frequently feel like outsiders, Emily, who appeared earlier in this book, being one example. She lives in the small mountain town in British Columbia where she grew up. She felt like an outsider as a child, excelling in all sports when girls were supposed to be docile and "feminine." Strikingly beautiful, she thought herself ugly. She thought her mother had no interest in her.

Miserable, Emily left the mountains for the prairies: she could not have traversed a more startling geographical distance if she had left the country. She did well, even selling some of her art as she had hoped. "Actually I had quite a few friends there, knew a lot of people, had a full time job." But she could not exile herself. "I missed the mountains, the trees, the rocks. I missed my house." Now returned, she feels no more warmly received, and yet she is where she has chosen to be. The artefact that represents her migration and something like a sense of home is a Japanese fan from her lover, Jean, with whom she has lived for six years. Her home life represents a refuge because her partner "knows about some of the stuff." Like it or not, like other migrants, Emily's present life must incorporate, no matter how uneasily, the discomfort of her past and the tenuous present she is trying to create. As a German immigrant said, "You create a life, a collage of the different families and nations, your parents, your grandparents, and you keep your old things."

Indeed, many women are self-consciously seeking to keep "old things," not just in honour of their personal histories but as the artefacts of their ethnic identities, their family traditions, and the cultures they have inherited. They want to place themselves in a communal past. Sometimes they seek their personal history, rooted in family lore or in ethnicity, as a personal way of joining into a collectivity larger than the self. Some of them do so in a private way; it is for themselves alone. Others want publicly to identify with their pasts. Sherry believes she has Native ancestry and treasures that insight. It came as rather a surprise to her. She was delighted to find out that Native women thought she might have Native ancestry, rather than merely a Scottish and English background. As she put it,

> It's highly likely that there is First Nations blood in our family. But of course the family is so uptight that they would never confess it. I had questioned them about it because I had developed a really strong affinity for Native ritual, and I thought it was trendy, what everybody in the world is doing. But three years ago I went to a workshop, when bell hooks was here, that two Metis women were leading. My last name was a French name so they assumed I was Metis and talked about the Kootenay area and said, "There's no doubt. You shouldn't even doubt it." So they embraced me and I was really blown away by the experience because it's one of those events that changes your identity in one five-minute session. All of a sudden your whole identity is in question.

I've gone through a questioning process about it and have done some writing about it, but I've never done anything about it in public, and came to the conclusion that I didn't really need to. It's just a part of me that feels right. I don't feel it's appropriate for white people to co-opt Native things usually. But when they present themselves to me, I'm included. It's like the medicine man including me in the ceremony without question. It happens.

All this was prompted by a feather that was given her seven years ago for her birthday. It wasn't from someone close to her, she hastened to say. But it prompted her to tell us about the discovery of her connection to First Nations people. It also evoked the medicine man story: when she was up North a medicine man was doing a cleansing ritual with a woman and asked Sherry to guide the eagle feather through the ceremony. She was deeply moved and amazed at the outpouring of emotion from the woman. Afterwards, she went outdoors, looked down, and found a raven feather at her feet. The feather she talked about "is the first one, a representation of that experience and of feeling really connected with birds." Sherry has created a past, in a sense, that has more meaning for the life she has chosen for herself than the stories she actually inherited: "My grandmother on my mother's side truly felt that if you weren't British then you were certainly inferior. I've had trouble connecting to that part of my history." Her feather represents another set of possibilities, a self-defined heritage.

In Sherry's case, there may indeed be good historical reason for her connection to First Nations people. As a western Canadian of Scottish and French ancestry whose relatives began arriving in the region a hundred years ago, a genetic link is probable. Kelly, by contrast, has attempted to find such a link, to create it, simply from a desire for it. The object she showed us was, not surprisingly, a small eagle feather, tied by a leather thong with other feathers. Sadly, we know too little about her to speculate on her alienation from her own heritage. It certainly holds less appeal for her than Native mythologies. Does the adoption of Native emblems present an easy route to insight and introspection? Her narrative about the eagle feather, the easy way she has taken up a culture not her own, or at least the parts of it that are easily acquired, seems perilously close to what people currently call "appropriation." Without the discipline, hard work, knowledge, and historical sensitivity that commitment to a heritage requires, the trappings of spirituality are worn lightly. They do not warm one for long and are easily transformed to superstition.

These are feathers, as you can tell. The pouches are things that I've made. There's a story behind this that I just love. I was in a workshop and the woman, who was into guided imagery, said to me, "As you're leaving this special place of yours, I want you to look down at the ground and there will be a gift for you." I looked down and saw an eagle feather. Two weeks later I was in this New Age book store and I told the woman in the store about this, that I was convinced that I will receive an eagle feather, and this young Native woman came up to me and said, "I will give you an eagle feather." I was absolutely blown away. I had never seen her before. She said, "I don't live here and I don't know when it will be, but you will receive your eagle feather." I was just walking on cloud nine. About a year and a half later I got a phone call, and this young woman said, "You probably don't remember me, but I met you in a book store and I have your eagle feather for you." When I arrived she had this for me. It's a small wing feather, and she put two owl feathers with it, and she's bound it with doeskin and green beads. Green is the colour of healing. So this is where it started. It has been in my car since that day. There have been four times that I could have been in a really serious accident. I just swear that this surrounds my car with protection. So I'm not taking a chance. It hangs on the steering column so it rests on my knee when I drive.

In the last seven or eight years I have realized that there are four kinds of bird that are really powerful in my life right now. The owl and the eagle are two of them. So this is really, really special. The hawk, the owl, the magpie, and the eagle are my totems, I guess you could say. I have a book on animal and bird totems. My art room is full of feathers. This is my connection with earth and nature.

Our discussion of Kelly's self-anointing into Native spirituality is not intended to slight her, but is rather a despairing comment on our own culture, which has convinced some women that one can take on a heritage easily, like a new coat, and shed it at will. Native emblems like feathers seem particularly to satisfy a longing for connections with a past, and yet these are slender symbols on which to hang one's identity, without the historical context to accompany them.

Some women do find themselves in their heritages. They discover facets of themselves or explanations for their characteristics from some knowledge, even if vague and general, of their ancestry and of the traditions that may have helped shape their early lives. Peg spoke fondly of a ring from her grandmother, to whom she was not close and whom, she acknowledged, she did not understand. However,

> she is an important piece in the puzzle that went to make me up. She used to call me her poukeen. She was Scottish, the Nova Scotia connection. Somehow it makes you understand a little better who you are if you know your ancestors were Scottish and if you've been to Scotland – that's why I have this good hardy peasant stock body. My ancestors were not greyhounds!

Similarly, Samantha reads Debrett's Peerage, the listings of British family lines. Descended from Scottish aristocracy, she writes frequently about her family history, albeit incensed by its male bias, as a way of understanding herself. And Gerry treasures a set of commemorative plates decorated with a picture of the Anglican church in her home in Annapolis Royal.

> My mother got them for me. That was the church that I was christened in and confirmed in and married in. See, we were brought up in history. I did everything in my younger life in that church. It hangs in my dining room and I see it all the time. I don't know, though, whether it's going to mean anything to my children. It means more to me than to anybody else, because it was part of my childhood.

Her childhood and her ancestry, both far from her geographically, come together for her, no matter where she finds herself, to provide a sense of place and of her connections to that place. Maria, who was married in Mexico to a Canadian, brought bride and groom dolls with her to Canada.

> I brought these because my family comes from the south. These are the typical outfits when you get married. When you get married in Mexico, you have a godmother for everything – for cake, for rings, for toasts – a tradition to help the couple. My godmother of souvenirs ordered them to give to the people at the wedding. It has been the tradition to help out the bride and groom.

Maria's knowledge of her community strengthens and supports her in her marriage and in a new country. No matter how difficult the transition, she has the dolls to remind her of familiar faces and places.

Buffy cherishes the holy bundles that have been in her family for generations, reminders of the prestige and honour her family commands. They are placed on an altar of sweet grass, sweet pine, cedar, and sage; she smudges the sweet grass daily and nightly. As a teacher she wants to bring her veneration of the ancestors into the classroom, "to restore what has been taken away from the people." She is well aware that her strong sense of self and heritage is not shared by many Blackfoot children. She believes that just as she derives her persistence from the influence of her parents and grandparents, so can she bring those qualities to young people by reminding them of their lineage.

Rochelle, a Cree woman, also looks to the emblems of her First Nations origins to sustain her. At the time of our interview, she could not have her eagle feather and her shell with her, because she was living in a transition house where "there are too many energies, and you can't trust everybody." Nonetheless, "there are a lot of Natives in the house, a Mohawk from Ontario, a Yukon lady, an Okanagan, a Shuswap, and there's a Cree. The energy is kind of nifty." She had her sweet grass instead.

That's what the Cree people use in Saskatchewan. I'm trying to connect with Mother Earth and still trying to walk a straight line with people. The Mother Earth part is easy; it's the people part that's not so easy. My eagle feather is in storage at a friend's place. When I sobered up the last time, this guy that had stayed sober for about eight years gave it to me. You can't have your eagle feather around any sort of drugs, so I want to be sure about myself. He was maybe trying to help me with my healing. To get over all my anger and rage.

Like other women, Rochelle may be creating a tradition, or she may be trying to restore and find her place in a tradition that was shattered and severed.

Carole does not fit into millennia-old traditions. Instead, she knows that she and her family need to create new rituals and observances. A Canadian of European heritage, she is married to a Canadian of Chinese ancestry. "My mother said that my children will pay a price for our marriage in racism and prejudice. She was right, of course, and we have to counteract that by honouring both their cultures." Her precious object is a minute bracelet from her son's Chinese grandfather. She loves the smallness of it but it is, she acknowledged, his treasure. However, for her it provides a reminder of her commitment to respecting her son's heritage.

The bracelet is not to be worn, it's to be kept and passed down. Part of the choice I made in marrying interracially is that I know it's a constant struggle to honour both cultures, not to dishonour or minimize or kind of over-exploit one particular culture, so that one culture doesn't dominate in the child's life. This has been very much a part of our parenting work, what we talk about. How do we strengthen these children through diversity?

New traditions are in the making in this household, as they are in the life of thirty-year-old Aimee, who

An Irish ring from her Irish mother

has an Irish mother and African father. They separated when she was a baby, and Aimee was raised by her mother. Nonetheless, despite his departure, one of her treasures is a picture of her father. She went to see him in his country and met his family when she was twenty. "I hadn't been raised in the African customs, but I learned a lot about the traditions. I learned more about who I was. I liked to fantasize that some of them came to this country as slaves, and that upon going back I would complete the cycle." Clearly, she gains a strong sense of self by identifying with her African father and his family, and she feels entitled to know her paternal family as well as her maternal one. In fact, another of her prized possessions is an Irish ring with a heart on it, symbolizing love and friendship. Her mother got it for her on her first trip back to Ireland. Aimee told us that legend has it that an Irish prisoner who knew he would be executed made one of these rings for his family before he died, to keep Ireland's spirit alive. "So my mother, because it is very apparent that I'm of African descent but not very apparent that I'm of Irish descent, wanted me to have this ring."

Aimee's third cherished object is a carving of St. Martin, the patron saint of the poor and of interracial relationships. Aimee's partner, who is white, got it in Peru. Aimee's traditions came together when she told her mother about the gift. St. Martin, her mother said, is also the patron saint of healing. When Aimee's mother was a child, she broke her leg, and her mother, Aimee's grandmother, slipped a small statue of the saint into her cast so she would not walk with a limp, despite dire predictions. In fact, she healed well, and her family made her walk around as a miracle of St. Martin and collect money for him. With this story, Aimee made it clear that she can embrace every part of her heritage with great pleasure and a sense of wholeness, the richer because of its complexity.

Susan's heritage emerged when she showed us a white enamel saucer with a blue rim that she keeps on her dresser. It evokes a past of her own mingled with her mother's and her grandmother's, and it returns her to a moment in a childhood filled with lakes and picnics and summer afternoons.

This came from my mother's picnic set when she was a child. My mother grew up in Armstrong. We would go out and see her mother, whom I adored. She died when I was sixteen, very very sad for me. She was ninety-six when she died. When my grandfather died, she sold her farm and had a lovely little house built for herself in Armstrong, and lived there for another seventeen years by herself. I loved it. She had two pianos and an organ. She was totally deaf, but she could play the piano and sing in this horrible scratchy voice. All the neighbours could hear her.

Mom and Dad and I, when my son was new born, took a road trip because my cousin was getting married. We stopped at the old family farmhouse on the way. It had been turned into a granary. We went inside; there was grain all over. There was a cupboard full of old newspapers, from the turn of the century. There were pen pal letters to my grandfather. I don't know where those letters went. She found a mixing spoon, which I have; a green bowl, which Mom has; and this little plate. Only one of them.

Obviously, she was so thrilled when she found it, and she told me this story. For my Mom to pause and tell a story is very unusual. She was always very wired and busy. She actually sat down on the step and flew back in time. She had this memory of the picnic basket that used to contain the plate, with a set of eight plates and side plates and bowls and glasses with lids that screwed on. It was a wicker basket. She would go for picnics to Otter Lake or Mabel Lake with her mom and dad and siblings. She and her dad were very close. I have a photograph of my mom, about twelve, and my grandfather, swimming

in Mabel Lake. When I see that photograph, I think
of the story she told me about the picnics, and how
she was able to stop and pause and have a memory.
Her usual ways just fell away. She gave me this plate
later and I love it.

The saucer marks an unusual moment of closeness with
Susan's mother, a reminiscence of her grandmother as an
unusual woman, a moment of contemplation, and the
flood of memory. Three generations of women create a
community.

Roberta, a western First Nations woman, also creates
a line of women that gives richness to her life. She has
turned her narrative into a story of strength, and it pleases
her to tell the story and to fit herself and her sisters into
it. Her grandmother's wedding ring is her prized possession. Roberta wears it every day, and considers it "probably
the most important thing that I have." Her grandmother
married in 1905, and the ring was passed on to Susan's
mother.

I badgered her until I got it. When somebody asks
me why I wanted it so much, I just see pictures,
not words. I was in a group once where we did
visualizations for directions and one of the directions
was the direction of the elders. I saw this ring coming
through the years toward me. It brought with it – I
want to use the word experiences. I've always had a
hankering for it, ever since I was a kid. I don't have
a logical explanation for it. I have plans that my

daughter will get this ring, when she's of the age that she deserves it. She's only ten now, so I'll have to see. Thirty, that's when I got this ring.

I only met my grandmother once, when I was sixteen. I know more about her now than I did before. My mom is almost eighty and has been telling me stories I never heard before. She lived on a farm, was an orphan. Her mother died really young and her father took off. She had a difficult childhood. Ended up marrying a man somewhat older than her and having a ton of kids. What my mother is now remembering is why my grandmother was the way she was, which makes sense as to why my mother is the way she is, and why she did what she did in her life. Which comes down to how she raised me. I'm forty-six now, raising a daughter. My daughter hears all these stories too. And God knows where this ring will be in a hundred years.

The ring marks me as one of the line of females in this family. I'm kind of making this piece-together-picture in my head. I'd say I know about the indomitable will. My grandmother was handed over to be a domestic at a stranger's house at a very young age. My mother, she didn't have an easy life, was shot in the shoulder when she was eighteen and just about died. She ran away with a man who was married to the west, my dad. Lived in a little cabin, raising some children, not married for a long time. My dad's an alcoholic, which got worse over the years. She worked like a Trojan. But who said life was easy anyway. This ring is about carrying life on the best way you can. It takes a lot of strength. My mother would never give up. And now in her eighties she's getting more definite about saying to the family that we need to get along together.

My sisters and I will become the matriarchs of the family. We see ourselves as pretty strong women.

Roberta's ancestry has become as tangible as her grand-mother's heavy gold ring, a line of women tied together by the stories her mother tells, trying to be understood by her children. Disillusion is not absent from the sto-ries: "who said life was easy anyway?" But Roberta and her sister see the power their aboriginal ancestors bring them.

Maria, a social worker in a small western community, also looks back to a heritage of strength. She decided on her profession when she was a child in Mexico.

When I was six years old, I was very ill. I had sei-zures. My mother told one of the saints that if I survived, I would do my first communion in that church. So a week before the first communion we had to celebrate another child's first communion, and to bring a little present for those kids. They took us to where the people live in garbage dumps and we did a celebration with those kids. I'm thirty-nine now, and I still remember how much impact that had on me. I understand that I was poor, but there were others poorer than me. I wanted to do something to help people; what, I didn't know.

When I finished high school, my mom asked me what I wanted to do. My sister was going to become a doctor, so we couldn't afford another major profession again. So I started looking for different careers and I met a friend of ours who was going for social work. I decided that's what I wanted to be. We found a school which the labour union funded. That first year was hell for my mother. I was quite independent, and when I got to school, they told me, "This is your right; this is who you want to be," and so on. My mom wanted to take me out. She figured they were teaching me wrong things. In my mother's hometown, women are very strong.

Maria identifies herself as part of their tradition of strength. The thought of those women allowed her to continue to study, and later even to leave the country.

Women keep objects to remind them of the turning points and important moments in their lives, and of the people with whom they shared them. Laurie, an Anglo-Canadian, has carefully kept cards in their original envelopes – wedding cards, baby cards. "It really struck me that so many of the women writing me had commented in their cards on their first child, their first birth, its date, the baby's weight, everything. The day I got my daughter home from the hospital that was really special to me." Lorraine keeps a little music box, which has been on her children's birthday cakes every year for twenty-eight years.

She is making a tradition that moves beyond being English, toward being a woman among women.

Marta is active in the women's movement, aware of its foremothers and well versed in its history. In her everyday life she feels part of women's history, as well as of her family tradition. She brought out, as her first object to discuss, her mother's silver. A Danish immigrant to rural Alberta, her mother died when Marta was in her twenties. Both Marta and her sister keep her memory very much alive, not only by using her silver, with her initials boldly evident, but even by using it just as she did.

> My sister serves tea on Sunday nights. We were there recently for my mother's Sunday night dinner, which my sister does, and I asked my nephew's fiancée if I could have coffee. "No," she said, "your sister wants you only to have tea because that's what your mother had." So that's what we had. It had a real impact on her. The dinner was always Danish open sandwiches and fruit and tea.
>
> The silver was a wedding present before my parents came to Canada. I love using the silver because I always feel that my mother is there. She always used it as a way of talking about her family, since she and my dad were the only ones that came here. We grew up without extended family. But we got stories of them; when we used the silver there were careful preparations and we would lay out the silver ever so carefully. Like our friend Merry, who uses the china that belonged to her grandmother's

sister and who feels that her ancestors are right there working with her when she uses it. This magical realism stuff. I always feel that my mother is there.

When my dad remarried I wrote him a letter and wished him well and said that I thought in case he died before his wife he should make a will and designate the silver to us because it had meaning. That didn't happen; the marriage didn't last and his wife left. When he died, because the silver was important to all of us, we put everything on the table and we took turns selecting pieces. It was the thing that had some history and that my mother loved.

For so many women these tangible reminders are the most powerful ways of being with their mothers or grandmothers, seeing those hands use the object, wear away at it. They work with them in their imaginations. They revisit their childhoods, imaginations prompted by the objects they hold in their hands. Paddy, a playwright who lives on the west coast, has her grandmother's mother-of-pearl jewellery case.

It was the thought of its being so used that I liked so much. I could see her putting her thumb across that monogram that is now almost worn away. It's a symbol; my grandmother was a teacher in the days when it was almost a self-taught profession. She went to normal school and was not highly educated, but she valued education greatly. And also the case might have something to do with the stock, Scottish stock, the pride in the family, and the pride in each other. And enduring was a great virtue, more than charity or any other great virtue you could name. Endurance and hard work were great virtues. I like to show it to people and share it with them. I like people to look at it. It's not just for me to look at.

She is proud of her Scottish grandmother and wants people to know she is connected to her, almost literally, as she runs her own thumb across the monogram.

These objects can be hard to relinquish, even when it seems that the time has come to do so. Marta has the silver spoon and fork, with Hans Christian Anderson characters on the handles, that were her utensils as a baby.

I had no idea how much they meant to me until a few years ago. I thought to myself that now, surely, obviously, I am not going to have children. I should pass them on. I should give them to my nieces or my nephew. It was when my oldest niece had her first child, and I thought that this is the time that you starting handing things on to the next generation. So I got them out to do that; and I just couldn't do it, so I thought, well, one day I trust I will be able to do it.

Marta may fear, as other women have told us they do, that the children to whom she gives these precious items, laden with memory, may treasure the objects but not share the intensity of emotion she invests in them. Frieda recognizes something of the same fear when she contrasts the care she lavished on the few toys she had as a child in post-war Germany to "letting them fly around and get lost." Her tiny glass tea set is an example: "I took it out once in a while and played with it, and then put it back in its little box." In time, all these women will pass their possessions on to somebody they perceive will care for them, who will at least understand the love they lavished on them. For the time being, women mark family and community traditions in the hope those connections will continue.

There are other ways of creating community. Volunteer labour is a way of belonging to a group that is chosen self-consciously, a political group or a feminist setting or a labour union. These are affiliations of choice through which women attempt to connect with a heritage, not on the basis of family ties or ethnicity, but on the basis of shared values. Vivian was led into leftist politics out of abhorrence of the entrenched right wing. She keeps a photograph of the leader she hoped to depose, "just to remind me." She envisioned and worked for a more embracing society, and she identifies herself with a community of committed socialists. Similarly, Betty, who worked for the major employer in her town, a steel company, was active in the union.

I've been battling sexism for years. The computer is making work for people, but it's also taking a lot away. We had a discussion the other day about women losing their jobs. I remember one of the girls that worked in the plants with the men being cornered in an area of the work place, and these guys were threatening her because she was taking a man's job. But she was a single parent, and she said, "You work for your children and your wife. You're the head of your household. I am the head of my household." And they don't get it.

She too is making traditions, as is Joyce, who is justifiably proud of her work for Girl Guides and other groups. She showed us a twenty-five-year anniversary pin awarded by her community center.

This is probably one of the things I am most proud of in personal accomplishment. We were in this district at the very beginning. We were the pioneers. We could see this district opening up and there were no Guides or Scouts here. You do these things with others; and we started the community center and the United Church Women, and I was very active in the schools too. I wear this pin like jewellery. This certainly shaped my personal history, my community service through all the years, my involvement with my children. That was what I did best, I guess.

I recall as a child sometimes wishing that my parents would be involved; and I think that is one reason why I was. I remember one night in particular at my junior high school that Mother was there, and

I was just so proud. I'm sure that directed me to more involvement.

And indeed, Joyce has created a tradition: all five of her children are actively working for social and economic change through organizations like battered women's shelters, hospital systems, outdoor programs for children, and the schools. They are inheriting traditions.

At the time of our first interview, Julia blended traditional Protestantism with evangelical fundamentalism, questioning both and yet certain that the religious community is the one where she finds her place. In fact, religion prompted her commitment to a community that embraces everybody's children. Nearly fifty years old, a university teacher who is loved by her students because of her obvious interest in each of them, she knows all their names, their dreams. She has high expectations of them; she keeps jellybeans in her office for them. A mother, a wife, an activist in every setting, Julia sees her life as a quest. The search combines religious observance and what she would call spirituality – perhaps a sense of the divine – with an appreciation of everyday pleasures. Her quest is to fit into the religious traditions even while questioning them publicly enough that they may change. It is not easy, after all, to combine feminism with evangelical Protestantism, or now with Catholicism, to which Julia recently converted. Her infectious, joyful inquiry and her generosity may help make it happen.

Julia brought her objects to Elly's university office, which became the setting for the kind of conversation one usually has in living rooms and kitchens. Julia brings informality to all her encounters. She went to university in her late thirties, and loved it so much that she went on for a master's degree in communications studies. Her first object, then, begins at that point in her life: a tiny, light grey suede pouch on a thin suede strap, beaded with a cross in four colours and closed with a small crystal clasp. Occasionally she wears it around her neck.

My friend Mary made this for me. We met when we were students together, and disagreed on every point in every discussion we ever had. She is a former Catholic; I'm evangelical. She's into New Age. So this little bag is a blend of her and me. She gave it to me at a time in my life that was not particularly nice. My daughter had just disappeared and things were not happy in our home at all. The bag gave me a place, like a medicine bag, for me to try to restore some wholeness to my self, to my memories, to my family. Mary had no idea, no idea. The bag became like a story in which the Good Shepherd tells a woman to put things in a bag to remind her of her life and her journey. And these things become the jewels in her crown when she reaches the top of the mountain. Mary gave it to me for my birthday the year I graduated from university. It became my attempt to make something positive out of the rough times.

I put things into it. Sometimes they're there for a long time, and I wouldn't take them out, sort of like a touchstone, symbolic of things. The first thing I put in it was a tooth from one of my kids, from my daughter actually, with a little note to the tooth fairy saying, "Please can I have a raise?" It reminded me of a moment when there was such a thing as

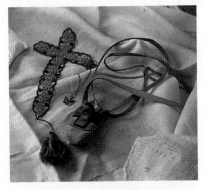

Heritage: A suede pouch, a beaded book-mark

innocence. There wasn't when I put it in there. I didn't even know if she was alive. Her little baby handwriting in there and her little baby tooth. You have to restore hope.

Now this little shell is from the beach in Hawaii where my husband and I went on our twenty-fifth anniversary. His mother bought us the tickets because we couldn't have afforded it otherwise. It is a symbol of our marriage, getting tossed on the waves, the way these shells do. And this little gold feather is just a cheap thing, but symbolic of an eagle feather my brother gave me when I graduated. He got it from women in the Blood tribe after he spent a semester down there teaching them. It symbolized their shared educational involvement, and his little note said that he was giving the symbol of shared education to me. That whole last year I wore this

Her grandfather heated water in a brass shell during World War I

pouch a lot, the year my daughter was gone. It had only the tooth in it.

She turned then to her other possessions. The one she discussed next was an old brass shell from World War I that her grandfather welded together and used to heat water throughout the war. It was in her grandparents' hall as far back as she can remember, and it is now in her own entrance hall. Her grandparents lived far away,

but were near in spirit. It's a link to a generation of young people I didn't know when they were young. My grandmother died in the late eighties. She thought that my daughter was me when my daughter was little. "My little fairy," that's what she used to call me. Here's another thing from her, a package of postcards sent her by her first fiancé from Belgium and France during World War I. I sometimes bring them in to show my students.

Then she presented her next items, her Bibles. The first one was given her at her confirmation, at thirteen. A note on the inside cover says, "Presented to our dear granddaughter." "It's the very first Bible I ever had. And look, it contains a Valentine from some kids I taught in Sunday school. Little notes about passages to read. A letter from my mother. A bill. Sermon notes. A postcard. I wear out Bibles!" The second Bible is older, given to its original owner in 1924. Faye became a friend of Julia's in her seventies, when Julia was twenty-three and her children were small.

She was my spiritual mother. Here's a birthday card from her. "To our adopted daughter." She loved my kids, spoiled them. She looked after the babies in the nursery at Sunday school. When she died her niece sent me her Bible. She had received it from her church when she left for Rochester, Minnesota to study nursing. Faye is one of the women my thesis was dedicated to.

And this little gold butterfly on a chain is really important to me. It was given to me by my best friend in the entire universe. We met when she was probably one of the most broken human beings I have ever met. In the first five years I knew her, she tried to kill herself at least three times. And we struggled along together. There were times when I was sick and she would come over, look after me, cook meals, look after my kids. She was a very dear friend through all her brokenheartedness.

The last time she tried to kill herself I was really ill. I had had a breast biopsy and was really bruised, had an infection, had to take drugs, the drugs made

A symbol of hope and friendship that survived many struggles

me dizzy and sick. I was just flat out. She phoned me; I said, "I don't want to talk to you, you bastard." I had kept telling her that God wasn't going to let her get off that easy. And I told her not to bother the minister unless she meant business.

She phoned him. And she is now the counselor at a church, a wonderful hospice.

So this is a symbol of hope and of friendship through horrendous struggles. At times we said, "Are we going to continue to be friends? Because this is too painful." And growing together. Times when we looked at each other and said, "I know you more intimately than I know another human being on this earth." What does that mean? Redefining intimacy. It was unusual for both of us because I moved a lot when I was a kid and she came from a really dysfunctional background. So she is one of the other women my thesis is dedicated to. Faye, my grandmothers, my mother, and Gail.

Julia preserves rituals even as she makes new ones. Catholicism's old traditions are new for her. Like the many other women in this chapter who move beyond the self to make common cause, she has become both heir to ritual and creator of new connections.

*A*utonomy may not be available to every woman, but those who are finding it are in the process of redefining women. While not seeking to separate from other people, they are writing their own stories, hearing their own voices, and expressing their own desires. They have been able to benefit from the new awareness first raised in the 1960s that suggested that women did not have to be defined by men or by "experts" or by myths — they could care for others, but they might also care for themselves. Women first began to give voice to their thoughts, feelings, and experiences in conversation with each other. Through these exchanges and from new feminist writing, they learned that issues of power, relationships of dominance and obedience, and the need for silence and secrets were not "natural" to women and men but were devised by cultures. Women began to think of themselves as agents of their own lives.

A recurring theme of this book, central to the lives of most women, is their commitment to relationships with other people. Most books about women, whether scholarly or popular, have highlighted the theme of women's connections. We also see, though, that women are creating other ways of being in the world. Our culture thinks about women principally as the caretakers of other people. This ideological construction of nurturance and unselfishness, of "the way women are," has prevailed in greater or lesser degree since the Industrial Revolution, when it became necessary for middle class women to wear on their persons and display in their homes the fruits of men's labour. In the presumably democratic societies of North America, women would display, both by the way they consumed and the way they took their places in society, the successes of their fathers and husbands so that men could comfortably differentiate themselves from each other without betraying their democratic commitment. Women were to do the emotional homework in families, leaving men at liberty to seize the main chance in the economy.

During the 1960s, despite the changes in North American economies and in household economies, the ideology that placed women in the private sphere and men in the public realm prevailed. That ideology, pertinent to women of all backgrounds, continued to define women as more emotional than men, more capable of nurturing, more desirous of relationships. Women who "had to work" were anomalous. However, women's roles, particularly their participation in the paid work force, were beginning to change during that decade, so that the difficulty of maintaining connections in families, with friends, and in voluntary organizations was intensified by what came to be known as the "double day." Women continued to need – and to be needed – to sustain men and families emotionally, even while ever larger numbers of them were out of the house in the paid labour force.

By the 1980s and 1990s, a large body of feminist scholarly literature lent support and credence to the belief that relationships were central to the lives of women. The economy's need for women's paid labour required them to be out of their houses for long hours on end, but women were still responsible for keeping family members connected. The scholarly literature provides validation for the culture's need for women to do the work of the emotions, but women also did that work because women, and their children, needed it.

We ourselves have been strongly influenced by that body of literature. Both of us came to understand women's lives as focused more around creating and sustaining connections than around individuation and separation. However, as we interviewed women for this book we began to understand these relationships as playing a role in women's growth toward autonomy, their search for wholeness and uniqueness within themselves. We will not suggest that they have succumbed, because of their paid work force involvement, to the myths of competition and individual success, although some of them have. Striving only for material success does not describe the lives of many women. Rather, we have found that women crave a space for themselves – a space that they can call their own. The work of relationship and connection and the work of individuation and separation proceed together. Relationships are not sacrificed to autonomy but become the means through which self-understanding and wholeness are achieved.

This chapter, then, acknowledges the individuation dimension of "women's work" and supports their needs for privacy and solitude. Yes, women seek connections, but they also seek a sense of their own wholeness as individuals. We hope that they will feel freer to acknowledge those needs, if only to themselves, and perhaps to make more room in their lives for themselves alone. Young women are still taught that such desires are selfish: we think not. Older women, sometimes reluctantly but more often joyfully, admit that this mythology has less and less meaning as they increasingly claim their lives as their own. Yes, their lives are laden with emotional commitments, but women are also increasingly acting on their own desires for themselves. They have always learned to live out their own needs, certainly, but there is a change. Women are allowing themselves to be the actors and directors of their own lives, refusing the definition of self as simply the sum total of a woman's relationships and substituting for it an understanding of the development, partially through relationships, of a strong and independent self.

None of this is to say that women are abnegating relationship: from our evidence, not in the least. However, they are making decisions and taking actions – sometimes publicly but more often privately, silently, and knowingly – that are allowing them to know themselves. They are refusing to be constructed by the expectations and ideologies of the culture or of their families. Women are actively shaping their lives.

Many women continue to define their own joy as connected to that of others. Joyce has spent her whole life

taking care of parents, children, and the community. "I can
say proudly that the central theme in my life is my family,
my parents, and so on. See, these are baby books and the
wedding book and the cookbooks. That is how I think
about my life. This is the continuum." She spoke happily of
being enmeshed in these connections. Lorraine, too, finds
great meaning in having been a single mother struggling
to maintain herself and her children. Her daughters are
now in their twenties, and they obviously understand and
appreciate her efforts on their behalf.

> On a Mother's Day just recently, my daughter was
> home this one time and I was on night shift. They
> both woke me up at two o'clock and told me to go
> have a bath. They had made me a bath filled with
> lilacs in vases everywhere, and candles. And they
> gave me a lilac tree for Mother's Day. The Mother's
> Days until then had been days when they were still
> kids, and this time it was them working together; an
> incredibly treasured memory. The smell of the lilacs.
> It was beautiful.

Another prized possession, a small square red rock, also
speaks of her intense devotion to her daughters but adds
what she learned about herself through caring for them.

> One Christmas in the last five or six years we
> were talking about how they hated stews and any-
> thing that was of Crock-Pot consistency. I worked
> twelve-hour shifts and would use the Crock-Pot a

lot. Shortly after that conversation, I was out walking and saw this rock. It reminded me of a piece of stew meat. The rock reminds me of the conversation we had about stew and the Crock-Pot. And another Mother's Day I came home from a night shift and on the coffee table, which they had put right in front of the door – they had to rearrange everything – was their picture, right there, and a card and three little roses. I opened up the door and bingo! There it was.

The authenticity of her devotion is clear, but so is the role that these strong connections played in learning who she was and accepting her independent choices.

None of the three of us do things because we have to. We do them because we want to do them. When you come off a night shift you're tired. Boy, I open the door and I can still visualize the warmth and the feel of walking in and saying that the most important thing is, yeah, I am a mom. My children are my treasures. And this book: Tracy gave me that as a little kid. The mother bunny and her two little babies. "This is us, Mom, this is Dawn and me and you. This is our family. This is us."

Similar dedication may exact a high price when it emerges only from a sense of duty. Jindra told us about her grandmother's life as she showed us the picture of her that she treasures. When her grandmother came from

Czechoslovakia for a visit, they connected because the old pictures allowed them to explore the important subjects of their lives. Jindra regrets that her grandmother did not have a happy marriage, "but she stayed because she thought she didn't have any other choice. She also talked a lot about her parents and their struggles." Fortunately, Jindra recognizes that "through understanding or treasuring the things that are passed on to us, we understand ourselves as well." She preserves her grandmother's artefacts and her stories; her grandmother is assured that the young woman loves her and that the duty she exercised all her life has its reward. And Jindra recognizes that she herself has other choices.

Peg's mother-in-law conveyed her commitment to her family by keeping a diary about her son's life that gives Peg certain insights into her husband. She, in turn, gets some sense "of what that family was about. The family and his life come forward to connect with your family. It's all specifically about this person that you love, and understanding his early life helps you to have more of a connection with him."

Marg has lived a life intimately connected with others: with her family, certainly, but with her community as well, both as a public health nurse and through her volunteer work as an artist. None of her connections have precluded defining her own needs. Marg lives on a west coast island with her husband; they raise sheep for wool and sell produce from their organic garden. She paints in watercolours and has a studio that is open to the public on weekends. Visitors are warmly greeted by Marg and Tony and often get a tour of their beautiful old farm with its apple, plum, and walnut trees; its donkey, flower gardens, sheep, and chickens. Their log house, now with a brown-red metal roof, is one of the oldest in this section of the island, beautifully and comfortably renovated inside with a modern kitchen and a glassed-in fireplace that heats the house. They moved here fourteen years ago, leaving a thriving business in a big city to work this farm and become part of a vibrant community. Marg's connections to other people seem to come naturally to her; relationships are an important component of what she needs.

We spoke at her dining room table, in a small dark room looking out at trees and shrubbery, and below them over the pasture. We were surrounded by Marg's family history: plates, pictures, glass-fronted cabinets. The daily events of her life take place in the presence and the memory of the people to whom she is connected.

The first object she showed us was a piece of wood that came from her grandparents' house, which was completed in 1907.

> My grandfather built it. The last thing he did was to sign that piece of wood and put it against the wall in the bathroom, the last bit of moulding he put in the house. Theirs was my first home. I lived with my grandparents until I was four, so I have a lot of connections with their home.
>
> I don't know what drew me but I went down to Westminster, and I had the strangest urge to walk up the lane toward my grandparents' house. I didn't

know the people who were living there at the time, but I had a very strong urge. It was in the fall, and I was feeling nostalgic – I get that way in the fall, I've lost a lot of my family in the fall – but I walked up the lane and looked in the yard. I explained who I was and said I just wanted to see the fruit trees and the house. She asked if I'd like to come in, but I said no. I knew there had a been a lot of renovations, and wanted to remember the house as it was. The outside was pretty much as I had remembered it. Her husband came out to join us. They looked at each other and the woman said, "Well, we have something that I think you should have." When they renovated the bathroom, just a few months before I got there, they found this board and saved it. Isn't it strange that I would walk up the lane that day, and that they would be there? It was the baseboard of the bathroom; see, it says my grandfather's name, and then "December 16, 1912, owner and builder of this" and "house" was obviously on the next plank. It was a very solid house and I always felt very secure there.

This white jug is one of two things that remind me of my grandmother. I like it so much because it represents the simplicity of the time. After I was four we left, but we'd go there every Sunday for dinner. The simplicity of this milk jug represents that time, when everything in my childhood was not complex. You accept everything that goes on, somehow. I feature it in a lot of my watercolours – fill it with flowers. I feel a real connection with it. The other thing: my grandmother knew that as a child I always admired this plate with Bobby Burns on it. They came from Aberdeen. They had a plate rail in their house; there it sat and when I was a little girl I used to look at the faces on the plates. So she put a little adhesive on the back that said, "Margaret Anne. This is for Margaret Anne."

Memories of childhood are suffused with whiteness, like this plate. It's no accident that Marg became a painter.

My early childhood was very happy, and it's all connected with light. The light coming through the kitchen window, dotted swiss curtains halfway up the window, big deep windows, and the light dappled with pear trees and cherry trees outside in the yard.

My grandmother always made porridge when I stayed overnight, on the wood stove. In fact, I have this plate too, the porridge plate. As I look around here, I know I'm really lucky to have all these objects.

You know, the other thing that reminds me of is that friends come into play in this too. My grandfather died first, and my grandmother when she was ninety-one. A friend of mine had come down to her house when they were sorting through her things and getting rid of them. My aunt and uncle who were looking after her possessions had put a lot of things on the big table, the many things that were going to a rummage sale. My friend looked at me and said, "You know, you shouldn't let these go. You should ask your aunt and uncle if you can keep some of them." So I did that. And I said, "Oh, Vivian, thank you." To have that objective opinion there, when you're upset emotionally, not really thinking into the future. I was so pleased that she'd said that.

Marg's knowledge of herself emerges from her connections. Another profound love is gardening, and she learned that from her connections too.

A lot of my memories of that time are gardening ones. I didn't realize until much later, when our children were born, that I really love gardening. The smells: a narrow garden along their house, filled with lily-of-the-valley. And the smells and joys of the kitchen: my grandmother cooked scones. Every time I went for a visit, she went right into the kitchen, made them, put them in the wood stove, and they would be fresh to eat with butter and her jam. She did this until my children were young, into the sixties. Finally the family decided that the wood stove was too dangerous for her, that she had to switch to an electric. Really, thinking now, why would she at that age be able to switch to a new stove? So she made them hook up the wood stove in the basement, and she'd go down there and cook her scones.

More smells flooded her memory, from her move when she was four to a house with a garden her father put in. "He grew roses; that was his specialty, when he had time. So again the scents come in." He was too busy to garden much, said Marg, because as a teacher he got very involved in the teacher's federation.

And this pen reminds me of him. He used to write on cards. After he died I found a number of cards that he wrote philosophical sayings on. So I put together a couple of books, one for my mother's things after her death, and one for my dad's. There was a real connection with fountain pens in those days; you wrote your essays and your letters [with them]. Another fountain pen of mine I was given when I went into nursing. Here is one card. It says, "Indeed, hard work is the price which life demands for the best hours, and its choicest gifts. It is these hours and these gifts which we earnestly desire for all Canadians." He read that in the *Winnipeg Free Press* in 1941.

Losing both parents, you tend to go through things very carefully and be selective about what you are keeping. When I was eleven, they found out my dad had a brain tumour, so he was ill for almost five years before he died. During that time my mother not only had to look after my sister and me, she learned to drive a car and went back to school and became a teacher herself, knowing that would be the best thing she could do, to be at home with us in the summer and to match our hours to take care of us.

My mom was a great reader. This book belonged to her when she was in high school. It was a selection of poetry. I love poetry also. It has in here the poem "Ulysses," which has been a big factor in my life. I loved English all through school, but I had an English professor in university who opened the doors of poetry for me. On the very first day I understood what poetry was all about; and I had missed all that through high school. I often think about that poem in times when I feel a little discouraged.

It became ever clearer that Marg is self-defined, knowing well her wishes and her dislikes, because of the ways she has been connected with people – family, certainly, but just as influential, her professors at university. Through her sociology professor she discovered *The Prophet*.

His thoughts on marriage and childhood were so compatible with the way I felt. You know how you find these writings through your life, like Virginia Woolf's *A Room of One's Own*, and when I had my children, in early marriage, Lindbergh's *Gift from the Sea*. This professor took a group of 1950s young women who had not been brought up to speak in school. We would sit in the classroom, just sitting there. I hoped no one would ask me a question in case I didn't know the right answer. This was the way my schooling was. So when I got to university I thought I could sit there, absorb, and read. Here he had this group of forty of us in the nursing class. Nobody said a word. I was one of the worst. I couldn't think of anything either. He lit his pipe, put his feet up, crossed his legs, and said, "Fine, we'll just sit here till somebody breaks the ice." We started talking about books and ideas; this was right up my alley, and I scooted to the library.

I get really cranky if I don't have a good book to read. I'm busy doing other things but every once in a while I have to stop and I have to read. My mother was a great reader. In fact, her family was always after her. She'd rather read than do dishes, so I get it honestly.

As for nursing, in a way it was a bad decision for me to make. It was very traumatic. The worst part was the actual physical care of another person. But women my age didn't quit. Once you set your path, you didn't quit. I never, never discussed my terrible times with my teachers. I just suffered through them. But I kept my white pen and my cap, though the rest of my uniform is gone.

That sort of brings me up to our marriage, so I've put my rings in my little white leather case, although my engagement ring came in a little silver case. I keep them together when I take them off. We knew each other for so long before we got married. We met when I was fifteen, and right away I fell in love with him. He would laugh, but the first date I was so comfortable, with his sense of humor, and his wonderful laugh, and his outgoing spirit, which I did not have. I was very reticent. I couldn't have sat and talked to you like this in 1958. My goodness, no. I had a great time in the sixties on the verge of change, with all the new readings and going to meetings where women were talking about a new way of thinking, a little more freedom. But it's interesting: I distinctly remember our wedding day and leaving the reception. I felt absolutely and totally free. When we left in the car, I left without a backward glance and absolutely knew it was the right thing for me to be doing. I don't know if many women can say that. It was just perfect. It felt just right. I had this wonderful sense of adventure, and driving off I had this absolutely great feeling. You never forget that. It doesn't happen very often in your life. You can feel whole and real. So I wear my rings a lot, actually. I'm always putting them on and taking them off.

When I first met Tony he was playing in a dance band. I would go with him to sit and be what they now call a groupie, I guess! We visited at intermission; the band had a favourite place they'd go and listen to after hours jazz, so we'd sometimes go there. We were very late, which probably upset my mother. Tony's being a musician had a very strong impact on our marriage. Double bass he played, and his trumpet. He sold them when we moved to the island. When they went out the door I have to admit I shed a few tears, because music was so much a part of our life.

Marg's art too, very much her own expression in water-colours, has its origin, in her mind, with other people. When her children were young she made time for reading, despite being very busy, and began drawing. A friend suggested an oil painting class; they began together and only Marg continued. Her sister gave her a book of watercolour paintings and instruction,

> ... and it all clicked, there again. This book is one of my favourite things from my sister. This photo ties in with the water colour book, because it's a family grouping, one of the last photos where we were all together, because after that we lost my mother and then Tony's mother and then my sister, who was only forty-three. She died of breast cancer.
>
> So often, you adapted your skills and ability to your situation. I felt isolated at home, I did a bit of nursing, did some prenatal teaching, worked for a while on Saturday in a doctor's office to keep my hand in, volunteered for four or five years in a family planning clinic. But I could not go on working on a full-time basis because all our family were working people, so there weren't any family members to look after the children, and there weren't any daycares.

Now Marg raises sheep and spins wool and paints and reads and is a grandmother and a wife. She pursues all of these as choices of her own. Marg is self-conscious and clear about her values and her desires. Life has meaning. "You can use thinking and memory to provide commitment to sane and healthy values. All your senses can be engaged in your aesthetic and in connection with the world you inhabit. You can bring beauty to the world. The world is beautiful." Each object that Marg discussed was a cue, evoking its context. Each released a flood of reminiscence and showed her the choices she has made and the relationships she has used to form her knowledge of herself.

In the scrapbooks she has made, Marg also keeps the histories of other people. Like an archaeologist, she discovers their depths through their artefacts. Each possession – and all of them are kept right around her, visible in her everyday life – produced a moral story or a fable; she interrogated each to make meaning. And the answers, most often, were that meaning emerges when one commits oneself to other people and when one fulfills one's duties in an exigent way, not sloppily or haphazardly but consciously. Marg's objects and stories imply that if you fulfill your commitments to yourself, you will discover your own competence: you will make perfect light scones and jam. You can sign your name when you have completed your house.

The path toward becoming autonomous, whole inside oneself, is slow and sometimes arduous because a woman's desire for a place of her own, whether literal or not, is all too often construed as selfishness. And yet, women struggle toward defining themselves rather than being defined, toward hearing their own voices, toward knowing their own desires. The project may start with small insights and small gestures. Something as simple as owning and driving a car can represent a step in that direction. Sharon, for example, at sixty-five is uncomfortable driving and intends to take driving lessons because her car symbolizes freedom. Laurel keeps the windshield washer blade from her first car, emblematic of her first forays toward independence. Countless women showed us their car keys as one of their treasures: invariably they signify freedom. Helena is an adult student in university and beamed with pleasure, saying that while she loves her three children, nothing, makes her feel as much in love as sitting in her van, high above the other cars, feeling as if she owns the road and owns her own life.

Divorce is an event that often propels women into independence. It often offers them the chance to make choices about their lives and about the kind of people they want to be. A woman of eighty said that one of her prized possessions is her divorce papers. She is proud of her courage, many many years ago, in leaving a very bad marriage to an alcoholic man, despite being ostracized for it. Raising her children alone was not a bad thing because she believed that "having a man around only hindered the proper upbringing of the family." Her divorce allowed her, after the children were grown, to become best friends with a man she could love who was kind to her. Betty was also freed to know herself by divorce. One of her prized objects is a musical score.

> I come from a musical family. I grew up singing, but I stopped and raised four children and two husbands. My therapist asked, after that, what I always had wanted to do, what I never had the time or money to

do. That was an easy answer for me: to take singing lessons.

She now performs as a soloist in small concerts. Maria, divorced in 1979 after twenty-two years of marriage, said, "That's when my real life began. I made my own friends." These friends have become something of a family for her, and the object that represents her family of choice is a blue ceramic bowl from one of them. Clearly, marriage need not impede women's autonomy, but when it does, and when they have escaped it, they treasure the sense of self they proudly gain.

Traveling alone was cited frequently as an expression of women's responsibility and commitment to themselves. Many of them are amazed at their capacity for boldness and for listening to their own desires. Jeanine's passport reminds her of backpacking for a year when she was twenty-one, going to Europe and places as remote from her Canadian experience as Turkey and Libya. All her luggage was stolen on that trip, and all she has left is an expensive silver ring she bought in Norway. She treasures it because, as she said, "I hardly ever buy something very special for myself." Jindra showed us a piece of black coral from her first solo holiday. "I see it as an independent step. That is why I love it." Aimee has a piece of batik that she bought in Africa when she traveled, alone, to meet her birth father in Sierra Leone. "I dropped out of university because I was in social work and became very disillusioned. My travel life really civilized me, because it was the first time I had been by myself."

Buying things for themselves, indulging themselves, comes hard to many women. It seems selfish, too self involved. And yet its delights include, more than the possession itself, the knowledge that they have heard their own voices. Gabrielle is only sixteen and is thrilled with the green summer dress she bought for herself with her own money. "It's one of the nicest things I have. I can be Miss Fashion Model in it!"

"This is a wallet that I got with my own money when I was about six years old," said Laurie. "I thought it was the most beautiful thing in the world." Heather's prized object is her collection of china figurines in a glass cabinet. She could not justify spending family money on them but always said that she would buy them if she had her own money. After her youngest child left home, she began to work for pay and to indulge her desire. Sherry, once an accountant and now an astrologer, has a watch she bought for herself, which she imbues with almost magical qualities.

When I was little my mom gave me a gold watch that had been my dad's wedding present to her. I could never make watches work. I have some sort of an energy thing. She was always accusing me of winding it backwards because I couldn't make it work. It would go fast, or slow. She'd put it on and it would be fine and she'd do one of those "Oh, what's the matter with you" kind of things. I was maybe six or seven. So I never wore a watch until I was about thirty. I decided for my birthday – it was the first year I was on my own after I had separated from my husband – to buy myself an expensive gold watch. And it has worked ever since!

Liz's ring, which she bought for herself on her first trip abroad without her parents, has also taken on magical qualities. She described being "encased in France in a school with high walls." She escaped and saw the silver and lapis lazuli ring.

It became the one thing that I brought back from France with me. Years later, having divorced my first husband, I was living in an apartment. Above the sink was a small shelf where I would put the ring when I washed the dishes. I sometimes forgot it there. One night I went out with friends to go bowling, got into the car, realized I had forgotten my glasses, came back into the apartment. My door was open, unlocked, and I knew I had locked it. And I could hear the bed squeaking. "Why," I thought, "would someone go into my bedroom and be in my bed?" I walked in, couldn't see anyone, walked into the bedroom, nobody in the bed. I got down and looked under the bed and sure enough: there was a burglar, a young man six feet tall. I hauled him out by the scruff of his neck, stood him up beside the telephone, and said, "You stand right there and don't you move." I called the police, gave them a description, and then told them he was standing right here. The policeman thought I was out of my mind. He could have a gun. I asked the kid if he had a gun. He said, "No, but I have this knife." So I said, "Give me that knife." And he did, and he waited there with me until the police came and arrested him. They took him down to the station and searched him. Sure enough, this ring was in his pocket. He'd broken it, trying to get it on his finger. That was the first day I recognized that as a woman I was more powerful than any man.

Women expressed the joy of self-knowledge and of the ability to say, in one way or another, "This is who I am." At the time of our interview, Angelina was buying a house and was about to unpack her possessions after years in storage. She looked forward to this process because of what it could tell her about her newly independent self. "I can revisit all these things that I've had put away for so long. I have my own place and I'll see who I am." She wants to find that out. Perhaps she will no longer acquiesce in the definitions imposed on her by others.

Sherry is also finding out who she is. One of her favourite objects is the pair of pants she wore at our interview – loose, cotton patterned pants she made herself.

Obviously favourite pants wear out and I've been madly mending these, trying to keep them going. Eventually they will wear out. But it took me a long time to accept the fact that I really love clothes. I've spent so much of my life rebelling against the wealth and superficiality I grew up with. I tried to rebel through dress. And finally I came to accept the fact that I like clothes, but that the clothes I like are kind of weird. Sometimes it's a painful thing because I go around dressed exactly the way I damn well please. But I don't feel badly about it. I think for a long time it was a rebellion, and now it's a genuine part of myself.

Such self-knowledge often remains very private. People seeing Sherry in her pants would surely not guess at the saga of self-understanding that accompanies them. Such revelations require more trust than people usually bring to public interactions. Even in their private spaces, people are not usually as confident as Nancy is about leaving her journals on her desk. "[My husband] has always told me that he respects that privacy, and I trust him. I leave them out and trust that he won't look, and it is important to me that he doesn't." She feels entitled to her privacy and knows it will be preserved.

Murie also keeps her secrets, sometimes almost as publicly. In the photographs of her children, she sees the drama she does not share with others.

I like this picture very much. You can tell so many things from a photo. This one is the only one with much of a smile. It's not your stereotypical photo. For so many years – because I had a difficult childhood and a difficult marriage, had all these children, was emotionally damaged and intellectually under-developed – for so many years of my life all I ever felt was pain. But now when I look at this picture I begin to remember the good times. People look at our family and idealize it. They say, "Oh, isn't that a wonderful family." Well, now I'm beginning to say, "Yes, it is a wonderful family." Just because I felt a tremendous amount of pain doesn't mean that *they* did. I still don't know quite why I got divorced. It was a deep need. I needed to get out, after twenty-nine years. So that picture is precious to me because it is my past life.

Murie's present life emerges out of her own needs, many no doubt still unknown. She is willing to look at herself, to seek a self she can claim as her own. Her final object was a small stone sculpture.

It's a monument. If I photographed it and enlarged it no one would know. It could be Stonehenge. "Monuments" is a better word than "symbols." The little rock piles, my monuments, are all over my house. People come in and say it looks like a museum and I'm smiling to myself because I know what it represents to me.

Murie is creating her own new life as an artist.

Sylvia told her story as a long saga toward wholeness within herself, even while her life is intertwined with the lives of the people she loves. She has come to a strong sense of a separate self with great difficulty, for so long having apologized for having needs of her own and more often not acknowledging them at all. She distracted herself successfully from hearing her own voice by attending to her obligations and commitments to others. It worked. For years she hardly had a voice. For all that she was vibrant, enthusiastic, beautiful, and joyous, she could also be deeply, if invisibly, sad.

Sylvia's narrative represents the culmination of the insights she began to derive after her daughters grew up. Living in a Los Angeles suburb as a seemingly perfect homemaker, volunteer, and paid worker, she only came to say the word "I" when, at about fifty-five, life's brevity and unpredictability impressed itself on her. The collection of her prized possessions speaks eloquently of a nearly thirty-year movement toward voice. She begins began in a slightly ironic tone:

> Not because I love shopping, but ...! One of my objects is my Broadway credit card. It was the first card I ever got for my own credit, on just my name. I didn't have to put my husband Fred's name or my parents. It was when I first started working around 1980. I went to the department store and didn't put anyone else's name on the application. I was very thrilled when I got it in the mail. I'm not even that crazy about The Broadway, but I appreciate that they gave me a credit card. Penney's, of all stores, had turned me down earlier, because I had tried it on my own. Now, people get credit cards like nothing. Left and right they're getting them. High school: Lynn got a Visa when she was in high school. First

Card, it was called: would you like a thousand dollars worth of credit? So, at Penney's in 1975, when Fred and I separated for a while, I couldn't get credit on my own.

That was around the same time when I was working and had insurance for that breast biopsy I had. I was the one with the insurance; my job was providing our insurance, but I had to put Fred's name as responsible for the bill. So The Broadway gave me my first credit card, for my own credit.

Her story took another turn. The department store had acknowledged her existence as an autonomous and responsible person. Now she affirms her own presence, admittedly in a very small place. "This is my purse. It is the only thing that is strictly mine. There is nobody who goes into my purse – not Fred, not the girls. Everyone knows that no one goes into my purse." Her identity is affirmed by that purse; her boundaries in one small realm are inviolable.

If they want something out of it, they bring it to me. I have no secrets in there, but I love that it's my purse. It can be messy, it can be neat. It can be heavy, it can be light. It's usually heavy and sometimes if people hand it to me they go, "What have you got in there?" I have my wallet, which sometimes has a lot of change in it. I've got keys. I've got my cell phone. I have things for my grandchildren. Every now and then I buy a little purse and go, "Who am I kidding?" and then go back to a big purse.

That's why it was so awful the time I was working in the school and my wallet got stolen. It was the biggest invasion, because even my own family doesn't go into my purse. And someone went in and took out my wallet and it was found later dumped in the trash without the credit cards. Really, there aren't many things that are yours alone that you don't have to share. So that shows my independence.

Spoken like a woman with obligations! And in a sense, she was laughing at herself, because her next possession, as she said,

... kind of represents that someone takes care of me. It is the gas tank in my car, which Fred has kept full for however many years we've had cars – which is just the opposite of independence. One time I almost had to do it. It was when Mother was in the hospital from her car accident and I had to go to the west side to the hospital. It was unexpected that I'd need that much gas – and I'd made extra trips, on my lunch hour and the night before. I pulled into a gas station that was only self-serve, and I was struggling. This man comes up and says, "Would you like me to help you with that, honey?" And I go, "That'd be real nice!" So that's the other end: I like to be taken care of too. I could have said my wedding ring, but I chose the gas tank instead. It's really funny. Fred

always says, "Is there any gas in the car?" after I've
taken a trip. And I say, "Yeah, it's right around half,"
because I don't even look; that's how bad it's gotten.
I don't know if it's because he's so nice, or because he
likes to: but that's OK, whatever the reason is.

Sylvia moved on to talk about the jewellery making and
design for which she discovered she has a talent about
five years ago. She began the work for fun and found that
making wooden pieces gratified her creativity and filled
her with happiness. She handed me a five-inch teak heart
carefully carved and polished, gleaming warmly, hung
on a leather thong.

This one is not the best of them, but it was in the first
group of them that I made. It's not as nice as the ones
we make now, but it will never be for sale, because
that's what started the hearts. I make quite a bit of
money on these necklaces. But it blows me away that
somebody wants to buy something that I've done.
Whenever somebody stops at my booth and oohs and
ahhs and then someone comes by says, "Oh, this is
just what I want for my birthday," or a tourist likes
it, I think, "Someone in New York is wearing one
of the hearts" and they say, "I was at this art show in
southern California, this lady makes them." There's
something just very nice about somebody appreciat-
ing what you've done and thinking that it's worthy
of spending their money on. Even if they don't buy,
they may stop and touch them and want to talk about
them.

I started this as a game, essentially, and I gave one as a gift to someone at a party. Somebody else saw it there and said, "You know, that's beautiful. Do you have any more of them? I would love to buy one." I went to her house the following week with the ones I had and she bought five. She helped me a lot, this one woman. She told me about shows, and she helped me by wearing them everywhere she goes. She opened doors to shows to me too, private ones in hospitals, which are great shows.

And now, here's a flyer for one of those craft shows. But this one is called Artisans of Southern California. It is a fine arts show, and when they accepted my pieces they sent me one of their announcements, which was very beautiful. It had my name on it and it said, "Exotic Wood Objects" next to my name. I thought, "Wow, I'm in this group of artists now!" I know I'll go there and feel outclassed because I always do at those things. Maybe I won't feel that way when my booth becomes a little more professional. But then I end up doing as well as anybody else.

Sylvia's hesitation was evident, her newfound sense of self less solid than it would become.

Now, my next object is my paintbrushes. I don't know how to express this, but it's important. It's not that my paintbrushes per se are important, but I was thinking that I use brushes for everything I do, whether it's the hearts that I varnish or the beads that I paint. And it's also that when I started doing the hearts I found that I do have creativity in me. See, when I started the hearts I did it with a friend. I thought she was the creative force, and that I was just doing what she was showing me, since she's an artist and an interior decorator and has confidence in her ability. And then when she moved, I found I was doing better things on my own. I'm grateful to her. She got me started and she's great about sharing what she knows. But I started doing so much better on my own, and I like it so much better on my own too. I'm not ready to say that I am an artist – but, you know, I may be selling myself short. I often say that I'm only following a pattern. A sculptor told me that I have talent, and he said, "What do you think happens when you go to art school or an art class? The teacher tells you the same thing. In fact, it's harder from a book than with a teacher." Still, I haven't got that confidence yet because I feel like I'm just copying. I always apologize for it, like for knitting or crocheting. When people say, "Oh, that's so good," I say, "Well, it's just a pattern that I'm copying." I'm getting where I'm not apologizing for the hearts, because I choose the woods, I design the hearts, I make most of the beads. People comment that it all goes together so well. So I know now I'm a little more than just a technician.

I am also good at something else, and that is selling. At one show, the man in the next booth asked

me, "What's your background in sales?" "I have no
background in sales." He told me I was very good,
that I knew when to start talking to a person, how
much to talk to them. If you say something too
soon, they walk away. But wait until they handle
the woods; and then I tell them right away they are
handmade, and I talk about the wood. I don't know
if that's who I was, but it's who I am becoming,
because I am getting confidence from it. And the
money that you make at the end of the day is like a
confirmation that you did a good job.

Sylvia's sense of self is expanding as she grows in confidence. She may not be entirely sure of her personal value
or of the power of her presence in the world, but she is
exploring them as she develops her creativity. She seeks
affirmation as many women do as they first begin to
experiment with individuality and independence. Is this
the opposite of being overly confident and self-centered,
strutting about the world, feeling like the anointed of
God? Most women are unlikely to become that way, listening, as they have learned to do, to the needs of other
people. Sylvia has not neglected any part of her complex
set of connections with people. Her friends, her children
and grandchildren, her husband, her parents – her day is
filled with her relationships.

Her next prized possession – no surprise – is her portable phone.

It's opened up this whole world to me! When I was
babysitting my grandchildren I could still talk on the

phone and socialize and do all the things I had to do, and still follow the children around. And I don't feel I'm wasting my time sitting and talking on the phone. I got the first one five years ago; it has been replaced twice. It afforded me the freedom of talking on the phone no matter what I was doing – and do it without guilt. I sometimes talk on the phone while I paint hearts. I probably need a phone that attaches to my ear!

Next she moved on to relationships and connections in the distant past. She treasures two poems that were written about her by a young man in college.

I can't even remember his name. Every now and then I read them even though I know them by heart. The first one goes like this.

Little girl with brown hair
Running wild through many men
Will some day look back to the day
When she could play and run away.

You can always remember the days when it didn't matter so much, do what you wanted and just…. I wonder, should I have married this man? And I don't even remember his name! I keep the poems in a box in my dresser drawer. It has other love letters from other people too. Not intimate love letters, but for some reason things I have not been able to give up. The box is a stationery box called Enchanted

Paper, the original box, which also contains something from another man at college. He played the piano really well but he didn't read music. He just wrote some notes on a page, a music page, and it said, "I wanted to give you something no one else would give you, so I wrote you a song." He was very talented. Sometimes I wonder if I should get rid of them, because they might hurt Fred's feelings. Not that he ever looks through my drawers. Probably would, though. Oh, well! "Smile, play, and run away." So that's that.

How do I represent what my grandchildren mean to me? A picture? No. That I have a crib in one of our bedrooms and a toy box. They're that much of my life. For goodness sakes, I got a toy box for them before their parents did because I was accumulating so many toys. In my desk in that same bedroom Haley has two drawers that belong to her where she keeps her books. So out of my three bedrooms, one belongs to my grandchildren. They come in and they know right where to go. In fact, when I pick them up at school, they say, "Which house are we going to?" Certainly they know that their house is their house, but my house is almost their house because they have their own place. They say, "I'm going to my room." That's a better way than a picture to represent them.

My other bedroom is my other possession. It's my back bedroom, which became mine when my daughter moved out. See, I always shared a room with my sister.

Even after she moved out it still had her bed and everything in it. And of course when you are in college nothing is yours. And then I got married so young; then all those years of being, what? a daughter, a sister, a wife, a mother. And then all of a sudden there was this empty room with no furniture. The first thing I put in there was an ironing board, because I thought, "This is my room and I'm going to leave the ironing board out." It represented that this was no one else's room, so if I wanted the ironing board in the middle of the room it could be there. It was kind of exciting, just recently, taking it down and putting it away, knowing that I don't need it anymore. And it still is my room. I can make the rules there and have it messy if I want. Right now I'm very excited about having it neat. My tool box is in there; that's another thing I bought on my own, after I started making the hearts. I realized I didn't have to consult with anyone if I should get this toolbox.

It is not the possessions in there that are important to me. It's the privacy. I really never had any before. I married so young, at nineteen, that I never had the chance to be alone. And it's such a thrill now because my family asks if I mind if they go into my room. Before that all I ever had was my purse. Certainly, I love my whole house, but the house is "ours." But here – sometimes I go in there late at night and make earrings, maybe turn on the stereo or watch TV in there. That's when I like to be in my room, late at

night. Sometimes I just look through my beads. I
have my stereo there, furniture, a phone of course;
if I had a refrigerator I could go in there and never
come out!

Sylvia began to contemplate the interview we had had.
Her words reminded us of the beauty of conversation. It
takes you places you never thought you'd go. It gives you
new thoughts.

When you asked me the question about my favourite
things, I thought there were no six things that would
define me. My scale was not going to be in there! So
I asked Fred, and he said that he should be in there.
Then I asked Christine, and she said, "Well, if it were
me, I would say my baseball glove, which is always
with me because you never know when there's going
to be a pick-up game." She suggested CDs or maybe
a favourite movie, but I don't have a favourite movie,
and I'm not really into music. I got discouraged, and
then all of a sudden – well, just look at these things.
It's been a nice experience for me. My family ended
up being in there, but somehow they're not there at
the very top, even though I feel that they are. I'm a
little surprised that they weren't, because if someone
had said, "What's important in your life?" I'd say,
"My family, my girls, my grandchildren." But here
are all these other things that I seem to like at least
as well.

Sadly, not long after the interview Sylvia's husband died suddenly and unexpectedly. She was consumed by feelings of loss. And yet, some time later, she has begun to find meaning in her life – not volunteer work, no, but gardening and maybe paid work, real commitments. Her developing sense of an autonomous self has been slowed, but she remains an individual who recognizes her value and allows herself to take up space. More and more she will speak in a loud voice. She will be heard. She is one of the people who are redefining women as connected but also as whole within themselves.

*T*he women we interviewed were selected using a "snow-
ball" technique. The first few were known to one of
us as friends, family members, or students. They suggested
other women they knew whom we had never met. Later we
focused on adding women who belonged to a minority group
that we particularly wanted to include and who were referred
to us by women we had interviewed previously. We sought
out the diversity that characterizes Canada, including particular attention to First Nations, immigrant, and refugee
women. Together, these groups account for nearly a third
of our interviews. We also interviewed especially for age,
disability, and social class, as well as for regional inclusion
and sexual orientation. As a result, we conducted interviews
in Ottawa, Calgary, rural Alberta, the interior of British
Columbia (an especially memorable road trip), and the west
coast of Canada and the United States. We were not looking
for "typicality," but for a diversity of experiences and narratives that could represent the wide range of women's lives
and circumstances.

Our first contact with a participant was usually by telephone, when we explained our project and asked for the
subject's participation. Not one woman turned down our
request for an interview – a fact that we think is quite

remarkable and that demonstrates the intrinsic interest of the topic and the ubiquity of women's practice as archivists. The interview often took place in the woman's own home, in the interest of her comfort and familiarity, but sometimes several women met at a neighbour's house, taking turns being interviewed and, in between, sitting in a group and chatting informally with one another. For the book, some women decided to use self-chosen pseudonyms while others preferred to use their own names.

At the beginning of the process, we completed a few interviews together, mostly to learn about each other's interview style, which we found to be similar. Both of us had previously completed qualitative research, and both had the same commitment to hearing women's own voices, whether in research or in counseling. Our questions in the interviews tended to be open-ended and non-directive. The conversation was usually initiated by our wondering in what order the woman might like to discuss her collection. Some women were very clear about a preferred order while others discussed the items randomly. Interestingly, by the end of the interview women often described a newfound unity among their possessions – a coherence deriving from a unifying core within their lives and experiences. We occasionally interrupted the flow of conversation to ask about where and how an object was kept, whether in public view or hidden away, to inquire about when she looked at it, or to ask about its ultimate disposition. Conversation about one object led easily into the next, and the session came to an end when the stories of her objects had been fully explored and there were no more objects to discuss. Most interviews lasted about two hours, though many went on much longer and a few were shorter.

Early in the process of interviewing, we decided that it was important to interview each other; the results of these interviews appear in the second chapter of the book. While we knew that our own commentaries would be biased by self-consciousness about the project, we also knew that we should be prepared to reveal ourselves to each other and to our readers, as our participants had done. We also thought that it was essential that we experience being interviewed on this subject, if only to sensitize ourselves to the demands that such an intimate process makes.

Most of the interviews were characterized by intensity of feeling. Emotions were evoked and memories flowed, sometimes painfully, sometimes joyously. Most women expressed pleasure at the end of the interview, no matter how difficult some parts of it might have been – in fact, several of them commented on the experience being a treat or "a marvellous piece of self-indulgence" that they had enjoyed very much. Plans were often made to sit down with a friend or a relative to share the stories again, in some cases to make sure that they were not lost with a woman's death.

The tapes were all transcribed with the participants' language unedited, except to delete conversational words such as "uhs" and "mmm's," which interrupt the flow of written narrative. We each read every transcript several times, and we met together to analyze them, placing anecdotes, narratives, and participants' comments into an arrangement of themes. We taped our conversations as we analyzed the documents, asking ourselves about the overt and covert meanings we were deriving from the conversations and making links across interviews to aspects of the process that seemed to recur in multiple narratives.

We believe – and we hope – that we listened very carefully, and that the themes we heard, which organize this book, emerged from the women's own words. We also recognize, however, the intensity and subjectivity of our own involvement with the material. In the end, of course, we were the ones who put this book together, who chose what to include, what to highlight, and what to pass over. The same interviews, done by other people, would inevitably have been different and would have been differently interpreted. There are no doubt meanings in the transcripts that we, through our own limitations, have overlooked or interpreted less fully than they might merit. Works such as ours are inherently and inescapably bounded by the authors' contexts. We do not apologize for this fact, especially as the process we are studying is itself a subjective, constantly changing one. Just as our narrative is personal and unique, so, too, the stories that women tell about the objects themselves are mutable. The keeping of these objects, and their use, seems to us to be first and foremost a developmental process for women. Accordingly, women's collections are not static – they change and grow as the objects they contain acquire new meanings, as grief is overcome, and as new experience requires that new items be added.

Our listening also grew from our immersion in the scholarly literature about women's lives – feminist psychology, narrative and biography, and women's history. We are especially indebted to the authors whose works appear in the selective bibliography we have appended. We have included many that are not specifically cited in the book because we read through them and sometimes found our thinking enriched by them. We believe that our work amplifies the literature that has nourished our growth as scholars and contributes to the intention of that literature to unearth women's invisible and often disqualified knowledge about themselves.

Elly is an historian and Kathy a psychologist, therapist and researcher. Both of us are feminists who have for many years placed women at the heart of our work and our writing, and we agree with Nielson's (1990) view that oral history is ideally suited to the purposes of feminist inquiry. The blend of our respective disciplines made for lively and multi-faceted discussions of the interviews and resulted in insights that were useful in other aspects of our work. For Elly, these involved a further development of her interests in archival materials and oral history. For Kathy, the participants' narratives indicated potential for a feminist approach to assessment and a useful adjunct to an existentially based psychotherapy that clarifies central sources of meaning through life review. Both of us see opportunities for the use of these objects to support mutually caring discussions among women and to deepen connections between mothers and daughters and grandmothers and granddaughters in particular. We feel a strong commitment to living an intentional life – a process that can be materially assisted by our awareness of the sources of meaning that are so clearly represented in our own collections of artefacts.

We have said very little about women's relationships with men in this book – perhaps an odd omission. Certainly, in doing the interviews we heard stories about men who were loved and who were loving, men like Kate's grandfather, and about how they shaped their daughters' and granddaughters' lives for better or for worse. Those stories were as strong in their emotional centrality to the women as any of the others we heard, but they were relatively few in comparison to the many, many narratives about mothers, sisters, grandmothers, and women friends.

There was, though, another pattern of interest in the stories some women told about men who had a lasting impact on their lives. A number of women saved something they had received from a man with whom they may have had a troubled relationship but who, through his particular gift, had shown that he knew and understood them. Such gifts were especially powerful when they included an indication that he had gone out of his way to choose something for her that expressed that understanding. In these relationships, understanding and affection was rare, so when it occurred, it moved them profoundly. Whether it was a father's special effort to mend a doll, or a grandfather's gift of a small glow-in-the-dark statue that he thought would give his granddaughter comfort at night, or a special book that showed a knowledge of her taste, the object still, often decades later, had the power to elicit tears. This realization of a wish to be known by a man in her life, and the gratification of being known, is especially powerful, it seems, in female/male relationships, perhaps most so between fathers and daughters.

In contrast, the many memories of mothers and grand-mothers were often, though not always, marked through treasured "objects of daily use." Such objects helped to recall a shared moment in time, part of a pattern of predict-able, reliable safety, security, and love. They evoked memory pictures that could return the woman to the comforts of her childhood, immersed in the community and in the company of the women in her family. Women who had conflicted relationships with their mothers usually did not keep such mementos as these, preferring memories of a grandmother or of a woman friend in their place. When a grandmother or mother had died early or was absent for another reason, it was not unusual for a woman to use an artefact of her life to weave a fantasy person around. Through communion with this object, the fantasy figure could be made to embody the archetypal mother – the powerful, caring figure who imparts knowledge and skills for living.

We have used many words and phrases in our writing to describe women's public and private roles as archivists and the uses they make of their treasured objects. Such objects are simultaneously gates to memory, historical artefacts, comforters, anchors, objects of attachment, transitional objects, continuity markers, symbols of the self, and objects of contemplation. They speak to women about personal development, relationship, achievements, losses, and the essential aspects of the self. They make it possible to con-nect generations of women, to manage moods, to find shelter in times of hardship and deprivation, and to work toward completing the unfinished business of formative relationships and events. They allow us to speak in a private code that simultaneously shares and conceals important meanings. No wonder women so often call them "treasures."

Selected Bibliography

Abelson, R. P. 1986. Beliefs are like possessions. *Journal of Theory of Social Behavior* 16:223–50.

Abelson, R. P., and D. A. Prentice. 1987. Beliefs as possessions: A functional perspective. In *Attitude structure and function*, ed. A. R. Pratkanis. Hillsdale, NJ: Erlbaum.

Ainsworth, M. 1989. Attachments beyond infancy. *American Psychologist* 44:709–16.

Anderson, K. 1990. Beginning where we are: Feminist methodology in oral history. In *Feminist research methods*, ed. J. M. Nielson. Boulder: Westview Press.

Baum, S., and R. Steward. 1990. Sources of meaning through the lifespan. *Psychological Reports* 67:3–14.

Belk, R. W. 1988. Possessions and the extended self. *Journal of Consumer Research* 15:139–68.

Belk, R. W. 1991. Extended self and extending paradigmatic reflections of identity: Gender and social-material position in society. *Journal of Social Behavior and Personality* 6:165–86.

Buss, H. 1993. Mapping our selves. Montreal: McGill-Queen's University Press.

Csikszentmihalyi, M., and E. Rochberg-Halton. 1981. *The meaning of things: Domestic symbols and the self.* Cambridge: Cambridge University Press.

de Beauvoir, S. 1973. *The coming of age.* New York: Warner.

de Grazia, V., ed. 1996. *The sex of things: Gender and consumption in historical perspective.* Berkeley: University of California Press.

Di Leonardo, M. 1987. The female world of cards and holidays: Women, families, and the work of kinship. *Signs* 12:440–53.

Dittmar, H. 1989. Gender identity-related meanings of personal possessions. *British Journal of Social Psychology* 28:159–71.

Dittmar, H. 1991. Meanings of material possessions as reflections of identity: Gender and social-material position in society. *Journal of Social Behavior and Personality* 6:165–86.

Faraday, A., and K. Plummer. 1979. Doing life histories. *Sociological Review* 27:773–92.

Formanek, R. 1991. Why they collect: Collectors reveal their motivation. *Journal of Social Behavior and Personality* 6:275–86.

Furby, L. 1991. Understanding the psychology of possession and ownership: A personal memoir and an appraisal of our progress. *Journal of Social Behavior and Personality* 6:457–63.

Gardiner, J. K. 1987. Self psychology as feminist theory. *Signs* 12: 761–80.

Glodi, K. A., and A. Blasi. 1993. The sense of self and identity among adolescents and adults. *Journal of Adolescent Research* 8: 356–80.

Graham, H. 1984. Surveying through stories. In *Social Researching: Politics, Problems, Practice*, ed. C. H. Roberts. London: Routledge & Kegan Paul.

Graumann, C. F. 1974. Psychology and the world of things. *Journal of Phenomenological Research* 4:389–404.

Guterce, A. 1991. Transitional objects: A reconsideration of the phenomenon. *Journal of Social Behavior and Personality* 6:187–208.

Hamer, J. H. 1994. Identity, process, and reinterpretation: The past made present and the present made past. *Anthropos* 89:1–190.

Heilbrun, C. 1988. *Writing a woman's life*. New York: Norton.

Heilbrun, C. G. 1998. *The last gift of time*. New York: Ballantine.

Hill, R. P. 1991. Homeless women, special possessions, and the naming of "home": An ethnographic case study. *Journal of Consumer Research* 18:293–310.

Hirschman, E. C., and P. A. LaBarbera. 1990. Dimensions of possession importance. *Psychology and Marketing* 7:215–33.

Horwitz, J., and J. Tognoli. 1982. Role of home in adult development: Women and men living alone describe their residential histories. *Family Relations* 31:335–41.

Jelinek, E. 1980. *Women's autobiography*. Bloomington: Indiana University Press.

Jelinek, E. 1986. *The tradition of women's autobiography: From antiquity to the present*. Boston: Twayne Publishers.

Jordan, J., ed. 1991. *Women's growth in connection*. New York: Guilford Press.

Josselson, R. 1987. *Finding herself: Pathways to identity*. San Francisco: Jossey-Bass.

Josselson, R., and A. Lieblich, eds. 1995. *The narrative study of lives*. 4 vols. Newbury Park: Sage Publications.

Katymun, M. 1986. The prevalence of factors influencing decisions among elderly women concerning household possessions during relocation. *Housing Practice* 3:82–99.

Kamptner, N. L. 1991. Personal possessions and their meaning: A lifespan perspective. *Journal of Social Behavior and Personality* 6: 209–28.

Kaschak, E. 1992. *Engendered lives: A new psychology of women's experience*. New York: Basic Books.

Katz, C., and J. Monk. 1993. *Full circles: Geographies of women over the life course*. London: Routledge.

Kessler, R. C., and J. D. McLeod. 1984. Sex differences in vulnerability to undesirable life events. *American Sociological Review* 49:620–31.

Kleinman, A. 1988. *The illness narratives: Suffering, healing and the human condition*. New York: Basic Books.

Kotre, J. 1984. *Outliving the self: Generativity and the interpretation of lives*. Baltimore: Johns Hopkins University Press.

Krieger, S. 1985. Beyond "subjectivity": The use of the self in social science. *Qualitative Sociology* 8:309–24.

Lewis, M. 1991. *The exposed self*. New York: Free Press.

Lorde, A. 1984. *Sister outsider*. Freedom, CA: Crossing Press.

Martin, S. 1992. 0 Canada. *Canadian Living*, Jan., 124.

McCracken, A. 1987. Emotional impact of possession loss. *Journal of Gerontological Nursing* 13:14–19.

Mehta, R., and R. W. Belk. 1991. Artefacts, identity, and transition: Favorite possessions of Indians and Indian immigrants to the United States. *Journal of Consumer Research* 17:398–411.

Middleton, D., and D. Edwards, eds. 1990. *Collective remembering*. London: Sage Publications.

Mountain, G., and P. Bowie. 1992. The possessions owned by long-stay psychogeriatric patients. *International Journal of Geriatric Psychiatry* 7:285–90.

Mumby, D. 1993. *Narrative and social control*. Newbury Park: Sage Publications.

Nielson, J. M. 1990. *Feminist research methods*. Boulder: Westview Press.

O'Brien, T. 1991. *The things they carried*. Toronto: McLelland and Stewart.

Olsen, T. 1982. *Silences*. New York: Dell Publishing.

Perreault, J. 1995. *Writing selves*. Minneapolis: University of Minnesota Press.

Prentice, D. 1987. Psychological correspondence of possessions, attitudes, and values. *Journal of Personality and Social Psychology* 53:883–1003.

Rabin, A. 1990. *Studying persons and lives*. New York: Spring Publishing.

Redfoot, D. L., and K. W. Back. 1988. The perceptual presence of the life course. *International Journal of Aging and Human Development* 27:156–70.

Rochberg-Halton, E. 1984. Object relations, role models, and culti- vation of the seal. *Environment and Behavior* 16:335–68.

Ruddick, S., and P. Daniels. 1977. *Working it out*. New York: Pantheon Books.

Sherman, E., and E. Newman. 1977. The meaning of cherished personal possessions for the elderly. *Journal of Aging and Human Development* 8:181–92.

Smith, B. 1983. *Home girls: A black feminist anthology*. New York: Kitchen Table.

Walker, B. G. 1990. *Women's rituals: A sourcebook*. New York: Harper Collins.

Wappner, S. 1990. Cherished possessions and adaptation of older people to nursing homes. *International Journal of Aging and Human Development* 31:219–35.

Waring, M. 1988. *If women counted*. New York: Harper Collins.

Whitbeck, C. 1984. A different reality: Feminist ontology. In *Beyond domination: New perspectives on women and philosophy*, ed. C. C. Gould. Totawa, NJ: Rowmein and Allanheld.

Whittaker, E. 1992. The birth of the anthropological self and its career. *Ethos* 20:191–219.

Wolf, D. 1996. *Feminist dilemmas in fieldwork*. New York: Westview Press.